D1186845

RUGBY
A History of Rugby Union Football

Chris Rea **RUGBY**

A History of
Rugby Union Football

Hamlyn
London · New York · Sydney · Toronto

See preceding page Protection racket – the 1974 Lions forwards give a perfect demonstration of the blocking art against South Africa, and enable Gordon Brown to feed Gareth Edwards without hindrance

Published in 1977 by
THE HAMLYN PUBLISHING
GROUP LIMITED
London · New York · Sydney · Toronto
Astronaut House, Feltham,
Middlesex, England

© 1977 Chris Rea

All rights reserved. No part of this publication may be reproduced, stored in a retrieval system, or transmitted in any form or by any means, electronic, mechanical, photographic or otherwise without the prior permission of the Publishers.

This book was designed and produced in Great Britain by London Editions Limited, 30 Uxbridge Road, London W12 8ND

ISBN 0 600 37591 9

Printed in Great Britain by Chromoworks, Nottingham

To my wife Terry,
who now knows the difference between
a back and a front.

CONTENTS

6

FOREWORD by Mike Gibson

Any midfield back must tread warily. In complimenting the author I must tread even more warily, for the regard and respect I have for him has often been stretched by a sport which demands total commitment to winning on the field. Though I refuse to make any admissions as to my vintage, my first encounter with him was in 1962 as a member of Belfast Schools XV against Midlands of Scotland Schools, both of us purporting to play at fly-half. Recollection of incidents is uncertain but not the fact of a victory for Belfast Schools. Forewarned by his experience in Belfast, the Author side-stepped into the centre to develop an international career whilst I continued my pursuit of recognition as an outside half. Our understanding and relationship matured in indirect conflict, but fate edged me sideways to the mid-field in 1969. Our relationship was thus challenged and, in fact, almost foundered at Murrayfield in 1969 when in a desperate tackle to prevent Chris from attaining glory, I dislocated his shoulder. The result was pain and suffering, and a hastily re-arranged summer holiday at his own expense, having had to forgo a tour to South Africa with the Barbarians.

Why then subject friendship to a game in which a player can end up maimed for life? Why play such a game at all? Anyone reading this review of world rugby, its origin, history and development will find ready answers. We do it because we love a game which cannot be compared to any others. We do it because of the friendships formed. We do it not only because individually we like to play for our country, but more importantly because we want to win for our country. These themes, and the players behind them, are sharply portrayed in a review which no follower of this king of games should miss. I can do no more than thoroughly commend the insight into the game, not only as a game, but as it is played and recounted in many different countries.

'Black milk' or a 'drop of Bush' has caused drink to be classified as Ireland's second favourite national pastime, and a natural consequence of such is the desire to have the last word (even though I am involved in the Foreword to the book – that seems to reveal the nationality of the contributor!). Whilst the English, Scots and Welsh (the Irish always use that order of play) are able to use their full available talent and thus may be occasionally more successful, the Irish talent is diluted by the demands of gaelic and hurley. Sure, men in County Kerry are of such a size that Mervyn Davies would have been a scrum-half and Chris and I would have been golfers!

Autumn 1976

The man who started it all. This is the only known portrait of the Rev. William Webb Ellis and was published by the *Illustrated London News* on the occasion of a sermon he delivered during the Crimean War

Because William Webb Ellis was never able to tell his own story, it is upon the testimony of an Old Rugbeian, Matthew Holbeche Bloxam, that the Ellis legend principally rests. Writing in the school's *Meteor* on 22 December 1880 Bloxam described the incident which had taken place in the Close fifty-seven years earlier, and when a sub-committee of Old Rugbeians was set up in 1895 'to enquire into the Origin of Rugby Football' it relied substantially on Bloxham's evidence. So much so, in fact, that this famous plaque was installed in the Doctor's Wall in 1900

THIS STONE
COMMEMORATES THE EXPLOIT OF
WILLIAM WEBB ELLIS,
WHO WITH A FINE DISREGARD FOR THE RULES OF FOOTBALL
AS PLAYED IN HIS TIME
FIRST TOOK THE BALL IN HIS ARMS AND RAN WITH IT
THUS ORIGINATING THE DISTINCTIVE FEATURE OF
THE RUGBY GAME.
A.D. 1823.

Above In a letter to his mother in 1851, a pupil of Rugby School wrote, *'I think I told you that Gilbert who makes the footballs for us is going to send one to the exhibition. I went to see it yesterday and I really think it will be quite a conspicuous thing there. It is a house . . . built entirely of leather – at least you can see nothing but leather.'* William Gilbert was a native of Rugby and occupied a shop in St Matthews Street where he was a shoemaker and football manufacturer, chiefly to Rugby School, until he died in 1877. But on his death the business remained in the family and Gilbert Rugby balls are still in use throughout the world. At the time the letter was written, the ball was an inflated pig's bladder cased by tailored leather. The modern ball, inflated by a rubber bladder, has to comply with fairly rigid specifications

Overleaf Rugby School – the seat of learning where the game is reputed to have originated. This painting by George Barnard depicts a game in progress in the school grounds in 1852. Two features of the game which distinguished rugby from other forms of football were already in existence – goals were scored by kicking the ball over the crossbar, and the ball was of approximately oval shape

ONE WHO WAS INCLINED to take unfair advantages at football,' was how a school contemporary described William Webb Ellis, the legendary inventor of Rugby Football. The occasion which marked Ellis out as one of the most famous products of Rugby School in Warwickshire, occurred in the latter part of 1823, when he is reputed to have caught the ball in a match against Bigside, and instead of retiring and punting it back to the opposition as the rules of the day demanded, he continued running towards his opponents' goal, the ball still firmly in his hands. The immediate result of this piece of bravado was probably a severe caning, which could well have discouraged the young offender from ever again taking the field – there being no record of his further interest in the game he had donated to the world. In fact very little is known about the man himself. He was apparently a pupil of average intelligence at Rugby between the years 1816 and 1825, when he went up to Oxford, won a cricket 'blue' and then entered the Church. The last seventeen years of his life he spent as Rector at Magdalen Laver in Essex, but his death remained a mystery until 1959, when the late Ross McWhirter traced his grave to Menton on the French Riviera. The discovery was greeted with great jubilation in that part of Gaul – the grave was tidied up and the site was visited by the President of the French Rugby Fédération, the captain of the national side and a brass band. Respects had at last been paid to the man who is reputed to have given birth to one of the greatest team games in the world.

But the origins of Rugby go back much further – after all, men had been participating in handling games, whether it was with a pig's bladder or a human head, for hundreds of years. Among the Romans the gymnastic game of 'harpastum', which contained at least two features of rugby football, ball carrying and scrummaging, was highly popular. It was the Romans who also fashioned a game called Soule which was played in Brittany up to 1870. It was described as 'a hot, dramatic game with fighting, strangling and head breaking; a game in which a scoundrel could slay an enemy as if by accident.' The early press in Britain wasn't exactly favourable either – in Elizabethan times football was described as 'nought but beastlie fury and extreme violence', and the Puritan Stubbes, never one to go actively in search of pleasure, called it 'a bloody and murthering practice'. In Scotland, as early as the fifteenth century, the Stuart kings were issuing Acts of Parliament against the playing of 'fute ball' and other pastimes which were interfering with the training of men in more warlike pursuits. The clergy too frowned upon the waste of time and damage to property caused by the players.

The principal football festival of the year was held on Shrove Tuesday, and two of the oldest games took place at Chester and Derby. The Derby game, which gave rise to the term 'local derby', meaning a contest between neighbouring sides, was played by two teams of unlimited numbers whose object it was to impel the ball towards their opponents' goal. Glover, in his *History of Derbyshire*, describes the action thus – 'the struggle to obtain the ball, which is carried in the arms of those who have possessed themselves of it, is then violent, and the motion of human tide heaving to and fro without the least regard to consequences, is tremendous. Broken shins, broken heads, torn coats and lost hats are among the minor accidents of this fearful contest, and it frequently happens that persons fall, owing to the intensity of the pressure, fainting and bleeding beneath the feet of the surrounding mob.' Two other pastimes were of a similar nature – one was a game called 'hurling to goales', which had very little kicking but contained a great deal of carrying. The other was called 'camp ball', the object of which was to carry or throw the ball through the opponents' goals which were situated 80 to 100 yards apart. In the Scottish border towns

'On Tuesday last, the ancient Shrovetide diversion of football was played most lustily at Kingston-upon-Thames by two clubs, one called the Thames Street Club the other the Townsend. They began at eleven o'clock in the morning, and kept up the ball till five o'clock in the evening. The rule is to kick the ball throughout the town; and whichever club gets the ball nearest the meeting place at five o'clock, wins the game. There are no stakes but the honour of victory; and the parties dine together in the evening.' This extract from the local paper describes a football match played at Kingston in 1846 to celebrate Shrove Tuesday – the principal football festival of the year

of Hawick and Jedburgh a ball game was played, the essentials of which were carrying and passing, and it is recorded that in 1815 at Carterhaugh Walter Laidlaw, watching for an opportunity, lifted the ball and threw it wide to William Riddel, a speedy player, who at once ran away from the mass of players and was prevented from scoring by being run down by a horseman – an action which found no favour with the spectators.

Summing up in their most detailed work, *The Centenary History of the Rugby Football Union*, Ross McWhirter and U. A. Titley wrote, 'It can be concluded that some game of ball has existed in Britain at least since Roman times, and although such games have differed somewhat from each other, the common thread has been that they were "carrying" games'. And, as they further point out, 'This leads to the belief that the crude equivalent of the modern rugby game is probably the most ancient of all popular team sports of the present day.'

Like all worthwhile inventions, the rugby

idea spread, and spread quickly, at first through the preachings of Old Rugbeians, thence to the universities and to the schools. In 1839, Arthur Pell, a student at Cambridge, attempted to form a rugby club, although it failed to gain official recognition, and it wasn't until 1872 that the Cambridge University Club was formed. By that time the clubs of Guy's Hospital (1843), Liverpool (1857), Blackheath (1862), Harlequins (1866), Wasps (1867) and Oxford University (1869) had all been established, and were playing organized matches against each other. But the game itself was almost unrecognizable from the modern version – there were 20 players on each side, with points being scored only by kicks at goal. In order to merit a kick at goal, a player had to cross his opponents' line with the ball in his possession, and it was from this practice that the term 'try' evolved. After a touchdown, the crowd would shout 'a try, a try', indicating that an attempt at goal could be made. Gradually the word became an accepted part of rugby parlance, and it was first used in print in a newspaper report in 1873. Another feature of the game in those days was 'hacking' – a legalized form of brutality which enabled a player to kick lumps out of his opponent without fear of police proceedings. Some idea of what went on, even in school games, can be gleaned from an article written in the New Rugbeian in 1860 entitled 'My First Big Side': 'Fellows did not care a fig for the ball then except in as much as it gave them a decent pretext for hacking. I remember a scrummage down by the touchline near the pavilion. By Jove! that was something like a scrummage! Why, we'd been hacking for five minutes already and hadn't had half enough. Take my word for it, all you youngsters, if you just watch a fellow of the old school playing, and take a leaf out of his book, you'll get on a long site better than if you take up any of the fiddle faddle of the present day. My maxim is – hack the ball when you see it near you, and when you don't, why then hack the fellow next to you.' Others were less enthusiastic about the custom. In a letter to *The Times* in the late 1860s, a surgeon gave a list of rugby injuries that he had attended, most of which were the result of hacking: 'One boy with his collarbone broken, another with a severe injury to the ankle, a third with a severe injury to the knee, and two others sent home on crutches.' Another journal wrote the game off as 'a mixture of hacking, scragging, gouging and biting – it could never take rank as a drawing room pastime.' It was under such pressure that, in 1871, with the formation of the Rugby Football Union, the practice of hacking was made illegal.

In Scotland the game advanced, as it had done south of the border, through the public schools, and in 1858 the Edinburgh Academicals Club was formed, although it's thought that a schoolboy game was played at the Academy as early as 1851. By 1870, other clubs had been formed – among them West of Scotland, Edinburgh University, St Andrew's University, Glasgow Academi-

cals, Royal High School and Merchistonians, and it was from these seven clubs that the Scottish team was chosen for the first international against England at Raeburn Place in 1871.

The Irish, for their part, by some devious logic, claimed William Webb Ellis as their own, arguing that he was born in the County of Tipperary and not, as Ellis himself had stated, in Manchester. But there is no denying the fact that Trinity College, which was founded in 1854, is the oldest club in Ireland, and in all likelihood the game was played there sometime before that date.

Unlike the game in Ireland, Scotland and England, rugby in Wales was not fostered by men who had links with the universities and public schools. It was a game which appealed to the working man and afforded him the best possible relaxation after a week of hard toil in the pit. This was also the case in the North of England, but there the game was to take rather a different turn, as we shall discover later. South Wales has always been the stronghold of the game in the Principality, and by the mid 1870s Swansea, Cardiff, Newport and Llanelli had been established.

The pioneers of the game abroad were British businessmen and the armed forces. It was through young Englishmen working in the wine trade that the game in France flourished, and to this day it is in the South that the game remains most popular. The union game in Australia has always had to withstand fierce competition from the two other football codes – rugby league and rules football. Nevertheless, the Australians had two notable 'firsts'. They were the first Dominion to form a union – the Southern Union being established in 1875 – and they were the first country to undertake an overseas tour, when New South Wales visited New Zealand in 1882. The oldest club, Sydney University, was formed in 1864.

By natural progression the game reached New Zealand, and the man responsible for taking it there was C. J. Munro, a son of Sir David Munro, who was then Speaker in the

The early game centred around scrumming and hacking which were considered to be the real tests of manliness, but when hacking was abolished in 1871 many of the old school considered that the game was doomed. *'Dash my buttons! you haven't a chance of getting a decent fall in the present day; and we wonder no wonder either when you see young dandies "got up regardless of expense", mincing across Big Side, and looking just as if their delicate frames wouldn't survive any violent contact with the ball. Hang the young puppies! we shall have fellows playing in dress boots and lavender coloured kid gloves before long'* – an excerpt from the *New Rugbeian* Vol. 111 (1860)

By 1890 there had been sufficient changes in the laws to make it recognizable as the game which is played today: hacking had been abolished; the number of players in matches under Rugby Union auspices had been reduced to fifteen; the never-ending scrummages had disappeared, and the law which provided that a player had to release the ball on being tackled made the game considerably faster

New Zealand House of Representatives. Charles Munro had been educated at Sherbourne School, and on his return to New Zealand in 1870 he suggested that his town club in Nelson, which had hitherto played the league and rules codes, should give the rugby game a try. They did, they liked it, and that was the start of rugby in New Zealand.

Canon G. Ogilvie is given the credit for introducing the game to South Africa, suggesting to the young men of Cape Town that the game played by his old school, Winchester College, would provide a 'healthy form of winter exercise'. There are records of a game played between the Military and Civilians as early as 1862 – the game lasted an hour and three-quarters, and was then abandoned as a draw, 'because the wind had changed and this would have given the Military an unfair advantage which they were far too sporting to accept.'

These then were the countries where rugby took the deepest roots, but in the early days when the game was growing and spreading it did so aimlessly. What it needed most was direction, and this was to come with the formation, in 1871, of the Rugby Football Union.

2 THE ANTI PROFESSIONALS

Throughout the history of rugby the universities of Oxford and Cambridge have had a profound influence on the game's advance. Under the guidance of 'Harry' Vassall in the early 1880s rugby at Oxford flourished. It was Vassall who saw the possibilities of open play amongst forwards and backs. His theories about forward play are thought to have originated from the time when he was captain of the School XV at Marlborough and there were several serious injuries. The school, anxious to allay parental fears, decided upon a temporary alteration to the laws which forbade forwards to pick up the ball. This served to speed up the game and when Vassall later captained the Oxford side, the controlled dribbling and close passing of the forwards was a feature of their game, and a blueprint of the game we know today

Overleaf On 26 January 1871 thirty-two people representing twenty-one clubs met at the old Pall Mall Restaurant for the purpose of founding the Rugby Football Union – a body which was to give direction to a rapidly expanding game. At that initial meeting an Old Rugbeian, Algernon Rutter, was elected first president. Rutter lived until 1908, the year in which Twickenham was purchased

T HE MISTAKE MADE by the representative from Wasps on the night of 26 January 1871 is somehow so typical of the Rugby spirit. He should have been attending the inaugural meeting of the Rugby Football Union at the old Pall Mall restaurant, but he turned up instead at a pub of the same name, where he presumably stayed to sup a few pints of ale in the best traditions of the game. But there was nothing muddle-headed about the meeting itself – the business was completed in two hours, by which time the first President, Algernon E. Rutter, and the first Honorary Secretary, Edwin H. Ash, had been elected. Thirty-two people represented twenty-one clubs of which eight are still in existence – Black-heath, Richmond, Guy's Hospital, Civil Service, Harlequins, Wellington College, King's College, and St Paul's School. Although Rugby School was not represented, many of those present were Old Rugbeians, including Rutter and Ash.

With the formation of a committee, one of the priorities was to draw up a code of rules – a task which was intrusted to three Old Rugbeians – Rutter, E. C. Holmes, who had chaired the meeting at the Pall Mall, and Leonard J. Maton, and had it not been for the fact that Maton broke a leg while playing in a match, it is doubtful if the work would have been completed in time for the following season. It was an unfortunate but timely injury, as Maton found himself laid up with nothing to occupy his days, and in return for a large amount of tobacco, he agreed to prepare a draft of the rules in his own hand. This laborious task he completed by the early summer, and on 24 June it was approved at a special general meeting. There were fifty-nine laws, which included the abolition of hacking and the appointment of the team captains as sole arbiters of all disputes. This understandably led to some severe differences of opinion, and it prompted H. H. Almond, who umpired the first international between England and Scotland, to remark: 'When an umpire is in doubt, I think he is

justified in deciding against the side which makes the most noise. They are probably in the wrong!'

The match took place less then nine weeks after the foundation of the Rugby Football Union – the date was 27 March, the venue Raeburn Place, home of the Edinburgh Academicals. A year earlier, a game had been played at the Oval, supposedly between the two countries, but that had been conducted under Association rules, and only one member of the Scottish side came from a Scottish club. Another had the somewhat tenuous connection with Caledonia in that he came north of the Border occasionally, to shoot grouse. The game at Raeburn Place, then, was the result of a challenge issued by the indignant home Scots to the Sassenachs. Playing twenty-a-side, the Scots in blue, the English in white, victory went to the Scots after a 'titanic struggle' before a crowd of about four thousand. The Scots scored first with what would now be called a pushover try, which was goaled by W. Cross, but the first individual try in international

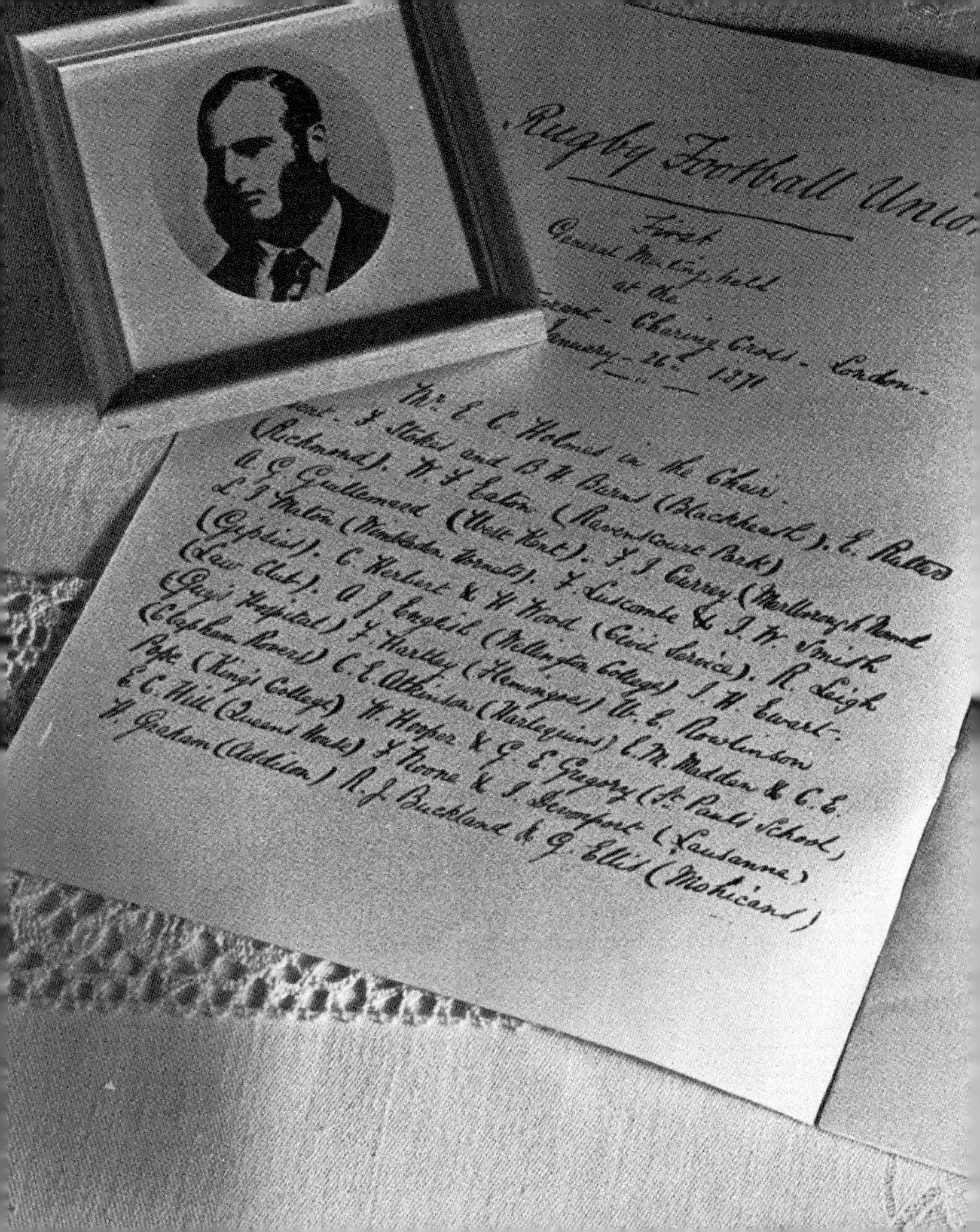

Rugby Football
First
General Meeting, held
at the
Charing Cross - London -
January - 26th 1871
Mr. E. C. Holmes in the Chair.
F. Stokes and B. H. Burns (Blackheath). E. Rutter
(Richmond). W. F. Eaton (Ravenscourt Park)
A. G. Guillemard (West Kent). F. I. Currey (Marlborough Nomads
L. J. Maton (Wimbledon Hornets). F. Luscombe & J. H. Smith
(Gipsies). C. Herbert & H. Wood (Civil Service). R. Leigh
(Law Club). A. J. English (Wellington College) J. H. Ewart
(Guy's Hospital) F. Hartley (Flamingoes) W. E. Rowlinson
(Clapham Rovers) C. E. Atkinson (Harlequins) C. M. Madden & C. E.
Pope (King's College) W. Hooper & G. E. Gregory (St Paul's School,
E. C. Hill (Queen's House) F. Noone & J. Davenport (Lausanne)
H. Graham (Addison) R. J. Buckland & G. Ellis (Mohicans)

J. R. Lancaster & H. Sefton Bryne (Wi...
H. Emanuel and E. H. Ash (Richmo...

———·———

The proceedings commenced with a few introductory remarks from
the Chairman who stated that the Meeting had been called with
the view of framing a code of Football Rules to be based upon the
Rugby system of Play, but before discussing this subject it would be
necessary to form a Football Society of the Clubs present——

The first Resolution ... then proposed by Mr Stokes (Blackheath Club)
"That in the opinion of this Meeting the formation of a Rugby
Football Society is desirable; that such a Society be formed forth-
with and that the co-operation of all Clubs be invited · This was
... ded by Mr E. Rutter (Richmond Club) and carried unanimously.

rugby was scored by the Englishman, R. H. Birkett, who also represented his country at the Association game. Unfortunately, the English captain, Frederic Stokes, failed with the kick at goal, and the score remained at one–nil. But the English XX had given a good account of themselves, and as the *Sporting Life* somewhat ambiguously put it, 'The English behinds were generally considered as having done their devoir remarkably well.' Revenge for England came a year later at the Oval, when they beat the Scots by two goals and two tries to one goal. So it was that internationals between the two countries became a regular feature, and an edge was added to their rivalry with the appearance of a trophy – the Calcutta Cup.

In January 1873, the Calcutta Club had been founded by Old Rugbeians residing in the city, but because of a lack of support, it went out of existence some five years later. There was, however, a good deal of money left in the kitty and the problem was what to do with it. Ideas ranged from a massive hooley to something slightly more permanent like the presentation of a trophy to the Rugby Union. The decision to make it the latter was a triumph for sobriety. So the cup, which is made from the silver of melted down rupees, was presented as an 'international challenge cup to be played for annually by England and Scotland'.

By this time Ireland had joined the international scene, but it wasn't until 1887 that they first registered a win over England. The Welsh entry to international rugby in 1881 was even more inauspicious – England won by seven goals, a drop goal, and six tries to nil, and considered it such a waste of time that they dropped the fixture for a year! Relations with Scotland were also becoming strained, and an incident in the 1884 match led to the formation of the International Board. The dispute arose over a try scored by the Englishman Richard Kindersley which the Scots claimed, with little justification, was illegal. Correspondence continued on the subject during the next year

when there was no game, and in 1886 the International Board came into being for the settling of disputes between all the countries and subsequently to make laws governing international fixtures.

The 1880s brought about a tactical revolution led by the universities of Oxford and Cambridge. The first University match had been played at the Parks in Oxford on 10 February 1872 with Oxford winning by a goal and a try to nil. But it was the 1881–2 season which brought the two clubs to the forefront – Cambridge with their brilliant but undisciplined individuals, Oxford with Harry Vassall. He it was who did most to give the game the shape it has today, with the accent on running and passing between forwards and backs. Gradually the mauls, which could last up to five minutes, went out of vogue, and the law of 1887, which ruled that a player must release the ball immediately after being tackled, served to speed up the game still further. The adoption by Wales of four threequarters instead of three completed the transformation.

The transformation would have been even greater if certain clubs in the north had been allowed to have their own way. The problem arose over payments to players for broken time, and in the industrial north especially, mill workers and miners were losing money by playing rugby – losses which were being made good by the clubs. This, of course, cut right across the amateur principles of the game, and the matter was brought to a head with the suspension by the Union of the James brothers, both of whom were Welsh internationals of humble means playing for Broughton Rovers. A General Meeting of the Rugby Union was called for on 20 September 1893 at the Westminster Palace Hotel, and although the northerners came south on two special trains to ensure maximum representation, their proposal, that players be allowed compensation for 'bona fide loss of time', was defeated by 282 votes to 136. The threat to the game's amateur status had thus been averted, the

Adrian Dura Stoop (third from
the left, middle row), one of the
legendary figures in English rugby
who applied much thought to the
techniques of half back and
threequarter play – a member of
the Harlequin club, he won 15
caps for England and was
President of the Rugby Union for
the year 1932–3. Standing
immediately behind Stoop is
C. H. (Cherry) Pillman who had
modelled his style of loose
forward play on Dave Gallaher,
captain of the 1905 All Blacks,
and employed the New
Zealander's tactics to maximum
effect during the British Isles tour
to South Africa in 1910

Above W. J. A. Davies, probably England's greatest fly half, won 22 caps between 1913 and 1923 and was never once on the losing side in an international championship match. He began his international career in partnership with F. E. Oakley, but within seven months of winning his first cap Oakley was drowned at sea in a submarine disaster. At the end of the war Davies was partnered by C. A. Kershaw who also represented Great Britain in the sabre and foil events during the 1920 Olympic Games at Antwerp

Left 'The Cabbage Patch', which was purchased by the Rugby Football Union in 1907–8 for the sum of £5,572 12s. 6d., provided excellent grazing facilities during World War I. Nowadays Twickenham, which extends over some thirty acres, can accommodate 72,500 spectators and is equipped with restaurants and twenty permanent bars. During the Middlesex Sevens it is estimated that 50,000 pints of beer are consumed.

anti-professionals had won the battle, and now they went flat out to win the war. So strict did they make the laws against professionalism that the northern clubs would have to conform to get out. At a meeting held at the Mitre Hotel Leeds on 29 August 1895, they chose the latter course. Twenty-two clubs, including the now famous rugby league sides St Helens, Leeds, Wakefield Trinity, Warrington, Widnes and Wigan broke away from the Rugby Union and formed the Northern Football Union. As it was to be proved later, the payments for broken time were only the first steps towards professionalism, and the Union game, therefore, owes no small debt of gratitude to the wisdom of men like the then RFU President William Cail, the Secretary, Rowland Hill, and Frank Marshall, who were instrumental in preserving the amateur code.

But the secession had a drastic effect upon the national side. Up until 1892, England, along with Scotland, had pretty well dominated the international scene, and had twice won the mythical Triple Crown (1884 and 1892) by beating the three other home countries in the same season. Not until 1910, however, did another Championship come England's way, and in the intervening period they lost to the 1905 All Blacks, the 1908 Wallabies and drew with the Springboks in 1906.

1910 – the year that France joined in the championship, playing all four home countries for the first time; the year that Twickenham was first used for international matches, and the year of the legendary half back, Adrian Dura Stoop. With a mother who was half Scottish and half Irish, and a father who was Dutch (naturalized English) there was a fair chance that young Stoop would represent some country or other, but a Rugby and Oxford education ensured that his background was an English one, and he joined the Harlequin club. As a player he had all the attributes which go to make the perfect fly half – speed off the mark, good hands, an immaculate pass and quite excep-

tional ability with both feet. It was as a tactician though, that he is probably best remembered. He brought a new dimension to back play, realizing the value of playing specialists in the key half back positions. Stoop's philosophy was based on attack, a practice he encouraged from the most desperate defensive positions. Never were his theories put to better use than in the 1910 game against Wales, the Triple Crown holders. Fielding the ball from the kick off, Stoop, instead of kicking safely for touch, elected to run, switching direction as he did so. The ball then travelled to J. G. Birkett and on to F. E. Chapman who was over for a try before a hand had been laid on him. Wales were unable to recover from the shock and lost 11–6. On that same day two other rugby greats blossomed into full maturity, Ronald W. Poulton (tragically killed by a sniper's bullet in World War I) and C. H. Pillman, who was to make his mark with the British side in South Africa later that year. But this was Stoop's match, and a letter to the press on 5 February summed up the feelings of many.

My dear Stoop,
If history should describe you as the saviour of your country, history will not lie, for that rare flash of genius which gave England a try in the first minute of the recent international with Wales undoubtedly turned the fortunes of the game. 'Apparently guileless yet full of guile', is how I heard a man describe you the other day. He had just seen you put into successful operation one of those seemingly simple ruses which are so terribly hard to frustrate. As in racing circles, the year is known by the name of the horse that wins the Derby, so, surely, shall 1910 be hall marked as 'Stoop's Year'. I would willingly surrender a seat in the 'Babble Shop' at Westminster to know and understand exactly how you felt on the night that Wales was beaten!

The Golden Era of English rugby
came between the years 1920 and
1928 during which time England
won the Grand Slam on four
occasions. Under the leadership
of the great Wavell Wakefield,
the English forwards reigned
supreme and the photograph
shows some of them relaxing at
half time during the 1923 match
against Wales. Wakefield stands
third from the right with his arm
around his back row colleague
Tom Voyce of Gloucester. A. F.
Blakiston, the third of that
famous back row trio, is to the
right of Voyce adjusting his
headgear

How fitting that England should beat Wales in that first international played at Twickenham on 15 January. Three years previously the site had been a market garden which was purchased by William Williams, a fine all-round sportsman, for the sum of £5,572 12s. 6d. At that time the Rugby Football Union had no settled base from which to operate, England's home matches being played at the Crystal Palace, Richmond, Blackheath and various provincial grounds. Williams, however, persuaded the Union that his 'Cabbage Patch' would make an excellent headquarters for them, and from that day Twickenham has grown from ten and a quarter acres to over thirty, accommodating massive stands, car parks, tea rooms and bars. It is to rugby what Lords is to cricket and Wimbledon to tennis. The first ever game played on the ground was on 2 October 1909, when Harlequins played Richmond, and before a crowd of 2,000 beat them 14–10. One journalist at least, was a man of vision, writing after the match: 'Twickenham will, in the course of time, become a real live rugby centre; it is a district that is growing, and the game played in such an entertaining way as it is by the Harlequins, will make rugby the recreation and sport of the young men of the neighbourhood.'

Alas for Harlequins and for Rugby, World War I was to take the lives of many of the country's greatest players – 26 England internationals and countless club players were killed, and the teams of the 1919–20 season were perforce experimental. But out of the next four seasons England were triumphant in three, winning the Triple Crown and the Championship (the Grand Slam). The 'Golden Age' had begun – at half back, the perfect blend, C. A. Kershaw and W. J. A. Davies, who played together in 14 internationals and never once finished up on the losing side; in the threequarter line, C. N. Lowe and H. C. Catchside, who gained his niche in rugby lore with a bionic leap over the French full back, L. Pardo, in the

1924 encounter, and with an expense claim submitted to the Rugby Union for a train journey from Newcastle to London. The fare amounted to £2 19s. 11d., which he rounded up to £3. This did not meet with the approval of the Union's treasurer, and Catchside received a cheque for the exact train fare. Nothing daunted, when he was next called upon to play at Twickenham, Catchside filled in his expense sheet thus:

Train Fare	£2 19s. 11d.
Toilet	1d.
total	£3 0s. 0d.

It was England's forwards who were kings amongst the gods – A. T. Voyce, R. Cove-Smith, G. S. Conway, A. F. Blakiston and the man described as the greatest England forward of all time, Wavell W. Wakefield. As Adrian Stoop had drafted a design for backs before the war, so Wakefield made improvements in the forwards' art some fifteen years later. Educated at Sedbergh in the days when a boy risked the cane if he heeled the ball anywhere in his own half of the field, Wakefield was quickly alive to the advantages of organized back row defence and solid scrummaging. He captained England 13 times in his 31 international appearances, was invited to captain the 1924 Lions in South Africa, and the 1930 Lions in New Zealand, but was unable to tour with either party. Today, with more than forty years of unbroken service in Parliament behind him, and a host of business interests, Lord Wakefield of Kendal still retains the same passionate interest in the game. The moments which gave him the greatest pleasure on the field came as a result of concentrated effort and planning. The first was in 1922 when his young and inexperienced Cambridge University side beat Oxford 21–8; the second, later that season, when he led the RAF, still in its infancy as a representative side, to victory over the Army and Navy. England's triumph over Wales in 1924, the first at Swansea since 1895, and their subsequent victories

Above Jeff Butterfield, the finest passer of a ball, played 28 times for England between 1953 and 1959, in which period England won the International Championship outright on three occasions. His centre partnership with the Harlequin Phil Davies proved to be highly productive both for England and for the British Lions

Above Dickie Jeeps, a tough and courageous competitor, was capped 24 times in the scrum half position. Strangely enough, his international debut was not for England but for the British Lions in the First Test against South Africa in 1955, and it wasn't until 1957 that he found a regular place in the England XV. Jeeps was at his best in wet muddy conditions clearing up behind his forwards. Here he sets his backs in motion in the match against France at Stade Colombes in 1958

Right England v. Australia, Twickenham 1958 – a match which will be remembered for its bitterness and for one moment of genius from Peter Jackson, who is here seen closing in on the Wallaby threequarter R. Phelps. Reduced to fourteen men early in the first half, England had fought back to level the score at 6–6 and it was well into injury time when Jackson got the ball with time and space to beat the Australian defence and touch down for the winning try

over Scotland, Ireland and France, was the third occasion for enormous satisfaction; the fourth was guiding Middlesex to their first County Championship title in 1929, this after he had scored the decisive try in the semi-final against Devon. Like all great men he remains modest about his achievements, but recalls ruefully that a reputation such as his did have its drawbacks. There was an occasion in a match at Twickenham when he spotted one of his team mates being kicked on the ground by an opponent. Running over to put a stop to the nonsense, he received an immediate apology from the transgressor who had been under the impression that it was Wakefield he was kicking.

It is a fascinating exercise to imagine what would have been the thoughts of William Webb Ellis if he had turned up at the Close one hundred years after his famous run, and had taken his place alongside the other 2,000 spectators at the game. It is unlikely that he would have recognized it as his own invention. He would have seen 30 of the country's finest sportsmen playing a game involving a number of complicated and mysterious ploys. Whatever he thought about the tactics, he could not have failed to have been excited by the spectacle. On the one side in this Centenary Match was the combined might of England and Wales, and facing them on the other side were 15 of the best from Scotland and Ireland. At half time the England/Wales XV were leading 9–6, and immediately after the re-start, they went further ahead with a try by the Welsh forward A. Baker, followed by a drop goal from W. J. A. Davies. By now there was no question of this being a mere exhibition – Scotland and Ireland fought back to level the scores, and with ten minutes left it was 16–16. Then England/Wales broke clear, Tom Voyce got the touchdown and W. G. E. Luddington converted to give them victory by 21 points to 16 – a fitting end to a unique match.

Possibly as a result of England's out-

Two of the greatest tries ever seen at Twickenham.
Left Alexander Obolensky, a Russian prince brought to England to escape the revolution, turned up on the wing for his adopted country in the 1935 match against the touring All Blacks. The photograph shows 'Obo' on his way to scoring his second try of the match – an effort which is recalled by Peter Cranmer who played alongside him that day: '. . . when Candler passed, Obo checked as the initial cover came across at him. Suddenly he saw an avenue to his left between the first and the second cover defence, and Obo just went like a stag through it, finishing at the north-west corner.'
Right Richard Sharp's try against Scotland on 16 March 1963 was another classic, revealing the speed and grace of the player. It all began with a flat pass from the base of the scrum; a dummy scissors with Mike Weston and Sharp was through the initial cover. With Jim Roberts to his left Sharp had one Scottish defender, Colin Blaikie, between him and the line. Too soon, Blaikie decided that Sharp would pass to Roberts and in that second Sharp had made his decision: 'I had no choice for my mind was made up for me. Blaikie committed the cardinal sin of not going for the man in possession. I was almost on top of him when I realized that although he was physically in front of me, his mind was on Jim Roberts. The memory of that moment is still vivid. I know I did the right thing.'

standing performances on the international field, the game was enjoying an unprecedented rise in popularity. Crowds of over 40,000 were turning up at Twickenham, which had now become the venue for the University Match, and for the Middlesex Seven-a-Side Tournament, but the men who had brought such glory to their country were not blessed with the gift of eternal youth, and one by one, they bowed out of the international arena. Sadly, England has never again seen their like.

The 1930s, although soured by the expulsion of France from the international Championship, did produce many memorable moments for England and several distinguished individuals – among them the exiled Russian prince, Alexander Obolensky, whose

two tries against the 1935–6 All Blacks at Twickenham have lost none of their brilliance from the distance of forty years. The second, in particular, must go down as one of the greatest ever scored on the ground. There was a scrum on the half way line in midfield, and behind the England backline Cyril Gadney, P. L. Candler, Peter Cranmer, R. A. Gerrard, and Obolensky was primed. England won the ball. From Gadney to Candler to Cranmer – a break by him, an inside pass back to Candler. By now the All Blacks cover was massing in strength, but there was the hint of a gap in midfield, just enough for Obolensky, now cutting diagonally across field from the right, to pierce. The All Blacks were caught on the wrong foot, Obolensky was over in the opposite

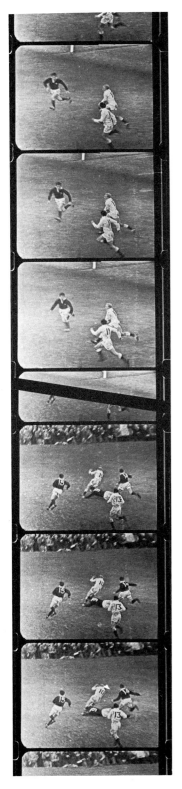

corner, and England were on their way to victory by 13 points to nil – their first win over New Zealand. How cruel fate was to be four years later when Obolensky, who had joined the Royal Air Force at the outbreak of war, was killed in a flight training accident in Norfolk.

The years immediately after the war were so dominated by Ireland and Wales that England had to wait until 1953 for another championship win and until 1957 for the Grand Slam. This was the era of David Marques, John Currie, Peter Robbins and Eric Evans in the forwards, and in the backs Jeff Butterfield, Phil Davies, Dickie Jeeps and the supreme artist P. B. Jackson of Coventry. In an age when defences lined up eyeball to eyeball, and the predatory wing forward roamed the field waiting to pounce on the merest suspicion of a break, the man who could somehow find his way past or through the morass of defenders was of inestimable value to his team. Peter Jackson was such a man. Not searingly fast, he relied on manoeuvrability to beat an opponent, and his desire to attack from any position on the field made him a great favourite with the crowd – so popular, in fact, that Ireland's Tony O'Reilly, another outstanding winger of the same period, was prompted to suggest that Jackson should be equipped with a unicycle and a set of juggling balls to entertain the crowd when play was not on his side of the field. Jackson is probably best remembered for the winning try he scored in the tenth minute of injury time against the Australians in 1957, but his personal treasure came seven years later, at a time when a spinal disorder forced him to the doctor's surgery after every match. The end of his playing career was close, but he geared himself up for one last effort, and took the field for Warwickshire in the County Championship Final against Lancashire. A try by him early in the match, and a pushover try in the closing stages were enough to give Warwickshire victory, and Jackson, at the age of thirty-three, retired a contented man.

Left A depressing sight for any side in opposition as Bob Hiller launches the ball into orbit. In his nineteen internationals for England he scored 138 points, and on each of his two Lions tours, to South Africa in 1968 and to New Zealand in 1971, he recorded a century. Perhaps England came to rely too much on his scoring power, but since his departure from the international game, England have failed to achieve any consistency in the Five Nations Championship

Right Easily the most photogenic of the current players, David Duckham of Coventry has been England's leading threequarter for the past seven years. His only misfortune has been to play in a national side which for the most part has lacked players of similar calibre and has been almost totally bereft of invention and adventure. His 36 England appearances make him his country's most capped back

The previous year, 1963, is worthy of mention, mainly in retrospect, because England has never since won the Championship. It was the year when Richard Sharp destroyed Scotland's hopes of winning at Twickenham for the first time since 1938, with a run which took him from the half way line, through the Scottish cover, and on past the full back Colin Blaikie to touch down for a score which is a worthy companion to Obolensky's effort in Rugby's Valhalla. Two years later, it was the Scots again who were on the receiving end of a sensational Twickenham try, when Andy Hancock ran 90 yards to deny the visitors their long awaited triumph. But since that time, England's displays in Europe have warranted scant attention, and, remarkably, their most noteworthy feats have been performed on foreign soil. In 1971 they went unbeaten through the Far East, twice beating Japan. In 1972 it was off to South Africa, self-consciously holding the 'wooden spoon' from the previous season's home campaign. The six provincial matches leading up to the test were cleared without defeat, and then, wonderful to relate, they beat South Africa by 18 points to 9, with Sam Doble, the Moseley full back, kicking 14 of the points. The following year they achieved an historic double in the southern hemisphere beating New Zealand in Auckland by 16 points to 10 after losing the three provincial matches prior to the international.

These performances overseas, and the glittering celebrations which accompanied the Centenary of the Rugby Football Union in 1972, an occasion which brought together the world's greatest players for a magical rugby tour, have tended to obscure the downswing in England's fortunes. The basic problem has been a shortage of top class talent – men like Budge Rogers, John Pullin, the elegant David Duckham, and Bob Hiller, have appeared all too infrequently. It was probably the uncannily accurate kicking of Hiller, in fact, which did more than anything else to paper over the cracks during the late 1960s and early 1970s. In his nineteen international appearances he kicked 138 points, and never was his value to the side more fully realized than in 1971 when he scored all 9 points against Ireland, and followed this with all 14 points against France. Without ever being a fitness fanatic (thirty seconds of continuous deep breathing was his idea of a hard training session) he, like those other great Harlequins, Stoop and Wakefield, did possess the gift of leadership – it's perhaps only coincidence that he too was an Oxbridge 'blue', and that England, generally speaking, has thrived when the universities of Oxford and Cambridge have been strong.

The recent decline in the playing standards at both these establishments has been principally due to the abolition of national service, which has meant a shortage of physically mature men, and to the mad scramble for university places, which has enabled dons to look for more than a good scrummage technique or a jinking sidestep from prospective students. The University Match used to attract a crowd of 60,000 at Twickenham, but now it has dwindled to less than half that number. There is, therefore, a very real danger that two of the most famous club sides in the world, which have produced so many internationals to successive generations, will have to lower their sights in the years that lie ahead. At the moment, for instance, they enjoy several rare privileges with a sizable representation on the R.F.U. Committee, and fixtures against touring teams – an honour granted to no other club sides in England.

Powerful pressures are now being brought to bear on the Union by some of the major or, as they prefer to call themselves, the 'gate taking' clubs to make radical alterations in the system of club representation on the Union Committee and, more significantly, to press for the establishment of leagues on a national basis. Many of them have become disenchanted with the National Club Knock-Out Competition which was instituted in 1972, and was expected to provide the com-

Budge Rogers, who first appeared
for England in 1961, still turns
out for his club, Bedford, and
continues to play with all the
enthusiasm which won him 34
caps. Here he makes a break
against Rosslyn Park in the final
of the Rugby Club Knock Out
Competition at Twickenham in
April 1975. Bedford won the
match by 28 points to 12

Police protection for Michael O'Brien following a flash of individualism during the charity international between England and France at Twickenham in 1974. But on this occasion it did not pay to advertise – having won £20 from his friends for his streak. Mr O'Brien was fined the same amount at a magistrates' court two days later

petitive edge thought to be missing from the English game. The first final at Twickenham was fought out (literally) between Gloucester and Moseley, the West Country side winning a hostile encounter 17–6. The second was a better advertisement for competitive football with Coventry beating Bristol 27–15, and as the outstanding club side in England, Coventry deservedly won it again the following year when London Scottish were their opponents. Now that a sponsor has been found (John Player, the tobacco company), it is considered that the competition will find more favour with the senior clubs, but sponsorship, however limited, brings its own problems, and many people within the game are uneasy about its encroachment upon an amateur preserve.

These are difficult times for the men who have to administrate an amateur game in an age of professionalism. The Mallaby Committee, set up by the R.F.U. in 1972 to consider the whole structure of the game in England, was aware of the pressures that are now facing the top players with squad training sessions for club, county and country, and advised that games should be played on Saturdays only, that club fixture lists should not exceed 45 matches per season and that squad sessions should be confined to the national side. Not since the Great Schism of 1893 when the 22 Northern clubs seceded from the Union, has that august body been faced with so many dilemmas. It is devoutly to be hoped that the present incumbents show the same degree of wisdom as their predecessors displayed more than eighty years ago, bearing in mind that the English character is anti-professional; its roots are with amateurs.

The Scottish XX which beat
England in the first official
international between the
countries at Raeburn Place,
Edinburgh, in 1871. The previous
year a game had been played at
the Oval but that had taken place
under Association Rules and few
of the Scottish side had any
connection with Scotland. The
match in 1871 was played before
a crowd of about 4,000 who saw
the Scotsman W. Cross give his
team victory with the conversion
of a pushover try

3 THE CANNYScots

SCOTLAND HAD MADE an encouraging start to international football with a win over the 'Auld Enemy' in their first encounter at Raeburn Place in 1871. This game can really be regarded as the source of organized football north of the border, but it was not until 1873 that the Scottish Football Union was formed. The founder members were the universities of Edinburgh, St Andrews and Glasgow, Edinburgh Academicals, Glasgow Academicals, West of Scotland, Royal High School and Merchistonians, while Edinburgh Wanderers and Warriston were admitted at the initial meeting. Dr Chiene of Edinburgh Academicals was elected first President and James Wallace, another Academical, was made Secretary.

In that same year, with each country having one victory apiece, the English again travelled north, this time to Glasgow, where they came up against a display of unparalleled gamesmanship. The Rev. P. Anton, who played in the Scottish side that day, was later prevailed upon to record the incident: 'Seeing the ground was to be sloppy, the English team went into a cobbler's to get leather soles fixed to their boots. I presume that the cobbler was nothing worse than a "Scots wha hae patriot". At any rate when the job was done the boots and the feet could not be got to correspond. There were two or three of the latter more than the former. What was to be done? the hour of onset was near. The missing boots not being found, the players put dress boots on bootless feet.' All credit then to the Saxons who gained a draw and obviously had some energy left to burn during the evening, it being noted that an England forward was picked up by his companions driving one of Her Majesty's mail carts round the town.

Although the game in Scotland remained largely the property of the schools, it swiftly reached the border towns of Langholm, Hawick and Galashiels where the side was an amalgam of men from Gala and Melrose. But this was an uneasy union and one which was alien to the lowland temperament. One night the men from Melrose carried out a raid in typical border fashion and when the good people of Gala awoke the next morning they found that their goalposts were missing Having established themselves at the Greenyards (presumably equipped with the Gala goalposts), Melrose found that they were running short of funds. It was then that Ned Haig, the town butcher, came up with a master plan to bring in the crowds – he invented the seven-a-side game, and in 1883 the first tournament was held in Melrose with the host side meeting their old rivals Gala in the final. At the end of the game the scores were level, but in extra time Melrose scored first and promptly decamped with the trophy despite loud protests from their opponents. Thus began the present day tradition of the 'sudden death' play off. There was no doubt though, that the truncated version of the game made exciting viewing, and soon it had been adopted in other parts of the country. In the south the principal Sevens event of the year is the Middlesex Tournament which has been held at Twickenham since 1926. Harlequins and London Welsh, each with seven wins and, as befits the country of origin, London Scottish (six wins), have been the most consistently successful sides down the years.

It was not until 1882 – eleven years after the inaugural match between Scotland and England, that victory went to the visiting side. The venue was Manchester, and the Scots won by two tries to nil. This was also the first international to be handled by a neutral referee. Scotland at this time had a good side – in the back line was W. E. McLagen who was to captain the British team in South Africa nine years later. He was renowned for the ferocity of his tackling, and was described by a colleague as being 'an ill tempered devil'. In the forwards were Bob Ainslie and Charles Reid, who played his first international whilst still a pupil at the Edinburgh Academy. The youngest player ever to have represented Scotland, his

Two early Scottish stalwarts – Charles Reid (right) and Mark Morrison (far right). Reid, who first played for his country in 1881 whilst still a pupil at the Edinburgh Academy, went on to gain 20 caps. Standing well over six feet and weighing 15½ stones he was a formidable forward. The Royal High School F.P. forward Mark Morrison captained Scotland on fifteen occasions and led the British Lions side to South Africa in 1903. Under his leadership Scotland twice won the Triple Crown, in 1901 and in 1903

frame belied his seventeen years, and at 6ft 3in and 15½ stone, he was his country's champion forward.

The second half of the decade was marred by the wrangling that went on between the home countries, and this period was perhaps the most disturbed in the annals of the game. First, there was the dispute of 1884 which subsequently led to the formation of the International Board. Then came the second period of discord in 1888 when the Rugby Football Union tried to introduce new laws without first passing them through the International Board. This was something that the other countries refused to tolerate, and matches with England were not resumed until 1890, when Scotland and England tied for the Championship. By this time Wales had been experimenting with four three-quarters instead of three, but until they beat England at Dewsbury in 1890 very little notice had been taken of the strategy. For the Scots, whose game was based on forward strength, this was tantamount to heresy. The great A. R. Don Wauchope, himself a back, wrote: 'I have always been a strong opponent of this new game. Forwards who are continually trying to play for their backs will invariably be beaten.' R. G. MacMillan, a fine Scottish forward of the time, was even more critical: 'The older players may be able to stick to the genuine game which they learned at the schools, but the younger ones will not be taught to put their heads down and shove, and will shirk and become loafers.' Rightly or wrongly Scotland ignored such warnings, jumped on the band wagon, and played with four threequarters, but many considered that Scotland had bartered her heritage, and that there was now nothing left in the game which was exclusively Scottish.

It took the Scots some time to settle into the new order of things, but they still produced forwards good enough to win games – forwards like Mark Morrison of Royal High School Former Pupils who captained his country on fifteen occasions, a number

The Calcutta Cup was presented to the Rugby Football Union by the Calcutta Club as a challenge cup to be played for annually by England and Scotland. Only very occasionally have Calcutta Cup matches also decided the fate of the Triple Crown and the Championship, but this was the case in 1925 when Scotland played for the first time at Murrayfield and beat England in an unforgettable encounter to win the Grand Slam for the first and only time in their history. The photograph shows the great Scottish forward
J. M. Bannerman kicking for touch in the match

Pages 42–3 Another scene from Scotland's Grand Slam year, this time in the match against Wales at Swansea where the Scottish winger A. C. Wallace evades a Welsh defender to score. Wallace, who later captained the Australian Waratah team to Britain in 1927, formed part of a magnificent Oxford and Scottish threequarter line, the other three being Ian Smith, G. P. S. MacPherson, and G. G. Aitken. It is interesting to note that the Scots did not at this time wear numbers – something which they regarded as a professional practice

Douglas Elliott, a raw-boned farmer who was the mainstay of the Scottish pack during the lean years when Scotland suffered seventeen consecutive defeats. In 1946, in his third season in club football, Elliot was picked to play for Scotland against the Kiwis, and he went on to win 29 caps without ever being dropped. Here Elliot gets his pass away before being tackled by John Kendall-Carpenter in the 1949 Calcutta Cup match at Twickenham which England won 19–3. Elliot played in seven Calcutta Cup games, but was only twice on the winning side

equalled by Arthur Smith and since passed by Ian McLaughlan. Morrison's presence in the Scottish side helped to secure two Triple Crown wins – in 1901 and again in 1903. Perhaps the hardest match of those two campaigns was the last match of the 1903 season against Ireland, who put up a fierce battle before yielding to a try by J. E. Crabbie. It was during this season that the Scottish selectors went along to have a look at a schoolboy from Fettes College who had been receiving rave notices. They very much liked what they saw and decided that Kenneth Grant McLeod was just the man they needed in the centre for the forthcoming game against Wales. Unfortunately the boy had barely reached puberty and his headmaster, Dr Heard, refused permission to allow his charge to play. McLeod's opportunity came two years later when, at the age of seventeen, he was picked alongside his brother L. M. McLeod for the match against the touring All Blacks, and by all accounts played exceptionally well. But for McLeod and for Scotland, the best was yet to come.

1906–7 was Scotland's 'annus mirabilis'. It began with a victory over the Springboks at Hampden Park in front of a crowd of 32,000. The day of the match was wet and bitterly cold, and in the words of W. A. Miller, the Springbok forward, 'every southerner in the vicinity was groping for his nose and shivering like a dude on a dentist's doorstep.' From the outset it was obvious that handling would be out of the question, the ball being 'as slimy as a sewer eel', but these were conditions ideally suited to the burly Scots forwards led by 'Darkie' Bedell-Sivright. Tries by Grant McLeod and A. B. H. Purves gave the Scots victory, and afterwards the Springbok captain H. W. Carolin was full of praise for his opponents, 'We were beaten to a frazzle by a wonderful pack of forwards. They took complete control of the game and our backs had no chance of showing their merit.' Encouraged by this performance, the Scots went on to beat Wales, Ireland and England to take the Triple

Wilson Shaw – the man whose genius helped Scotland to a Triple Crown win in 1938. Restored to the captaincy for the final match of the season against England at Twickenham, Shaw played an outstanding part in the game, scoring two tries and creating countless other opportunities for his colleagues. It was thirty-three years before the Scots were again successful at Twickenham, and not since that date have Scotland won the Triple Crown

Murrayfield massacre – an all too familiar sight for the Scottish players as the South African prop 'Okey' Geffin adds to the Springboks' ever increasing score with a successful goal kick.

The match, which was played on 24 November 1951, created a world points scoring record in an international, the Springboks winning by 44 points to nil. This was the lowest point of Scotland's rugby fortunes although it was to be another three years before they won a match.

Left By the 1960s Scotland had unearthed some massive forwards, and here a group of them sweep downfield, apparently unopposed, in a match against France in Paris. In the foreground are the two locks Frans ten Bos and Mike Campbell-Lamerton, both standing over 6ft 4in and between them weighing around thirty-four stones. To the immediate right of Campbell-Lamerton is the Howe of Fife prop David Rollo who equalled the Scottish record of 40 caps set by Hawick's Hughie McLeod (extreme right of picture). McLeod, who first played for his club at the age of 18, came into the Scottish side in 1954, five years before Rollo's first international appearance, but then the two continued in harness until McLeod's retirement in 1962

Crown for the fifth time, and to sit astride the rugby world. Their ascendancy was, however, a brief one and eighteen years were to pass before the mythical trophy was once again theirs.

Like the other nations during World War I, Scotland lost many outstanding rugby players, but there were the select few who leapfrogged the years and played for their countries before and after the war. One such man was the irrepressible Gala forward Jock Wemyss, who won his first cap against Wales in 1914. Then came the war and Jock went to France where he was badly wounded. He returned home minus an eye, but he always maintained that he played better with one eye than with two, and in 1920 Jock was recalled to the Scottish side to play France in Paris. When he got into the changing room he noted that there were only fourteen jerseys hanging from the pegs, and further inspection revealed that the missing one was his own. On enquiring of an official where it was, he was told, 'Don't be bloody stupid Wemyss, you got your jersey six years ago.'

By the early 1920s the Scots had effectively filled the gaps left by the war, and in 1923 they went to Cardiff and gained their first victory at the ground since 1890. A try by Eric Liddell, who was later to break the world record for the 400 metres and win a gold medal at the 1924 Paris Olympics, put them on their way. But the two Scottish heroes that day were J. M. Bannerman and A. L. Gracie. Continuous rain beforehand had given the impression that the River Taff had been re-routed through the Arms Park. If so, it was a fiendishly cunning Welsh ploy because the conditions were perfectly suited to Tom Parker and his forwards. Early in the first half they tested the Scottish full back Dan Drysdale in the air and on the ground, but despite the conditions he remained firm, and all Wales had to show for a great deal of effort was an Albert Jenkins penalty. In the second half Liddell got his try to level the score, but Wales were soon back in the lead with a try by Clem Lewis which Jenkins

converted. Twenty minutes left and with Bannerman and his forwards now imbued with the spirit which had so distinguished their ancestors at Bannockburn, the Scots moved over to the attack. L. M. Stuart cut the Welsh lead to two points, then, the final whistle just a breath away, Gracie received the ball, beat three defenders and was over for the winning score. But even crossing the line was a hazardous business in Cardiff with the crowds sitting so close to the touchline, and Gracie was conscious of knocking out a little boy's teeth as he dived to score. Fortunately, the boy was a Scots supporter and he was delighted to make the sacrifice for such a worthy cause.

Neither Gracie nor Liddell was in the side two years later when the Scots ran out at Murrayfield for the first time. No fiction writer could have set the scene more dramatically for the opening. It was the Calcutta Cup, and England, led by Wavell Wakefield, were the Triple Crown and Championship holders. But Scotland had already beaten France 25–4 with the fabulous Ian Smith scoring four tries. At the after-match dinner Smith was sitting next to an admiring Frenchman who asked him how many seconds it took him to run 100 metres. Smith, who had not been particularly attentive to the question, thought that his neighbour was referring to the number of tries he had scored, and answered casually, 'Oh four or five I think.' 'Mon Dieu, Mon Dieu,' gasped the astonished Frenchman. The Scots went next to Swansea, and with their famous Oxford University threequarter line of Smith, G. P. S. MacPherson, G. G. Aitken and A. C. Wallace in devastating form, they won 24–14. Ireland were next on the list, going down 14–8 in Dublin.

The prospect of the Grand Slam brought 70,000 people to Murrayfield for this inaugural match. But as the minutes ticked by in the second half it looked as if the huge Scottish support was going to be denied a night of revelry. England were leading by six points when the Scots hit back with a try in

Left One of the finest wingers to have played for Scotland, Arthur Smith, in his British Lions garb, prepares to deal with the attentions of a Northern Transvaal player during the tour to South Africa in 1962. Smith, who captained the Lions during that tour, was Scotland's captain on fifteen occasions, and finished his international career with 33 caps. His appearance in the Scottish side coincided with the end of Scotland's horrendous run of defeats

Above A look of eager anticipation on the face of the Scottish captain and No. 8 Peter Brown as he prepares to launch himself at the English line during the match at Twickenham in 1971. It had been thirty-three years since the Scots had last won on the ground, but this game was to bring to an end the dismal run, the winning points being kicked by Brown in the closing minutes

the corner by Wallace, which A. C. Gillies miraculously converted. Just one point in it now, and during the last fifteen minutes the Scots carried out a saturation raid on the English line. Players were falling to the ground in sheer exhaustion as the pace began to take its toll. With minutes left, the Scottish fly half Herbert Waddell, realizing that his threequarters had nothing left to give, let fly with a drop goal which sailed between the posts to give the Scots the Calcutta Cup, the Triple Crown and the Championship. This was the perfect baptism for a ground which today boasts one of the finest playing surfaces in the world, underground heating, and a world record attendance of 104,000 – that for the game against Wales in 1975.

The only blight on the 1925 season was the Scots decision not to play Cliff Porter's All Blacks – as European Champions they would have proved worthy opponents for the 'Invincibles'. Their refusal to play arose from a difference of opinion with the Rugby Union, who had made all the arrangements for the tour, despite the agreement that major tours should only be handled by the International Board.

Without ever reaching the heights of 1925, Scotland did produce some very fine sides in the thirties, notably the Triple Crown winners of 1933 and 1938. In 1933, of course, Ian Smith was still appearing on the Scottish wing, and when he ran on to the field at Lansdowne Road for the final match of that season, it was his thirty-second and last appearance for his country. Although he was injured early in the game, the Scots won and took their seventh Triple Crown. By one of those odd quirks of history Scotland returned to Lansdowne Road twenty-nine years later with another winger called Smith in their side, and he too was winning his thirty-second cap. This time it was Arthur Smith who went on to become the most capped Scottish back. 1938 will ever be remembered as Wilson Shaw's year, when he jinked and bobbed his way through the

The Scottish cap record stood at 40 until 1975 when Sandy Carmichael, the West of Scotland prop who had replaced David Rollo in the Scottish side in 1967, overtook the record previously held by both Rollo and Hughie McLeod. In this Calcutta Cup match at Murrayfield, Carmichael forces his way past the Bristol hooker John Pullin (No. 2), who is currently the leading cap winner in English rugby with 42. The Scots won the match 16–14, with full back Andy Irvine kicking the winning points in the last minute of the match

English defence at Twickenham to score the tries which made certain Scotland's victory. It was Shaw's greatest game for his country and fitting that he should be leading the side to their first win at Twickenham for twelve years. His first try, the result of a superb piece of opportunism, came when he snapped up a loose ball and swerved past the England full-back Parker to touch down in the corner. The second ensured a Scottish triumph and was simply the result of Shaw's genius as he ran thirty yards swerving and side-stepping through the English ranks. It was to be thirty-three years before the Scots won again at Twickenham.

The Scottish club system, as we have seen, was based on the schools, and only a minority of the clubs at this time were 'open', with the result that very few fresh ideas were circulating within the Scottish game. The former pupils' sides would consist of players who had been together since their schooldays, adopting the same tactics as men as they had done as boys under their games masters. Even the Border clubs tended to field home-grown talent, and so poor was the standard at the universities that the student from Edinburgh or Glasgow would choose rather to play for his F.P. side. Gradually this in-breeding began to affect the national team, and the Scots found it increasingly difficult to keep pace with the other countries. In addition, there was no equivalent in Scotland to the English County Championship, and many players found the gulf between club and international football too much for them. When Scotland, against all the odds, beat a much heralded Welsh XV by 19 points to nil in 1951, it was their last victory against Wales, or any other country for that matter, for four years. During this time they suffered seventeen consecutive defeats.

The search for talent was mounted on a massive scale, and in one season 30 players were capped. No country was safe from this manhunt, and cartoons appeared in newspapers and magazines depicting men in grass skirts and carrying spears, queueing up at

Murrayfield for a trial. But with such a tiny rugby playing community in Scotland, the national selectors have been forced to cast their net wide in search of suitable material, and they have not always been over particular about lineage. In recent years, for instance, they uncarthed the massive Frans Herman ten Bos who had been a pupil at Fettes College in Edinburgh. Finding very little in his name which would convince doubters of his Scottish blood, they searched further into his parentage. But they were out of luck – both his parents were Dutch and to make matters worse he had been born in England. The thought of ten Bos taking up where Marques and Currie had left off in the English second row was enough to convince the Scottish selectors that, on this occasion, Fettes College would have to act 'in loco parentis'. Throughout his playing career ten Bos had to take some fearful abuse from club secretaries who found it impossible to spell his name correctly in the match programmes. This was particularly the case when he went with an Oxbridge team to Japan, and in the programmes for consecutive games he appeared as, ten Oz, ten Bob, and tin Bin. But under the fourth alias, tan Pax, he obstinately refused to take the field. Then there was Peter Stagg, at 6ft 10in the tallest man ever to play international rugby, who was also of Dutch extraction and who claimed never to have heard of Scotland until he played for them. But the Scots got noble service from both – ten Bos played in seventeen internationals, most of them alongside the formidable Mike Campbell-Lamerton, while Stagg won twenty-eight caps and went with the 1968 Lions to South Africa.

To return to the troubled fifties, the nadir of Scotland's fortunes was surely reached when the Springboks beat Scotland by 44 points to nil at Murrayfield in 1951. By the time the All Blacks arrived three years later, however, there was light at the end of the tunnel. Admittedly the Scots lost the match, their fourteenth on the trot, but it was only by a Bob Scott penalty goal to nil. The side was led by the lowland farmer Douglas Elliot, who had been out of action for six weeks with an injury, but who had been the mainstay of the Scottish pack since 1947. He was rated as being one of the world's finest wing forwards by no less a person than Cliff Morgan – 'to be tackled by him,' recalls the Welsh maestro ruefully, 'was like being trapped in a vice.' Elliot's only flaw was that he occasionally required motivation, and as often as not a member of his own side would be detailed to provide the necessary stimulus with a well directed boot to the buttocks.

The game against New Zealand signalled the second international appearance of the Hawick prop Hughie McLeod, who went on to set the record for Scottish caps, beating the previous record held by J. M. Bannerman. It is a remarkable fact that the three leading cap winners in Scotland have all been props – David Rollo, the Fife farmer, who formed a lengthy and profitable front row partnership with McLeod and Norman Bruce, equalled McLeod's record of 40, and A. B. Carmichael, Rollo's successor in the Scottish side, has gone on to beat them both. Perhaps it is not so surprising, though, when you consider that the position requires the highest degree of physical maturity – a maturity born out of age and experience. Props are a strange breed whose satisfaction comes from the total domination of an opponent. Victory or defeat for them is not the result on the scoreboard, but the number of tight heads won or lost. Their pursuits tend to be physical rather than cultural, and Norman Mair, who played four times in Scotland's front row and is now rugby correspondent of the *Scotsman*, recounts the tale of one Scottish prop who was seen by some team mates to be admiring his impressive physique in the mirror – 'Look at Adonis over there,' observed one of them. 'What do you mean A donis?' retorted the prop indignantly. 'THE Donis.' The fact remains that props are the foundation of any side – without them little can be achieved and

Scotland have indeed been fortunate in having men like McLeod, Rollo, Carmichael and Ian McLaughlan at their disposal.

On 5 February 1955, a 14–8 win over Wales brought to an end the rash of defeats which had plagued Scotland for four years. By then, of course, some steps had been taken towards improving the standard at international level. First, there was a more consistent selection policy; secondly, some very useful players were beginning to make their presence felt – men like the late Arthur Smith, winner of 33 caps, and one of the finest wings to have played for Scotland. A man who devoted a great deal of time to the game, he was ever ready to advise and encourage players of the future, and university rugby in particular owes him a very great debt of gratitude. Looking back to that game against Wales in 1955, he remembered that most of the side were raw beginners and knew very little of each other's play. But the establishment of the Inter District Championship in 1953–4 helped to bridge the gap between club and international football, whilst giving the players a greater insight into each other's methods and ideas.

As the 1960s approached so did Scotland gain in confidence. There was a solid nucleus of tight forwards, loose forwards of the calibre of G. K. Smith of Kelso and backs like Arthur Smith and K. J. F. Scotland, who reached the height of his career in New Zealand in 1959 when he played in arguably the finest Lions back division ever fielded, and what's more played in every back position during the tour. But Scotland was a full back, and an attacking one at that. His intrusions into the threequarter line were models of split second timing – an example to all who have followed. Like another great Scottish full back, Dan Drysdale, he was a product of Heriot's School in Edinburgh – a school which has provided eight full backs for the national side. The latest member of the elite band is Andy Irvine, whose entry into international rugby was as dramatic and exciting as anything seen at Murrayfield.

An aerial view of the Scottish full back Andy Irvine, one of the most exciting runners in the modern game. He came into the Scottish XV against the All Blacks in 1973 and, apart from a brief interlude on the wing, has been his country's number one choice at full back. His 156 points for the Lions during the tour to South Africa in 1974 was a record for a Lions player in that country. Irvine's club, Heriots F.P., has a proud record of supplying full backs to the national team – he is the eighth to play in that position for his country. Previous incumbents have been Dan Drysdale, Jimmy Kerr, Ian Thomson, Tommy Gray, Ken Scotland, Colin Blaikie and Ian Smith

The Scots by nature are a pretty conservative lot – they are people who tend to be suspicious of change, and this has been apparent in their attitude towards rugby. In the past Scotland's administrators have dug their heels in about the wearing of numbers which they regarded as professional practice; about allowing players who have turned professional back inside the grounds of their former clubs; about substitutes, coaching and leagues. And yet in many areas they have been pioneers. The first international short tour, for instance, was undertaken by Scotland to South Africa in 1960. Led by Gordon Waddell, the London Scottish and Cambridge University stand off half, the side played three matches, losing one, the international, by 18 points to 10. Since then the Scots have travelled to the Argentine in 1969, where they played two torrid internationals, losing the first and winning the second; to Australia in 1970, where they went down by a record 23–3 margin in Sydney, and to New Zealand in 1975, where they played the All Blacks in conditions more suited to an aquatic extravaganza than to a rugby match, and lost 24–0. Admittedly, the short tour has its drawbacks in that players have to become acclimatized to the strange conditions far too quickly, but at a time when it is becoming difficult for employers to release international players who are called upon to take part in major tours, the short tour has an important part to play, and the Scots can take pride in the fact that they were the pathfinders.

In the matter of leagues, too, they have been successful. In 1971 the Scottish Rugby Union voted to a man against the introduction of competitive football, but did exactly the reverse when the subject came up for discussion the following year. Sensibly, though, they have proceeded with caution, and the early results have been encouraging. But in other areas the Scots have been reluctant innovators. Very much against the introduction of substitutes in international matches, it was ironical that they should be the first country to benefit when Gordon Connell was injured in the match against France at Stade Colombes in 1969, and was replaced by the Gordonian's scrum half Ian McCrae. There was no question that it won the match for Scotland, as the French attackers hit a threadbare Scottish defence. But the Scots, aided by some unbelievable lapses in the French handling, held out until half time when, battered and bewildered, they huddled around their skipper Jim Telfer. The sight of this prompted a French journalist to enquire whether they were holding a team talk or a prayer meeting. The winning try by Telfer after some good work by McCrae must have convinced him that the Scots were indeed in receipt of Divine assistance.

The Scottish Rugby Union has approached the whole question of coaching with much the same wariness, and when Bill Dickenson was brought in for the Welsh match in 1971, it was made clear that he was not a coach but merely an 'adviser to the captain'. To everyone else in the country, of course, he was regarded as the national coach, and perhaps the Scottish performance that day convinced the S.R.U. that coaching had a future. Leading 18–14 with seconds to go, the Scots looked home and dry. It had been a magnificent match with the lead changing hands several times. Unhappily for the Scottish following it was to do so once more before the final whistle. Out went the ball to the Welsh wizard Gerald Davies, who was over for a try in the corner. But with the conversion to come Wales were still a point behind. As it turned out, the Grand Slam depended upon the kick which was entrusted to John Taylor. Calmly, the London Welshman planted the ball high between the posts for what was later described as 'the greatest conversion since St Paul'. Some measure of consolation came Scotland's way later in the season when they went to Twickenham and registered their first win on the ground since 1938. The following week they played England again – this time at Murrayfield to celebrate the Centenary of

the first international between the two countries at Raeburn Place, and again the Scots won, by a record 26–6.

In 1973 the S.R.U. celebrated their Centenary in much the same way as England had done two years previously, by bringing together many of the world's top players for a short tour. In addition they held an outstandingly successful World Seven-a-Side Tournament at Murrayfield in which England beat Ireland 22–18 in the final. But the Triple Crown was last won in 1938, and the feat which would have greatly enhanced the Centenary season, once again eluded them. It eluded them two years later when they went to Twickenham for the last match of the season, having earlier beaten both Ireland and Wales. This time, alas, there was no Wilson Shaw to work his magic, the Scots were beaten and the chance was gone. Despite these setbacks there is a mood of optimism abroad in Scottish rugby – competition is keen, the national leagues are thriving, and surely the time is not too far distant when Scotland will, once again, produce a team to challenge the best in the world.

4 GREAT GAMES OF IRELAND

Ireland had made a poor start to international rugby; but the 1890s were to bring about a remarkable transformation in Irish fortunes with two Triple Crown wins. Photographed here is the Irish team of 1898, the year before the second Triple Crown triumph. Louis Magee, the most talented half back of the day, is seated on the ground on the right of the picture. It was his miraculous tackle on the Welshman R. T. Skrimshire during the 1899 match which saved the day for his side and brought the Triple Crown to Ireland

Although the Irish teams of the 1920s failed in their Triple Crown and Championship attempts, they did produce some very fine players and an interesting assortment of characters. W. E. Crawford for instance, seen holding the ball, was no great respecter of authority during his playing days, but was later to become President of the IRFU.

Like J. D. Clinch, another character of the period, Crawford won 30 caps. Clinch can be found on the extreme right of the back row bending the ear of a colleague whose boots appear to be in need of some immediate attention

For the great Gaels of Ireland
Are the men that God made mad,
For all their wars are merry,
And all their songs are sad.

G. K. Chesterton

ACCORDING TO POPULAR opinion the Irish play football because it appeals to their belligerent nature – a theory endorsed by J. J. McCarthy, one of the most entertaining of chroniclers, who wrote towards the end of the last century, 'Football in Ireland may be said to consist of three parts – Rugbeian, Associationist and Gallic. The rule of play in these three organisations may be defined as follows – in Rugby you kick the ball; in Association you kick the man when you cannot kick the ball; in Gallic you kick the ball when you cannot kick the man.' But in his opinion the Irishmen who turned up at the Oval on 19 February 1875 for the first international against England were in no fit state to kick anything – he described them as being 'immaculately innocent of training'.

While it may have been true that these Irish representatives fell some way short of physical perfection, it was also true that Irish rugby at this time lacked any real organization. A difference of opinion between North and South meant that international progress was hindered. The rift which began in 1874 came about when the Irish Rugby Union was formed in Dublin. The Belfastmen felt slighted and, in a fit of pique, formed their own 'Northern Union'. But five years later the differences were forgotten, the unions became one, and despite the social, political and religious upheavals down the years, they have remained united.

The inaugural meeting of the Irish Union was held on 14 December 1874 at Lawrence's sports shop in Grafton Street, Dublin, and at the meeting the Lord Lieutenant, the Duke of Abercorn, was elected President. Although the North then broke away to form their own union, there remained some measure of co-operation between the two, and at the first meeting of the Northern Union, it was arranged that 'physical assistance be given Ireland in the forthcoming international match which is to be played at Kennington Oval'. Not that this 'physical assistance' amounted to very much in the eyes of Jacques McCarthy, 'Almost everyone of the North men wore beards,' he wrote, 'and Ash was like Falstaff – "a mountain of Mummy".' This decrepitude apart it appears that there was a shortage of manpower – two Irishmen failing to turn up. It was only to be expected in the circumstances that Ireland would lose, and this they duly did by two goals and a try to nil. When the sides met for the first time on Irish soil ten months later, it was England who won again, this time by a goal and a try to nil. The game was played at the Leinster Cricket Ground in Dublin, and it was not until England's visit to Dublin in 1878 that Lansdowne Road was first used for a rugby international.

The previous year international relations had opened with Scotland, and on this occasion the match was played not in Dublin, but in Belfast. Neither the venue nor the match was much to the liking of the prolific McCarthy. According to him Belfast was a city of unceasing rain, which presumably suited the amphibious Scottish forwards more than it did the home side. At any rate, the Scots won by six goals and two tries to nil and, if McCarthy is to be believed, they were a pretty rough lot. He went on to point out, however, that Scottish aggression was not the sole reason for defeat. At the time the game was played the dispute between North and South was at its bitter height, and the South had contributed only two men to the cause, both of whom, in McCarthy's opinion might have been much better off at home in bed. He had a happier story to report four years later when the Irish achieved their first victory, beating Scotland in Belfast by a goal to a try. This time, McCarthy records, the sun was shining in the 'Northern Athens' and the Irishmen had learned the tactic of being first with

A caption from the *Picture Post* of 17 March 1951 sums up that season. *'This year, the title "Team of the Year" undoubtedly goes to Ireland. Apart from a superior record to their rivals the Irish team have done more to revive open fast play than any other international team.'* This was the year in which they won the Five Nations Championship, a victory which followed hard upon two Triple Crown wins in 1948 (when they won the Grand

their retaliation – 'they commenced fiercely, but when Spunner and big Jock Graham had gotten black eyes and a certain hot Scotsman had come second best out of an independent boxing match with David Browning, milder methods were adopted.'

Nowhere has Celtic rivalry been more intense than in the annual rugby encounters between Ireland and Wales, and the first match in 1882 set the trend. So disgusted were two Irishmen with the fury of the proceedings that they walked off the field, an action which may well have accounted for the Welsh victory by two goals and two tries to nil. The fixture was discontinued for a year, but in 1884 the two sides prepared once again for battle. Once again Ireland found themselves a couple of men short – this time it was simply that the players hadn't bothered to put in an appearance, and two Welshmen, F. Purdon of Swansea and H. M. Jordan of Newport, were loaned to the opposition for the afternoon. Their contribution to the game that day has not been fully documented, but as Wales won by a drop goal and two tries to nil, they presumably did nothing to embarrass the Land of their Fathers.

On the domestic front by this time the Irish clubs in both the North and South were getting themselves organized. The Leinster Senior Cup competition had been established in 1882 with Trinity being the first winners – a victory celebrated by 'blazing tar barrels, rockets, squibs and all sorts of jollifications by the students in the college square'. The Ulster Cup was established three years later, and North of Ireland were the initial winners. In Munster it was the Provincial Cup which went first to Bandon in 1886, and Galway Town were the winners of the Connacht Cup when it was introduced in 1896. Competition for the various trophies normally took place (and still does) in the last two months of the rugby calendar, and consequently cup matches produced the climax to the season. But the internationals provided the initial stimulus,

Slam) and 1949. Irish teams at that time owed much to the back row play of Des O'Brien, Bill McKay and Jim McCarthy, and to the brilliance of Jack Kyle at outside half. Here O'Brien and McCarthy lead a footrush in the 1951 match against England, which Ireland won 3–0; and after the match Kyle completes a joyful day for some young Irish fans

and by 1887 the Irish following desired nothing more than a victory over England.

Since matches had first started between the countries, Ireland had gone twelve consecutive games without a win. It was a sequence which was soon to end. The side of 1887 had the qualities of which heroes are made. One of their number, a gentleman by the name of John Macauley, made the ultimate sacrifice for his country. He had been chosen for the English game but had exhausted his annual leave. A quick glance at his Conditions of Employment told him that there was still one avenue left open, and that was to take honeymoon leave. Macauley did the only thing possible in the circumstances – he got married and arrived at the ground in time for the match accompanied by his bride. Another cavalier of that team was D. B. Walkington, a full back from North of Ireland who was so short sighted in one eye that he took the field wearing a monocle. It was written about him, 'he is as good as he can be on a bright day, but in the dark his sight tells terribly against him.' It must have been a bright day in Dublin for the match against England – the Irish won by two goals to nil.

The first fifteen years of international football in Ireland had contained more bad than good, but by the nineties things had improved. In that decade they won the Triple Crown twice, in 1894 and 1899, the Championship in 1896, and had the great good fortune to be able to call upon players like Sam Lee, C. V. Rooke, Tommy Crean, A. D. Clinch and Louis Magee. The match against Wales in Cardiff which gave Ireland their second Triple Crown was a tempestuous affair. So large was the crowd that it had spilled on to the pitch, and when the Welsh full back W. J. Bancroft was tackled into touch, he came into contact with some of the overflow and had to leave the field badly injured. It was a game of thrilling runs and last ditch tackles, and in the end it was a try by the Irish winger G. P. Doran which settled the issue. As the new century dawned,

however, it was Wales who forged ahead with four consecutive wins, and although the Irish record up to World War I was by no means a poor one, the Triple Crown escaped them until 1948.

In 1920, despite the 'Troubles' in the South which had grumbled above and below the surface between 1916 and 1922, England went once again to Lansdowne Road and won the first of the post-war encounters by 14 points to 11. But if the immediate post-war years were inglorious in terms of results, Ireland did at least contribute several characters to brighten the scene. One of them was the Lansdowne full back W. E. Crawford, who was first called to his country's colours at the relatively mature age of 28, and who went on to win 30 caps. Described by Wavell Wakefield as a 'brooding intelligence', he was reputed to possess the combined skills of a magician and a ventriloquist, and there were countless opponents who would testify to hearing a disembodied Belfast voice urging them to part company with the ball. As a sort of 'pater familias' he had some rare birds in his brood. There was, for instance, J. D. 'Jammy' Clinch, son of A. D. Clinch and a forward of considerable substance who had little truck with the finer points of the game. Like Crawford he won 30 caps, 7 of them against Wales, and he recalls with pride running on to the field at Swansea before a match and hearing the outraged appeals from the local support, 'Send that bastard off ref.' At no time in his career did Clinch ever lay claim to being the most mobile of players, and there was one occasion in particular when his comparative lack of pace was cruelly exposed. He was taking part in a charity match, and for some unaccountable reason found himself in the three-quarter line playing alongside that Scottish streak of lightning, Ian Smith. Whether by accident or design, Clinch succeeded in getting through the game without once giving Smith a pass, and at the after match function he was thanked profusely by the opposition

A balletic sequence from Ireland's match against England at Twickenham in 1964, featuring the Irish full back Tom Kiernan, whose 54 caps gained over a spell of thirteen years make him the longest serving full back in the world. During these appearances he scored 158 points, and as captain of the 1968 Lions in South Africa, he scored all but

three of the tourists' 38 points in
the four tests. In the background
of the picture is a youthful
Mike Gibson making his
international debut. He played
that day as an outside half and
helped his side to their first
victory at Twickenham since 1948

for his tactics which had won them the match. Unabashed, Clinch replied that while Ian Smith might be known in Scotland as the 'Flying Scotsman', he himself was known in Ireland as the 'Irish Mail', and that was only slightly faster than the Irish female.

By the mid-twenties, Ireland had gathered together a marvellous side. Apart from Crawford and Clinch there was George Stephenson – a devastating tackler and a fine runner. First capped in 1920 he played in the Irish XV without a break for nine years, until injury ruled him out of the game against Scotland. Alongside him in the threequarter line were the Hewitt brothers, Frank and Tom, and at half back a superb combination, Eugene Davy and Mark Sugden. In the forwards there were W. F. (Horsey) Browne and at number 8 George Beamish, who was to gain distinction as an air ace, and later became Air Marshal Sir George Beamish.

The Irish were the first international side to feel the weight of the 1924–5 All Blacks, but nonetheless put up a gallant display before losing 6–0. The following year they beat England, Scotland and France only to have their Grand Slam hopes dashed by Wales. The premature retirement of the Hewitts perhaps prevented the side from fulfilling the promise of that 1926 season when they shared the Championship with Scotland. At any rate, Ireland had to be content once again with a share of the Championship in 1927, and there was still no Triple Crown to show for all their efforts. By this time the team was beginning to break up, although many of them were still together for the game against England at Twickenham on 13 February 1929. Ireland's victory by 6 points to 5 was their first on the ground, and the result was in no small way due to tries by Davy and Sugden, and to George Stephenson who brought off a try-saving tackle in the dying seconds despite having several ribs fractured earlier in the match. The relieved Irish supporters demonstrated their joy at the end of the game by throwing their seat cushions around Twickenham in what one newspaper described as 'a spate of uninhibited hibernianism'.

Like England and Scotland, Ireland suffered a slight regression in the 1930s after the glories of the previous decade, but there was one outright Championship win in 1935 – the first for thirty-six years. How fruitful those years would have been for Ireland had it not been for the presence of Wales! Seven times they had proved to be the final obstacle in the way of Ireland's Triple Crown hopes, and four of them were in the 1930s. In 1939 there was one last chance for them before the whole of Europe was plunged into war. They began their campaign at Twickenham and beat England 5–0. Then on a rainy day in Dublin they triumphed 12–3 over Scotland, but before 30,000 people at Ravenhill in Belfast, hopes of the Triple Crown dissolved as the Welsh forwards completely outplayed their opposite numbers to lay the foundation of a 7–0 win.

A casual observer going along to Lansdowne Road for the unofficial international against England in 1946 might have been forgiven for not knowing too much about the young outside half who was playing for the Irish XV that day, although a glance at the programme notes might have given him some insight into the future. 'JACK KYLE. Age 19. The discovery of the season. He was on the Ulster Schools XV two years ago and proved himself to be in the top class by his great display for Ulster against the Kiwis in November, subsequently confirming that form against the Army. A particularly straight strong runner, he looks to have a brilliant future.' Two years later, with Kyle's assistance, Ireland won the Triple Crown and the Championship for the first, and up to the date of writing, the last time. As had happened so often before, Ireland faced Wales in the final match of the season, having already beaten the other countries, and with France now happily restored to Championship status the season carried the additional incentive of the Grand Slam. The

All Willie John McBride's considerable determination is concentrated into breaking free from the clutches of England's Budge Rogers during the 1969 match in Dublin. McBride was then half way through an international career which brought him a world record number of caps, five Lions tours, and just about every honour that the game can bestow. In his autobiography McBride concludes, *'Many great things have happened in my life, but I can say without hesitation that nothing has occurred of greater importance than that I was privileged to wear the green jersey of Ireland. May what it means, and what it stands for, and its glory never fade!'*

Welsh side contained many great names – Haydn Tanner, Bleddyn Williams, Ken Jones, Billy Cleaver and Rees Stephens. But Ireland had Kyle and he was in irrepressible form. After thirteen minutes he broke through the Welsh defence to send Barney Mullan charging over the line for a try, and although Wales equalized, it was a try from Ireland's Chris Daly which released the frustrations of half a century. Between 1948 and 1951, Ireland played seventeen matches winning eleven, drawing two and losing four; they won the Grand Slam once, the Triple Crown twice in successive years, and the Championship three times.

Kyle, of course, was not the only star in the constellation at this time. There was the skipper Karl Mullen at hooker, a magnificent back row trio of Jim McCarthy, Bill McKay and Des O'Brien in the forwards, and in the centre Noel Henderson. But the direction came from Kyle whose great strength lay in his breathtaking acceleration over the first twenty yards and an uncanny knack of knowing where and when to breach the opposing defence. Nowadays this self-effacing man lives and works as a surgeon in Zambia, and only rarely does he make the journey home to his native Belfast.

Kyle won his last cap in 1958, by which time another personality had installed himself in the Irish side. He was the Old Belvedere winger A. J. F. O'Reilly of the sharp wit and even sharper brain who is now

Above The Has Bean – the end of Tony O'Reilly's extraordinary international career, a career which had begun in 1955 and had brought him glittering success both at home and abroad. Then business had intervened, and proving himself to be equally successful in this sphere, he rose to become President of Heinz. On his way to that exalted position he was recalled to the team after a gap of seven years for the 1970 encounter with England at Twickenham, and here he is, boot bandaged, lending his weight to the Irish cause. England won 9–3

Right Two of the best – Mike Gibson of Ireland and Mervyn Davies of Wales in opposition at the Arms Park. Since he first came into the Irish side in 1964, Gibson has become recognized as the outstanding threequarter in modern rugby and, along with Jack Kyle, the most complete footballer ever produced by Ireland. Davies, who, in Colin Meads' opinion, was the finest of the Lions forwards in 1971, developed into the world's leading No. 8 and captained Wales to their Grand Slam triumph in 1976 before illness cut short a magnificent career

Right Alan Duggan, captured on film by the late Dermot Barry for the *Irish Times*, flying in for one of his thirteen international tries – the highest try tally by an Irish winger

President of Heinz – an immensely success-ful and wealthy man. Between 1955 and 1963 he won 28 caps and went on two Lions tours establishing try-scoring records on both. But in that latter year, he suffered a series of injuries, and with his business com-mitments occupying more of his time, he disappeared from the international rugby scene. The Irish selectors however, had not yet finished with him and, unbelievably, he was resurrected for the match against England at Twickenham in 1970 – fifteen years after winning his first cap. Perhaps it was considered that prosperity in business was an accurate barometer of a man's playing ability, but whatever the reasons, when Bill Brown withdrew from the side on the Thursday before the match, O'Reilly was the man chosen to replace him. As the team piled out of the bus for the Friday training session at the grounds of the Honourable Artillery Company, a chauf-feur-driven Rolls Royce bearing O'Reilly to his ordeal slipped silently through the main gates. There was something Gilbertian about the whole affair, but the next day it was put into perspective when O'Reilly arrived at the ground to find a telegram awaiting him. It had been sent by Johnny Quirke, the former Irish scrum half, and it read, 'Heinz beanz are haz beanz'. The match itself was completely undistinguished both for Ireland and for the 'Bean Baron'. He recalls with alarm the one occasion when he was forced into activity – 'I found myself at the last moment reduced to bravery. A long English footrush was terminated when quite out of character – I dived at the feet of the England pack . . . As I was emerging from momentary unconsciousness, I heard a loud (and let me confess) Irish voice shouting from the popular terrace; ". . . and kick his bloody chauffeur while you're at it!".' (Sean Diffley: *The Men in Green*.)

The continued influence of the univer-sities in Irish rugby has meant that the national side has often looked more like a collection of Mensa members than a football

'Big and ignorant – that's all that's required of a second row forward' – one of Ray McLoughlin's theories which might bring some dissent from Willie John McBride, standing to his right in the picture. Both men made their international debuts in the same match – against England in 1962 – and both went on to give magnificent service not only to their country, but also to the game

team. O'Reilly had with him in the 1950s and early 1960s the Cambridge 'Blue' Andrew Mulligan – an entertaining combination both on and off the field. They were followed by the Connacht prop Ray McLoughlin, a man with an intelligence quotient of around 180 and mathematically perfected scrummaging technique. He was made captain in 1965 and brought some much needed discipline to the Irish side, but his thinking tended to be on a higher plane than the average individual, and the appointment was not an entirely successful one. Perhaps he attempted to achieve too much too quickly.

He had as his lieutenant that year a young Cambridge student C. M. H. Gibson, who on his international debut the previous season had played no small part in Ireland's first victory over England at Twickenham for sixteen years. On that occasion he played as a fly half, but it is as a centre that he will probably be best remembered – especially in New Zealand with the 1971 Lions where, under the astute coaching of Carwyn James, he was able to demonstrate the full range of his skills both in attack and in defence. Most of all it was his defensive genius which marked him out as the outstanding back of the tour. Alex Vesey in his biography of Colin Meads quotes the great man as saying, 'the real king of the Lions was Mike Gibson. He was the defensive rock on which our ship foundered. I would say that eighty per cent of our back movements came unstuck through Gibson's quickness, courage, dedication and skill.' That, coming from one of the world's most famed forwards, is no mean praise. He is, along with Kyle, the most gifted natural rugby player ever to have played for Ireland, and certainly ranks as one of the greatest of the present-day footballers.

Ireland has never lacked leaders of quality. The first Irishman to captain a Lions side was Dr Tom Smyth, who took the 1910 British party to South Africa. Of the last five Lions teams to tour South Africa in fact, four of them have been led by Irishmen, while Karl

Mullen (1950) and Ronnie Dawson (1959) have skippered Lions sides in New Zealand. In South Africa, after Smyth came Sam Walker in 1938, R. H. Thompson in 1955, Tom Kiernan in 1968, and the man in charge of the unbeaten side in 1974 was Willie John McBride. He was making his fifth Lions tour, and when he retired from international rugby the following season after thirteen years, he had amassed 63 caps – a world record. One of the outstanding lock forwards of all time, he could not have finished his career on a higher note. Having helped his country to an outright win in the 1974 Five Nations Championship, he led the Lions unbeaten through South Africa – how sweet this success must have been after his disappointments with previous Lions sides in that country. The following season it was the Irish Centenary, and although Ireland failed to achieve any honours, Willie John celebrated his penultimate appearance with his first try for his country. It was in the game against France, and when McBride dived in triumph over the French line near the end of the game the Lansdowne Road crowd could contain themselves no longer. They ran on to the field to pay tribute to the man who had given them so much pleasure throughout the years. 'The show must go on', was one of McBride's favourite phrases when the going began to get a bit rough on tour, but when he walked from the field at Cardiff on 15 of March 1975 having made his 63rd and last appearance in an Irish jersey, it was clear that the 'show' had lost one of its brightest stars.

5 MEN OF THE VALLEYS

A. J. Gould (top) and W. J. Bancroft (middle) were both legendary figures in the early development of Welsh rugby. Gould, who won 27 caps, was instrumental in getting Wales to adopt the four threequarter system. Any doubts that he himself may have harboured about the system were dispelled in 1893, when under his captaincy Wales won the Triple Crown for the first time. His rugby career was brought to a premature end in 1897 when he retired following allegations of professionalism made by the other home countries. W. J. Bancroft, a fearless full back, was capped 33 times in that position – a record which stood until 1976 when J. P. R. Williams, who possesses so many of the old master's qualities, created a new record of caps for a Welsh full back. Gwyn Nicholls (bottom), was known as Prince of Centres. His presence in the Welsh side coincided with an unequalled run of success. He postponed his retirement to captain Wales in their memorable match against the All Blacks, and was still playing the following season when his club, Cardiff, recorded a remarkable 17–0 victory over the Springboks. Willie Llewellyn, who played alongside Nicholls in the national side, said simply of him, *'He was the perfect player.'*

RUGBY, LIKE SINGING, is a national instinct in Wales; the harmony of a male voice choir is musically flawless, and yet how many can actually read the dots on a sheet of music? Similarly in the early days of rugby before squad sessions, coaching and the like, the village team took the field every week and played as practice and experience had taught them. It was Gwyn Nicholls, a prince amongst centres, who wrote, 'In an ideal Welsh game you really see fifteen great chess masters working in partnership and without consultation, each man intuitively knowing not only the best thing to be done, but that the other fellows know it also, and are falling or have fallen into their place accordingly.'

Quick of mind and muscle, Welshmen tended to be short and wiry with their centre of gravity closer to the ground than rugbymen from other countries; hence they developed the art of dodging, and from the outset the game in Wales was based on attack. When a member of the Swansea side of the 1890s was asked about the defensive qualities of his team he replied, 'I couldn't tell you. Ever since I've been playing for the club we've been attacking.'

Although it is essentially a game of the people with many of its greatest exponents coming from the working classes, it appears that rugby was brought to the Principality by young Englishmen with a public school and university education. At the beginning of the 1870s there were no official rugby clubs, but by the 1880s all the main towns in the industrial south proudly boasted a team. Of the major clubs Neath was the first to be formed in 1871 followed by Llanelli, Swansea, Newport and Cardiff. Interest grew, large crowds came to watch matches, and the establishment of the South Wales Challenge Cup in 1887 added the competitive edge. The local rivalry on the terraces was often more heated than the exchanges on the field, and one final between Cardiff and Llanelli had to be abandoned after a disillusioned group of supporters had made off

Above The 1930s produced several outstanding Welsh players following the depressions of the previous decade. The best British full back of the era was the London Welshman Vivian Jenkins, seen here taking a pot shot at goal in the 1934 encounter against Ireland. It was in this match that he made history by becoming the first full back to score a try in an international

Top right It takes a good deal more than a spot of cold weather to discourage the Welsh from playing their rugby. Prior to the match against England in 1893, Cardiff Arms Park was completely frostbound and there was speculation as to whether the English side would actually make the journey to Cardiff. But arrangements were already in hand to burn coal fires in braziers and when the England team went to the ground on the eve of the match they saw *'50 fire devils blazing furiously, with hordes of small boys darting in and out among them like devil dancers.* Despite the conditions, the game was played and victory went to Wales 12–11. The same method was used sixty-three years later in an attempt to get the ground fit for the game against Scotland

Right On 28 September 1935, Swansea took the field against Jack Manchester's All Blacks with two schoolboy half backs – W. T. H. Davies and Haydn Tanner. Both played brilliantly and helped Swansea win the match 11–3. It was only the second time that the All Blacks had been beaten in Britain in sixty-five years and it ensured a place in history for both youngsters. Willie Davies joined the Rugby League ranks and won the Lance Todd Memorial Trophy, awarded to the outstanding player in the professional game. Tanner remained an amateur and won 25 caps, 12 of them after World War 11. He is seen here playing for Cardiff against Harlequins at Twickenham

with the match ball. By 1887 the first class clubs had retired from the competition, but during its brief existence the Challenge Cup had done much to stimulate the Welsh feeling for the game.

It was with a certain amount of envy that the Welsh watched the success of the international matches between England, Scotland and Ireland, but without an official governing body it was not possible for them to participate. In March 1880 a meeting was held at the Tenby Hotel in Swansea, and the South Wales Football Union, which had been formed some five years earlier, was dissolved to be replaced by the Welsh Rugby Union. The Earl of Jersey became the first President, and Richard Mullock, an outstanding administrator of the day, was appointed Honorary Secretary and Treasurer.

Having obtained the necessary credentials, Wales made haste to join the international circuit, and on 19 February 1881 they played their first representative match against England at Blackheath. Not only did they lose the match by seven goals, six tries and a drop goal to nil, but they lost the fixture for a year. An article in the *Field* gave a fairly accurate summary of the Welsh effort: 'Looked at from whatever point, it is impossible to congratulate the team on their first match with England, unless it was in their pluck in coming so far with the prospect of almost certain defeat.'

Such was Welsh resilience, however, that their first international triumph came against Ireland at Lansdowne Road the next year. In the light of subsequent events it seems unbelievable that the Irish could fail to take the game seriously. Only four of the team originally selected took the field, and by the end they were reduced to eleven, two having been injured and two having walked off in disgust. Victory against England came eventually in 1890, and by this time the Welsh ingenuity was having a profound effect on the game's development. The four three-quarter system, originally the brainchild of Cardiff, had been adopted by the national side, and thanks to the presence of players like A. J. Gould of Newport and Cardiff's F. E. Hancock, the conversion from three threequarters was a smooth one. When Wales beat England at Dewsbury in 1890 it was clear that the system had a great deal to commend it.

Turning out at full back for Wales that day was W. J. Bancroft, small in stature but fearless of character. Possessed of an unwavering self-confidence he would lure opposing forwards towards him and then, 'with the speed of a darting snipe', would change direction leaving the heavy-weights leaden footed and hopelessly stranded. There was more than one international forward who would willingly have sacrificed a couple of caps for the pleasure of dumping Bancroft into the front row of the stand. No one practised more assiduously than he did, and such devotion to duty brought its own rewards, as was demonstrated in the match against England in 1893 – the 'Brazier Match' as it came to be known.

For most of the week leading up to the event there had been a heavy snow and hard frost, which had transformed the Arms Park into an ice skating rink, and in an effort to improve the situation coal fires in iron braziers had been placed over the playing surface. The day of the match dawned still bitterly cold but the ground was declared playable. The English forwards with the wind at their backs began in great style, and despite a hat trick of tries from Arthur Gould, it looked as if the result was going to be in favour of the visitors. But an English blunder in the closing seconds gave Wales a penalty and a faint hope of victory. Bancroft walked over to his captain Gould and said, 'Arthur, I'm going to drop it.' Thereafter, Bancroft recalled, 'To his remonstrations I merely repeated the statement. The crowd were getting restive, and Gould finally threw the ball on the ground and walked away. Before the ball had travelled ten yards to its journey I shouted to my skipper now standing in the centre of the field with his back to

me, "It's there, Arthur," And, of course, it was.'

The historian W. J. T. Collins in his book *Rugby Recollections* wrote, 'In my opinion the greatest pack who have put down their heads in a scrummage since 1889 were the Welsh eight of 1893. Every man among them (with the exception of Day) was highly intelligent.' Collins was quick to point out, however, that what poor Harry Day lacked in brain he amply made up for in brawn, and he continued, 'They stood up to the relentless vigour of the English; held and rolled back the close-dribbling and usurping Scots and quenched the fire of the Irish.' So it was that Wales won the Triple Crown for the first time.

This success proved beyond doubt the value of the four threequarter system and it marked a personal triumph for Arthur Gould, the man who had helped in its development. Gould continued to play for his country until 1897 when he retired – a retirement which was forced upon him. As his playing career was drawing to its close, his many admirers wished to acknowledge his services to the game and they collected about £600 which was used to purchase a house. While this may have been an innocent enough gesture to the Welsh, it was blatant professionalism to the other home countries at a time when the slightest hint of a breach in the amateur code touched the nerve ends. This particular episode led to a dispute, and Wales played only one game that season – against England. Gould himself resolved the matter by retiring.

The years between 1900 and 1911 were the most successful over a sustained period in the history of the Welsh game. Apart from occasional interference from Scotland, Wales had things very much their own way. Out of forty-three matches played during that period they lost only seven; they won the International Championship outright on six occasions and six times won the Triple Crown. The most remarkable game during the first decade was the one against Dave

The Cardiff tradition against touring sides is a proud one with victories against all three major countries: New Zealand, South Africa, and Australia. A crowd of 53,000 came to the Arms Park to watch the club play the 1951 Springboks, and with minutes to go Cardiff led 9–8. But a try in the dying seconds by 'Chum' Ochse saved the game for the tourists. The picture shows action from earlier in the match when the Welsh centre, Bleddyn Williams, dived over Van Schoor to score Cardiff's only try

R. H. Williams the Llanelli lock forward of ideal proportions who won 23 caps and went on two successful Lions tours, proving himself to be the best all round forward in the country. Between 1954 and 1960 he played in some wonderfully talented Welsh sides, but was never fortunate enough to be part of a Triple Crown triumph. In fact during this period Wales had only one outright win in the Championship

Jones the Sprint – Ken Jones winning one of his 44 Welsh caps in a match against Scotland. He was twenty-six years old when first called to his country's colours in 1947, and the following year he won an Olympic gold medal for Great Britain in the 4 × 100 metres relay. He finished his international rugby career in 1957 with a cap record which endured for nineteen years

Gallaher's All Blacks at the Arms Park in 1905. The tourists had gone unbeaten throughout the country, and everywhere the deeds of Wallace, Deans, Seeling and Gallaher were being talked of with admiration. Now they came to Cardiff to meet a Welsh XV which was not entirely bereft of talent. At centre threequarter there was Gwyn Nicholls who had intended to retire at the end of the previous season but had been prevailed upon to lead his country against Gallaher's men. With him there were Rhys Gabe, Percy Bush, Dickie Owen, A. F. Harding and G. Travers, great players all.

When the team took the field the ground was packed to capacity and many of the thousands locked out were mounted on nearby trees, telegraph poles and buildings, hoping to catch a glimpse of the proceedings. The All Blacks began nervously giving away several penalties from which Wales gained nothing; then Owen, Cliff Pritchard and Gabe combined to put Teddy Morgan over for a try which went down in the record books as being the only score of the game, although to this day there are still those who are prepared to argue the fact. Later in the match when the New Zealander Bob Deans burst for the Welsh line he was tackled by Gabe; Deans and his colleagues insisted that it was a score, Gabe and his colleagues were equally adamant that it was not. The immediate argument was settled by the Scottish referee Mr John Dallas who ruled no try. Deans, even on his deathbed, maintained that he had crossed the line only to be pulled back by Gabe and sundry other Welshmen, and it was a view supported by many including the All Blacks manager G. H. Dixon who stated, 'Deans dived over and grounded the ball well over the chalk mark.' Gabe, not to be outdone in the after-match quotes, offered his side of the story; 'I knew it was touch and go whether or not he had scored. But as he kept struggling to move forward, I knew that he had not reached the line.' As for Mr Dallas he was doubtless relieved that he was spending the

night in Cardiff and not in Timaru. Let us reserve the last word for an impartial witness, the *Scotsman* reporter who wrote: 'I was within six yards of the spot where the New Zealanders scored the disallowed try. It was the unanimous verdict of a goodly number of Welsh supporters and also my own, that no fairer try has been scored on the football field.'

The Golden Era of Welsh rugby came to an end in 1912, when Wales suffered three defeats in five matches, and it was evidence of their recession when those great half backs Billy Trew and Dickie Owen chose to play for their club Swansea rather than travel to Ireland with their country.

The economic depression of the 1920s brought apalling hardship and poverty to Wales and this was reflected in the results of the national XV; of the thirty matches played against the home countries during that decade only eight were won. Surprisingly enough, little blame could be attached to the forwards, and the Newport pack in the immediate post war years, with Tom Roberts, Tom Jones and Jack Whitfield outstanding, was the best in the land. It was the backs who lost their attacking urge, and significantly enough in those thirty matches a mere twenty-eight points were scored. An exception was Albert Jenkins, a tinplater from Llanelli, where at least one man claimed that he went to his Maker happy having seen Jenkins play football. Unfortunately, because of lack of support, he was never able to play as well for Wales as he did for his club, and his reputation outside the Principality remained something of a myth. The one year when he might have enjoyed support, he played in only one match, against France. It was the 1921–2 season; Wales had recalled the diminutive Tommy Vile and J. M. Lewis; and Swansea's Tom Parker was leading the pack. With their help Wales finished as Champions and, but for a draw with Scotland, would have won the Triple Crown.

Apart from this there was precious little

else to excite the men standing for hours in the employment queues, yet despite the misery the community spirit in Wales was a unifying force, and the dramatic societies, choirs and rugby clubs never lost their appeal. W. Rowe Harding, the Cambridge University, Wales and British Lions winger (later to become a distinguished Judge), described the typical Welsh supporter of the decade: 'He is usually a small sallow man, emotional, talkative and, if need be, abusive. He probably has a scarf of outrageously clashing colours, a cloth cap which accentuates the dead whiteness of his face which perhaps does not see daylight for forty-eight hours in the week, and if it is an international match he wears a leek of gigantic proportions and smells of leeks and beer in about equal strength.' Harding had the misfortune to be playing in the Welsh side at a time when both England and Scotland were exceptionally strong and in the 1924 match at Inverleith the Scots beat Wales 35–10. The following day the Welsh team were taken by coach to see the Forth Bridge. 'Take a good look at it lads,' said T. D. Schofield, a Welsh official, 'because it's the last time any of you will see it at the expense of the Welsh Rugby Union.'

During the bleak years of the depression, many promising young players who might well have represented Wales were tempted north where the rugby league clubs were at least able to offer some financial reward, although in most cases it was pitifully low. Moreover there had been since the war a basic change in strategy which had escaped Welsh notice. While Wakefield, Voyce, Blakiston, Clinch and others had brought a new dimension to forward play, and backs like McPherson, Smith and Stephenson had introduced sophistication to the three-quarters' technique, Wales stuck by the patterns of play which had brought them so much success prior to 1912. Now, finding themselves lagging behind the other countries, they were forced to adopt an ultra-defensive approach, a legacy which was

carried over into the next decade. There was, however, one important difference – the Welsh teams of the 1930s contained some extraordinarily fine players.

Despite destructive wing forwards and tight defensive marking, Wales produced backs of quality like Vivian Jenkins, Wilf Wooller, Cliff Jones and Haydn Tanner, an eighteen-year-old schoolboy when he first played for his country. In the forwards were Watcyn Thomas, Archie Skym, A. M. Rees and Arthur Lemon, who got his revenge upon an Irish forward, who boasted, 'Oi'll make an orange of him,' by knocking that same gentleman cold before the match had ended. The new decade was only a year old when Wales won the International Championship, and two years later in 1933 there followed a first win over England at Twickenham. But it was the visit of Jack Manchester's All Blacks in 1935 which caused a stir in the Valleys. The little boys who had sat at their fathers' knees, and had listened to the tales of Deans, Gabe, and all who had taken part in the 1905 epic, were men now, and with Cliff Porter's side having beaten Wales in 1924, they came in their thousands to the Arms Park for the decider. The early forward exchanges were furious, but the Welsh pack led by Arthur Rees played well enough to supply Tanner, Jones and Wooller with sufficient possession to win the match by the odd point in twenty-five.

After World War II, Cardiff were fortunate in having at their disposal a ready made team with players like Tanner, Bleddyn Williams, Jack Matthews and Billy Cleaver. This was the glamour side of Welsh rugby, and crowds of 40,000 were no exception for club matches at the Arms Park. The tradition went back many years, especially against touring sides. In 1907 they did what Wales had failed to do and beat the Springboks 17–0, and then in 1953 they completed the 'double', beating the New Zealanders 8–3. The years between 1948 and 1958 brought a regeneration of talent within the club and famous old names were replaced by pro-

A spectacular try by A. E. I. Pask, the Abertillery No. 8, in the 1966 match against England at Twickenham. Wales finished the season as Five Nations Champions, but it was one of the most unimaginative periods in the history of the game, with the forwards dominating the proceedings

mising new ones. Into Tanner's place came Rex Willis, Alun Thomas replaced Jack Matthews, and a bow-legged sprite from Trebanog called Cliff Morgan stepped into Billy Cleaver's outside half position.

Like so many of Wales' greatest players, Morgan grew up alongside the harsh realities of the coal pit, but despite the poverty, there was a great deal of happiness, and there were few who would have chosen any other way of life. As with many families in that environment, Morgan's parents were determined that he should have the education which they had been denied, and soon he left his native valley to take up his studies in Cardiff. It is a remarkable fact that five international half backs were weaned in that valley on the fringe of the Rhondda, and Morgan has an amusing theory about the reason for this. In the little villages, with their narrow streets and terraced houses, there were no pavements, so that when you stepped out on the road you had to be careful to avoid the traffic; if you stepped off the road you were in the river, and when you tried to get out of the river you found yourself on the railway line. The result was that people had a nervous awareness of the dangers which were always at hand and developed an instinctive move away from trouble.

Morgan's move to Cardiff was a happy one both for himself and for his new club. Playing alongside established stars such as Bleddyn Williams he quickly matured into one of the greatest of fly halves. In a game which has given him so much it would be churlish, he feels, to select one moment which stands out above all others, but from a personal point of view the memory of the Lions 23–22 win over the Springboks in the First Test at Ellis Park in 1955 will remain with him always. During his eight years in the national side, Wales won the Championship outright twice, the Triple Crown once, and his premature retirement from the game coincided with a decline in Welsh fortunes on the international field.

'I'll tell you a story,
Tis a strange and weird tale,
Of a factory in my valley
Not fed by road or rail;
It's built beneath the mountain
Beneath the coal and clay
It's where we make the outside
halves,
That'll play for Wales one day.'
Thus wrote the Welsh minstrel
Max Boyce in a poem dedicated
to the outside halves who have
played with such distinction for
Wales down the years, and here
are four quality post-war
products – Cliff Morgan, Cardiff
(top left); David Watkins,
Newport (bottom left); Barry
John, Cardiff (top right); and
Phil Bennett, Llanelli (bottom
right)

It would have been hard, however, to maintain the standards set during these years and hard for Wales to produce the same calibre of player. Apart from Morgan and his Cardiff team mates, there were many others who gave magnificent service both to Wales and to their clubs. There were C. C. Meredith, Rees Stephens and Roy John from Neath; Terry Davies and Clem Thomas from Swansea; Lewis Jones and Rhys Williams from Llanelli; and Bryn Meredith and the incomparable Ken Jones from Newport. Before the outbreak of World War II, Jones had played some rugby, but he was better known as a sprinter, and in 1948 he won an Olympic gold medal in the 4×100 metres relay. The previous year, at the age of twenty-six, he made his debut for Wales against England at the Arms Park, and ten years later he made his forty-fourth and last appearance for his country against Scotland. He remained the most capped Welshman until 1976, when his record was overtaken by Gareth Edwards.

Alas, the supply of class players was not infinite, and by the end of the 1950s Welsh rugby had lost the spark which fired the British game and the next few years were the most arid in the history of the sport. Once again the laws encouraged a negative approach in which the only attacking gambit was the kick, and apart from a brief but refreshing spell when D. O. Brace was in the side, the Welsh game lacked any sort of adventure. The introduction of Clive Rowlands at scrum half brought success in terms of results, but few admirers. A fine tactician and captain, Rowlands used the laws to maximum effect and was able to play almost exclusively to the Welsh strength which rested in forwards like Alan Pask, Haydn Morgan and Brian Price. Sadly, backs of the stature of Dewi Bebb and David Watkins were for the most part neglected, and Watkins eventually turned to rugby league where he has given long and productive service to Salford. Ironically his last season in the union code, in 1967, was probably his most enjoyable.

That was the year when Wales met England with a teenager called Keith Jarrett making his first appearance at full back, and he marked his international debut by scoring nineteen of his sides thirty-four points. The story is told that after the celebrations Jarrett arrived at the bus depot to find that he had missed the last bus home. But this being Wales he was immediately recognized as the hero of the day and the inspector was duly called. 'Get a bus out for Mr Jarrett,' he instructed, 'and make it a double decker – he might want a smoke on the way home.'

In the Welsh team that day was Gareth Edwards, another youngster in his first season of international rugby. Edwards's ability at an early age was enough to convince a wealthy Englishman that he should be given a chance to develop his talents in the best possible atmosphere, and the anonymous gentleman paid for the boy's education at Millfield, one of the most expensive schools in Britain. From there Edwards went to Cardiff; by the time he was nineteen he had played for his country; and at twenty he was the youngest player to captain Wales.

He was joined at Cardiff by a slim young outside half called Barry John, and that was the start of one of the most profitable half back partnerships in the history of the game. There were Grand Slam wins in 1969 and 1971, and in that latter year the two reached new heights with the Lions in New Zealand. Although they combined so smoothly on the field, their attitudes to the game were poles apart. Edwards was, and still is, a competitor; John was an entertainer. Their styles too were totally different; Edwards has always based his play on aggression, using his strength to get him through opposing defences, while John would ghost his way past bewildered defenders, occasionally employing his sleight of hand to bait opponents. But it was his kicking which really put him in a class of his own; it was the pinpoint accuracy of his tactical kicking which destroyed the New Zealand full back Fergie

Clive Rowlands is seen here
running with the ball, but it was
as a tactical kicker that he gained
his international reputation. With
Rowlands as scrum half, Wales
had a Triple Crown, a
Championship and a share in the
Championship to show for three
seasons' work, but in 1966
Rowlands was dropped and his
place went to A. R. Lewis of
Abertillery, the captaincy going to
A. E. I. Pask. His playing days
over, Rowlands returned as
coach to the Welsh side in 1969

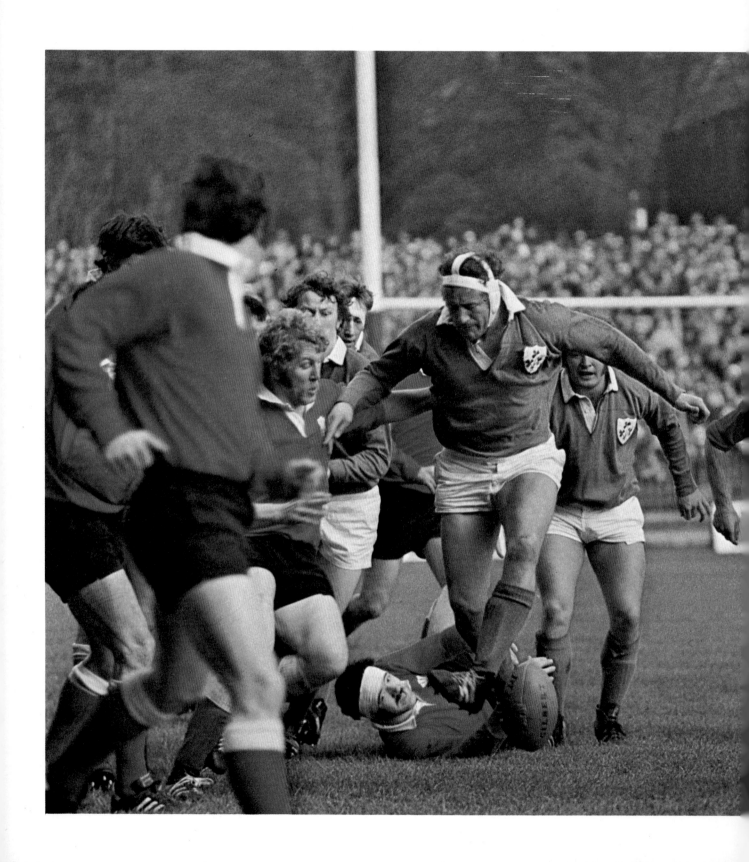

Left Irish forwards on the attack in the match against Wales at the Arms Park in 1975. Leading the rush is the Irish prop R. J. McLoughlin who has successfully overcome the challenge of Mervyn Davies (on the ground)

Above Scottish forwards on the retreat in the 1976 match against Wales in Cardiff. On the left, Alistair McHarg, George Mackie and Gordon Brown race back to cover a loose ball

McCormack in the First Test at Dunedin in 1971, and put the Lions on the way to victory; and it was his goal kicking throughout the tour which enabled him to break all sorts of records. Without being arrogant he did have remarkable confidence in his own ability, and when he made an unbelievable hash of a crucial goal kick in the Fourth Test at Auckland, he was the least perturbed player on the field. He accepted that mistakes were part of the game and he knew that his next attempt would, in all probability, be successful. When he returned from New Zealand he considered that he had achieved as much as he could do in the game, and he retired at the end of the 1972 season to become a rugby writer and commentator.

Edwards on the other hand continued, and has since proved himself to be the most complete footballer in the world today. His performance with the 1974 Lions in South Africa set new standards of scrum half play, and his partnership with Phil Bennett (another quality product from that fly half factory in the Valleys) both for Wales and for the Lions has realized as much as did his association with Barry John.

When Wales won the Grand Slam in 1976, their seventh, it underlined the abnormally large contingent of top class players in the Principality. At full back was J. P. R. Williams, whose love of combat and total disregard for danger makes him the most exciting of the present day players. On the wing was the quicksilver Gerald Davies, one of the few with the priceless ability to sidestep either way at speed. Captaining them from the No. 8 position was Mervyn Davies rated by Colin Meads as being the outstanding Lions forward in 1971, and it was a tragic loss to the game when he collapsed with a brain haemorrhage in a cup match with his club Swansea at the end of the 1976 season. While it is expected that he will make a complete recovery, he will probably never play rugby again, a grave blow to Wales who will find it hard to replace him. Nevertheless, John Dawes who is now applying the

Left The 1967 season had been a dismal one for Wales. Beaten by Australia, Scotland, Ireland and France, they brought in a new full back, K. S. Jarrett, for the last game of the season against England, who were in line for the Triple Crown. Jarrett had left Monmouth School only a few months previously and was playing club rugby with Newport, mainly as a centre. It was a spectacular debut for Jarrett, who scored nineteen points with five conversions, two penalties, and a try, and Wales won 34–21. Two other Welshmen have scored nineteen points in an international – J. Bancroft against France in 1910 and Phil Bennett against Ireland in 1976, but Jarrett's feat remains unique in rugby history because it was achieved on his first international appearance. He continued to play the amateur game until 1969 when he switched to a career in Rugby League – a career that was to be cut short because of illness

Above Probably the most gifted rugby footballer in the world today, Gareth Edwards ranks with Haydn Tanner as the greatest of Welsh scrum halves. He came into the national side as a nineteen-year-old in 1967 and the next year became the youngest player ever to captain Wales. Since that time he has broken the Welsh cap record, became the world's most capped scrum half, taken part in three Lions tours, and shared in three Welsh Triple Crown wins. His total of eighteen tries in international matches for Wales is also a record, and one of the most breathtaking efforts was this one against Scotland in 1972, when he ran the length of the field to touch down ahead of his pursuers, Jim Renwick and Louis Dick

same intelligence to his job as Welsh coach as he did to his captaincy of Wales and the Lions, appears to have an abundance of young talent ready to answer the call, and with England, Ireland and Scotland currently in the doldrums, the principal challenge to Welsh supremacy in Europe is likely to come from France.

Further afield Wales have not enjoyed quite the same consistency. Like good wine, the Welsh take some time to settle down, and the late U. A. Titley once wrote, 'Welsh players are best at home before their own crowd. They are inclined to be homesick (a rather extraordinary thing when one thinks of the mining valleys) and to brood together in a knot. Moreover, since they brood in Welsh, it is difficult for ordinary mortals to know what it is all about.' In 1964 Wales went to South Africa for a four match tour which included one international. With twenty minutes of play remaining the score was 3–3, but then a drop goal from the Springbok fullback Lionel Wilson broke the deadlock and South Africa won comfortably 24–3, the biggest margin between the countries. Wales, in fact, are the only one of the International Board countries never to have beaten South Africa.

An unsuccessful and unhappy trip to the Argentine in 1968 was followed the next year by a prestigious tour to New Zealand. Wales left as Five Nations Champions and Triple Crown Winners; they had a hefty set of forwards and a back division of great skill. The All Blacks, on the other hand, were considered to be a far weaker combination than the side which had crushed British opposition two years previously. In retrospect the itinerary which faced the tourists was much too ambitious, including as it did three internationals, two against New Zealand and one against Australia. The first international was played on a wet May afternoon at Lancaster Park, and New Zealand won 19–0; but this was only an appetizer for the second match in Auckland which the All Blacks won 33–12, with Fergie

Left Two of the world's finest scrum halves, Gareth Edwards of Wales and John Hipwell of Australia, about to come face to face in the game at Cardiff in 1976, which Wales won 28–3

Above Phil Bennett about to tear the Japanese defence to shreds in the 1973 match in Cardiff

McCormack scoring 24 of the points – a world record for an international match.

The Welsh had experienced disasters before, of course – their very first international against England in 1881 could hardly be otherwise described. They had overcome the shock of that setback with determination, and now they set about the task of recovering their lost prestige. 'Coaching' became the password to success, and the Welsh flung themselves into the venture with enthusiasm. Coaching was organized on a national level, mini rugby was introduced as an insurance for the future, and Welsh aptitude for the game did the rest. When the Lions left for New Zealand in 1971 there were thirteen Welshmen in the party and a Welsh coach.

It is this very attitude to the game in Wales which has remained unaltered since the men of Newport, Swansea and the other towns in the south decided to trade in their footballs for the rugby bladder; the hywel remains, the Arms Park (now renamed the National Stadium) continues to provide the most emotional moments in sport, the only difference being that there's more of Max Boyce and less of Cwm Rhondda, and most important of all, the Welsh have retained their passion for the game. Is there a more knowledgeable crowd in the world than the one at the international ground in Cardiff? Each man, woman and child is a walking

encyclopaedia of rugby trivia, and woe betide the person who is not equally well acquainted with the facts.

There was an occasion some years ago when Andy Mulligan, the Irish scrum half, was invited, along with several other distinguished guests, to sit on a sports forum at Treorchy. Before the evening's proceedings got under way it was pointed out by the chairman that this was a sports forum and not a sports quiz. 'In other words,' he said, 'we don't want any bloody silly questions like who did what to whom and when, etc.' Having thus spoken he duly declared the forum open, and the first questioner arose. Mulligan recalls that he was wearing trousers with nine-inch bottoms and a blazer so

Straight from the coaching manual – Cardiff and Wales winger Gerald Davies gives a perfect demonstration of how to make the ball available to a colleague despite being tackled in possession. In actual fact the two defensively minded Irishmen in the picture can count themselves fortunate to have got hold of their man, because Davies is one of the few present day players with the ability to sidestep either way without a noticeable reduction in speed. Another in the list of world class players in the current Welsh side, Davies was honoured with the captaincy of his club in their centenary season

The Grand Slam – the highlight of the 1976 season was the meeting of Wales and France in Cardiff. Both sides were unbeaten and the result would almost certainly decide the outcome of the Five Nations Championship. With time running out, Wales, already Triple Crown holders, were ahead by six points, but the ball was with the French winger, J. F. Gourdon, and he was striding out for immortality. Only J. P. R. Williams stood between him and the Welsh line. The race was on – the two met just inches from the line and Gourdon was bounced into touch. Wales had won the Grand Slam for the seventh time

heavily encrusted with gold braid that he positively listed to one side. Beneath the blazer badge was inscribed, 'WALES 1950 **TRIPLE CROWN WINNERS**', and, barely visible alongside, 'Supporters XV'. Having managed to get himself on an even keel, the Welshman announced that his question was for Mr Mulligan. 'Who was it who scored for Neath-Aberavon against the 1927 Waratahs?' A hush fell over the audience as Mulligan attempted to re-emphasize that this was intended to be an evening for discussion rather than for the performance of phenomenal feats of memory. But his interrogator stood his ground and eventually Mulligan was forced to confess ignorance. 'Do you WANT to know?' demanded the

man. 'Yes,' replied Mulligan, not daring to give any other answer, 'it was bloody me!' he shouted to his own delight and to the obvious approval of the assembled gathering.

A scene from the All Blacks match against England at Eden Park, Auckland, in 1973. Sid Going, the New Zealand scrum half, takes the ball from behind his scrum and prepares to kick, watched closely by his opposite number, Jan Webster. Having lost the three provincial matches prior to the Test, England won 16–10

6 ALL BLACK POWER

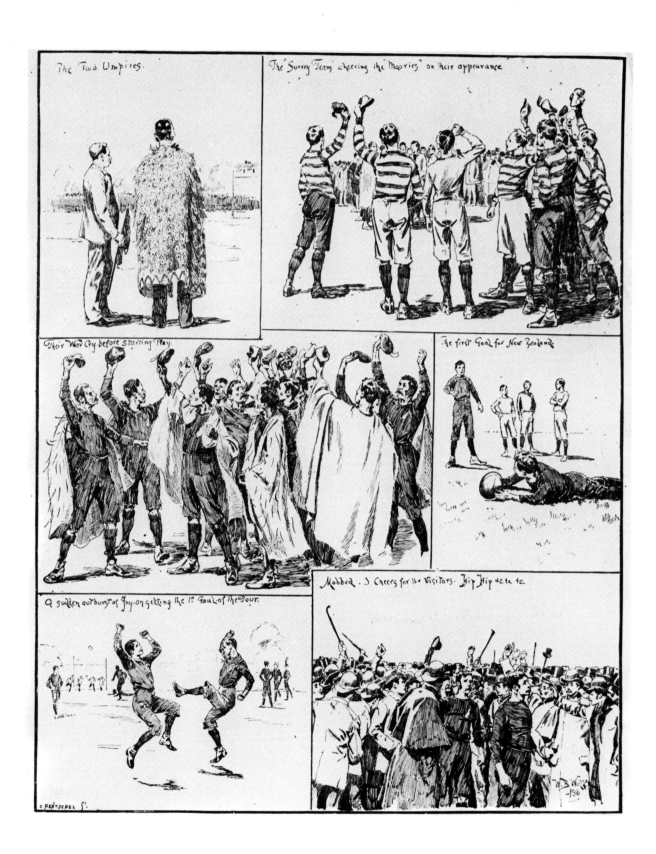

The Two Umpires.

The "Surrey" Team cheering the "Maories" on their appearance

Their War Cry before starting Play.

The first Goal for New Zealand.

A sudden outburst of Joy on getting the 1st Goal of the Tour.

Mobbed. 3 cheers for the Visitors. Hip Hip etc etc.

The first-ever touring team from New Zealand to Great Britain was the Native side of 1888. They played a total of seventy-four matches, winning forty-nine of them, losing twenty, and drawing the remainder. Here are various scenes depicting the tourists' first match against Surrey at Richmond

Overleaf The Match of the Century? – certainly one of the greatest ever seen at Cardiff Arms Park, where the All Blacks and Barbarians turned on the most amazing exhibition of rugby during the final game of the 1972 tour. The Barbarians won with one of their tries coming from Fergus Slattery, whose head can just be seen through a mass of All Black cover

IS IT POSSIBLE that one of the most famous nicknames in the sporting world was the result of a type-setter's mistake? In 1905 the New Zealand rugby team were making a first visit to the British Isles – with spectacular success. Everywhere they went the crowds thrilled to their brand of open football, with the forwards every bit as gifted in their ball-handling skills as the backs, and it was after one such display by the forwards that a sports editor dreamed up the headline 'ALL BACKS'. But because of a typographical error, the heading which actually appeared the following day read 'ALL BLACKS'. That is one version of how the name originated. The other, which sounds far more likely, is that J. A. Buttery, the rugby correspondent of the London *Daily Mail* at that time, bestowed the name upon the team because of their uniform. The black jersey with silver fern leaf and black cap with silver monogram had been proposed some twelve years earlier by T. R. Ellison, before he took a New Zealand side to Australia, although it's thought that the Native side which played 74 matches in Britain as early as 1888 turned out in all black strip. Whichever version is the right one, the name endured, and to wear the All Black uniform became the ambition of every rugby playing youngster in New Zealand.

The turn of the century brought an enormous advance in the game's organization both at home and abroad. In 1901, the Governor of New Zealand, the Earl of Ranfurly, let it be known that he intended to present a cup for competition within the colony. The Ranfurly Shield (which to the embarrassment of all concerned, originally depicted soccer posts and a soccer ball) became the premier trophy for inter-provincial competition.

The first official international was played on 15 August 1903 against Australia, and victory went to New Zealand by 22 points to 3. The first points were scored by Billy Wallace, one of the game's immortals, and to Albert Asher fell the honour of scoring

New Zealand's first try.

The announcement that New Zealand was going to make a major tour of Britain in 1905 was greeted with more than a little interest. A British side under the captaincy of the Scotsman Bedell-Sivright had just lost a series in the Dominion, and there was a general feeling that New Zealand had something rather special to offer the rugby world. Apart from Billy Wallace, who was to score 246 points from 26 matches on tour, the side contained players such as Jimmy Hunter who scored 42 tries – a record that has never been threatened. Another was Jimmy Duncan, who had captained the side in Australia two years earlier. During a match he always wore a tweed cap on his head which apparently served a dual purpose. In addition to covering his bald pate, it would occasionally come in handy as a decoy, and whilst the opposition were frantically mauling for Duncan's headgear, he would be off up the field, the ball tucked safely under his arm.

Then there was the captain Dave Gallaher – a controversial figure on tour because of his tactic of playing outside the scrummage as a 'rover'. In those days the New Zealanders played with a seven-man scrum, having two men in the front row, three in the second and two in the back. This enabled one forward to play as an extra scrum half, which was thought to be unfair play in Britain; but it was not considered unfair when five years later, the Englishman 'Cherry' Pillman adopted the same tactic in South Africa with such great success.

The journey by boat from New Zealand lasted six weeks, and immediately on arrival the team made for Newton Abbot where they were to play their first game against Devon – Champions of the South West. Circadian dysrhythma (jet-lag to the layman) was a term unknown in those days, and if the players were feeling the effects of their long journey they certainly showed no sign of it. They won by 55–4, with Billy Wallace contributing 28 points (made up of 3 tries, 8

conversions and a penalty). So surprising was the result that when news of it reached London many newspapers thought that there had been a mistake in transmission, and printed the result the other way round. But there was no mistake, and in their first six matches the tourists scored 231 points with only a drop goal against them. The first side to put any sort of brake on their early progress was Surrey, who eventually went down 11–nil. But the star turn of that game was the referee, whose efforts will ever be remembered by kind permission of Mr Buttery. This was his verdict which appeared the following day in the *Daily Mail*: 'The finest artists are said to shut their eyes when whistling their hardest, and judged on this hypothesis, the referee must have had his eyes closed on and off for the greater part of the game. The fantasia commenced in the first minute and continued, with brief intervals for respiration, throughout. As for the game – there was no game. It was an exposition of the power of music to tame even the New Zealand Rugby footballer.' The soloist's name was Billy Wallace, the founder of Twickenham

By the time of the Scottish international – the twentieth match – the All Blacks had scored 612 points, with just 15 against. They beat the Scots 12–7, the Irish 15–nil and the English by the same margin – and so to Cardiff Arms Park for the Welsh game, the All Blacks still unbeaten, the Welsh confident of being the first side to beat them. The plain fact is that Wales won 3–nil and inflicted upon the All Blacks the only defeat of the tour, but never has any match generated such controversy, and even now arguments still range whenever Welshmen and New Zealanders meet. When the All Black Bob Deans was tackled in the act of going over for what would have been the equalizing try, the referee, Mr Dallas, clad in his ordinary walking clothes, was apparently far behind play. After the match, Deans sent a telegram to Mr Buttery: 'Grounded ball six inches over line. Some Welsh players admit try.

FIXTURES.

Date.	Opponent.	Ground.	Result.
Sept. 16	Devon	Exeter	55pt. to 4
,, 20	Cornwall	Redruth	41 ,, 0
,, 23	Bristol	Bristol	41 ,, 0
,, 28	Northampton	Northampton	32 ,, 0
,, 30	Leicester	Leicester	28 ,, 0
Oct. 4	Middlesex	London	34 ,, 0
,, 7	Durham		16 ,, 3
,, 11	The Hartlepools	Hartlepool	63 ,, 0
,, 14	Northumberland	North Shields	31 ,, 0
,, 19	Gloucester City	Gloucester	44 ,, 0
,, 21	Somerset	Taunton	23 ,, 0
,, 25	Devonport Albion	Devonport	21 ,, 3
,, 28	Midland Counties	Leicester	21 ,, 5
Nov. 1	Surrey	Richmond	11 ,, 0
,, 4	Blackheath	Blackheath	,,
,, 7	Oxford Univers'y	Oxford	,,
,, 9	Cambridge ,,	Cambridge	,,
,, 11	Richmond	Richmond	,,
,, 15	Bedford	Bedford	,,
,, 18	Scotland	Edinburgh	,,
,, 22	West of Scotland	Glasgow	,,
,, 25	Ireland	Dublin	,,
,, 29	Munster	Limerick	,,
Dec. 2	England	Crystal Palace	,,
,, 6	Cheltenham	Cheltenham	,,
,, 9	Cheshire	Birkenhead	,,
,, 13	Yorkshire		,,
,, 16	Wales	Cardiff	,,
,,	Glamorgan		,,
,, 23	Newport	Newport	,,
,, 26	Cardiff	Cardiff	,,
,, 30	Swansea	Swansea	,,
	Total Points up to date	461	,, 15

AGES, WEIGHTS, & HEIGHTS.

BACKS.

	Age.	st. lbs.	ft. in.
W. Wallace	27	12 0	5 8
E. Harper	27	12 7	5 11
E. Booth	26	11 10	5 7½
G. W. Smith	33	11 12	5 10½
H. Abbot	23	13 6	5 7
F. Roberts	23	12 4	5 6
R. Deans	21	13 9	5 10
J. Hunter	26	11 8	5 9
W. Mynott	29	11 0	5 7
W. Stead	28	13 0	6 0
G. Gillett	28	13 9	5 8
H. D. Thomson	24	16 9	5 9
R. McGregor	23	11 3	5 9
Manager—MR. DIXON.			

FORWARDS.

	Age.	st. lbs.	ft. in.
D. Gallaher (Capt.)	29	13 0	6 0
W. S. Glenn	27	12 7	5 11
S. Casey	22	12 4	5 10
A. McDonald	23	13 6	6 0
W. Johnstone	22	13 7	6 0
C. Seeling	22	13 10	6 0
G. Nicholson	26	13 0	5 11
G. A. Tyler	25	15 6	5 10
J. Corbett	25	13 9	5 11
F. Newton	23	15 0	6 0
F. Glasgow	25	13 3	5 10
J. O'Sullivan	22	13 7	5 10
W. Mackrell	23	12	5 10
W. Cunningham	29	14	6 11

No touring team has generated more interest or more controversy than did the 1905 All Blacks in Britain. Under the captaincy of Dave Gallaher they won all but one of their thirty-two matches, scoring 830 points in the process. Gallaher's tactic of playing outside the scrummage as a 'rover' brought some adverse reaction from the British public, and here (top right) he overlooks a scrum in the match against the

Midland Counties at Leicester.
The other great point of discord
arose during the international
against Wales in Cardiff when the
New Zealander Bob Deans had a
'try' disallowed. Arguments still
rage to this day about the rights
and wrongs of the decision, but in
the diagram (right) sketched by
Billy Wallace, there was no doubt
in New Zealand minds that a try
had been scored. In a message
(far right) written by the
Welshman Teddy Morgan and
sent to Wallace during a dinner
in 1924, it appears that the All
Blacks had every reason to feel
aggrieved about the decision

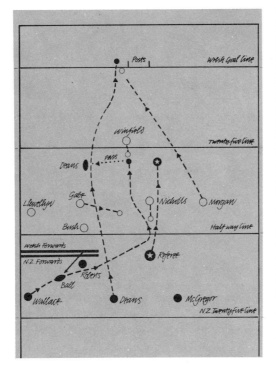

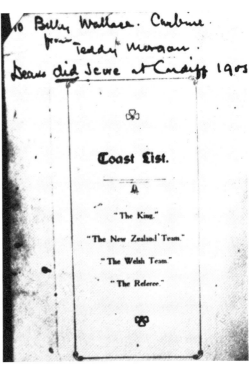

Hunter and Glasgow can confirm was pulled back before referee arrived. Deans.' Dr Teddy Morgan, the man who tackled Deans, is reputed to have told a medical colleague at Guy's Hospital that Deans had scored, and at a dinner after the All Blacks game against Wales in 1924, Morgan, who was sitting next to the New Zealand captain Cliff Porter, wrote a message to Billy Wallace on Porter's menu card: 'Deans DID score at Cardiff 1905.' That is the New Zealand side of the story. The Welsh account is somewhat different, but ever since that day the countries have been united in discord.

It was to be nineteen years before the All Blacks returned to Britain, the interval containing a lengthy tenure of the Ranfurly Shield by Auckland, a shock win in the same competition by the little fancied Hawkes Bay, World War I, and a first visit by South Africa. The year was 1921 and the Springboks, under the captaincy of Theo Pienaar, lost only two matches – to Canterbury and to New Zealand in the first of the three internationals. It was in the first test at Dunedin that the All Blacks winger Jack Steele scored one of the most extraordinary tries in the history of the game. Play was inside the New Zealand '25' and the ball was flung awkwardly out to Steele – so awkwardly in fact that it went over his shoulder. But by some amazing sleight of hand he clamped the ball on to his back and, in a self-imposed half-nelson, he set off for the Springbok line amidst near hysteria from the crowd. The South Africans squared the series in Auckland, and in the decider at Wellington perverse weather conditions prevented either side from scoring, but enabled both sides to emerge from the series with honour.

Sights were then set towards the British Isles once more. Trials were held in the North and South Islands, after which the North met the South and routed them 39–8. At the end of it all the touring party was selected and the selectors, confident that they had done a good job, sent their men on a trial spin to Australia. Not everything

When Cliff Porter's All Blacks left for Britain in 1924 they had the good wishes, if not the confidence of their country behind them. They were not expected to do particularly well. In the event they returned with the finest record of any touring side, having won all thirty of their matches in Europe. One of the stars of the tour was the Hawkes Bay full back George

Nepia, seen below in classical goal kicking pose. The one blight on the tour was the match against England at Twickenham when the All Black forward Cyril Brownlie was sent from the field by referee Albert Freethy. The forward exchanges were described as 'lively' and the picture on the right shows a lineout from an early part of the match

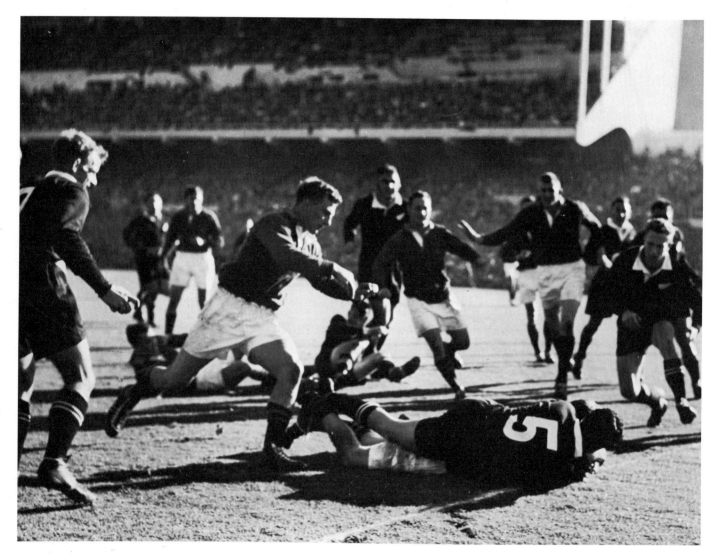

Since 1928 the All Blacks have
five times toured South Africa,
but have never succeeded in
winning a series. In 1960 they
played the Springboks in the
Second Test at Newlands, and
despite this narrow escape, when
Terry Lineen just managed to
prevent the South African John
Gainsford from scoring, the All
Blacks won 11–31 to level the
series. But with the series
depending upon the final test, the
Springboks won 8–3

The All Blacks have a happier tale to tell in home matches against the Springboks, and when Peter Jones crossed the line for a try in the final test at Auckland in 1956, the All Blacks had beaten South Africa in a series for the first time. The match over, Jones was brought out to make an historic broadcast to the waiting nation

went according to plan, though, and the All Blacks lost one of their matches to New South Wales. When the team returned home and were promptly beaten 14–3 by Auckland, there was an outcry – 'the worst team ever fielded', and 'a disgrace to its predecessors', were amongst the kinder of the newspaper headlines. As it was, the 'worst team ever fielded' turned out to be Cliff Porter's 'Invincibles', who went unbeaten through Great Britain and Ireland, and the names of George Nepia, A. E. Cooke, Mark Nicholls and the Brownlie brothers will endure as long as the game is played. The first international was against Ireland, and despite a strong wind which conspired to blow against the All Blacks throughout each half, they won 6–nil. Against Wales there was to be no repeat of the cliffhanger nineteen years earlier, and the tourists won 19–nil. The Scots declined to play, despite having one of the best sides in their history, which left England as the only obstacle in the way of the All Blacks' triumphant progress. The weather was fine, the going heavy, as the referee, Mr Albert Freethy from Wales, started the game before a crowd of 60,000. The All Blacks forward, Read Masters, later recalled that their opponents that day took their responsibilities very seriously indeed: 'Through the over kneenness of one of the England forwards, heated play was in evidence from the first scrum and many subsequent scrums, whilst in the general tight play, arms were swung freely. Thrice the referee issued a general warning to both packs and appealed for calmer play. Then came the climax! The game had progressed about eight minutes, when after some loose play following a lineout, the whistle sounded followed by the remark "You go off". Our horror can be imagined when we realized that the remark had been directed at Cyril Brownlie. Jock Richardson, our captain, appealed to the referee, but Mr Freethy, who seemed to have completely lost his head for a minute, remained firm, and one of the most good-natured men in our team had to retire.'

Masters continued, 'If England had any chance of winning, and up to that stage it certainly appeared that they had, it was reduced to a minimum now. We were determined to avenge the unjust charge made against Brownlie – that he had kicked the leg of an Englishman who was lying on the ground – and a new spirit seemed to obsess us.' That 'new spirit' produced something extra from players like Nicholls, Cooke and Maurice Brownlie, who took it upon himself to restore the family honour with an inspired performance, culminating in a try which required him to barge his way through most of the England team to reach the line. In the dressing room afterwards, Brownlie turned to his team mate Jim Parker, who had been up in support during his surge for the line, and said quietly, 'Jim, I wouldn't have passed it out for a hundred pounds.' The All Blacks had won 17–11 and finished the tour with a record that may one day be equalled, but never can be bettered.

Four years later, the All Blacks were on their travels again – this time to South Africa. Because of the apartheid laws they were unable to take with them the outstanding talents of players like George Nepia and Jimmy Mill, but it was generally supposed that this was an unusually fine side, stronger even than the 'Invincibles'. In New Zealand and Australia at this time there was the restriction of no direct kicking to touch outside the '25', but Nepia had perfected the art of dropping the ball into touch on the first bounce, thus gaining huge distances, although positioned outside his own '25'. The story is told that in practice, he would spread a white handkerchief on the turf a yard or so inside the touchline, and hour after hour he would aim his torpedo kicks at the target. Alas, there was no one with such astounding accuracy in the 1928 touring party, and without a reliable line kicker the All Blacks frequently lost acres of ground by failing to adapt to the unfamiliar conditions and tactics. All the more remarkable then that their finest tactician, Mark

Nicholls, should spend three out of the four internationals waving a flag on the touchline. It wasn't until the final test at Newlands, with the All Blacks 2–1 down in the series, that he was recalled – and mainly because of his astute play and accurate goal-kicking the game was won and New Zealand shared the series. The experiences of the All Blacks in South Africa should have convinced officials back home that the tactics employed by their players were out of date. They were still playing with a detached wing forward, leaving only seven men in the scrummage, which left them hopelessly outmanoeuvred by the powerful and well-drilled Springbok pack. Defeat in a three-match series the following year against Australia still failed to get the message across, and it was not until 1931 that New Zealand changed to a three-man front row.

The 1930s were years of mixed success for New Zealand rugby – defeats by England and Wales in 1935 were followed by a lost series at home against the Springboks two years later, and because of the war it was twelve years before the All Blacks made a return visit to South Africa, although a tour had been planned for 1940. At that time Mr Ted McKenzie was sole selector of the national side, and was instructed by the New Zealand Union to submit his team to them by 31 December 1939 – if the war was over by that time!

When the war was over, it was a case of making up for lost time. In 1945–6, the New Zealand Army team (the Kiwis) toured Britain. This was followed by a victorious series against Australia, and then the hunt was on to find the thirty best players for the long awaited tour to South Africa. Maoris were still omitted and the selectors, mindful of the thrashing that the All Blacks forwards had received in 1928 and again in 1937, were determined that the emphasis in 1949 was going to be on weight. The result was that several of New Zealand's finest forwards who failed to match up to the physical requirements were not even considered for selection.

A comforting sight for the All Blacks, but not for their opponents and certainly not for the ball, as Don Clarke's boot makes contact to send over yet another successful kick, this time in the Third Test against France in 1961. Clarke scored 17 points that day, and in his 31 international appearances he scored a total of 207 points
Overleaf One of Clarke's more remarkable feats was the drop goal he scored from a mark in the match against England at Lancaster Park in 1963. The ball travelled 60 yards and made victory certain for New Zealand

Above left and right Two moments from the career of Colin Meads: first, the loneliness and anguish as he walks from the field, having been sent off by referee Kevin Kelleher in the 1967 match against Scotland; and second, in more typical style, as he turns to look for support in the 1964 match against the Barbarians at Cardiff Arms Park. The man tackling Meads is the All Black prop, Ian Clarke, who was that day chosen to play for the Barbarians in honour of his services to the game

Other contenders, more ambitious but perhaps less honest, whose chances of going to South Africa were as slim as their bodies, suddenly appeared in the trial programmes a good two or three stones above their actual weight. Nevertheless, when the team was selected under the captaincy of Fred Allen, there were very few who had any violent objections to the men chosen – the forwards were big, the backs were fast – the fortyniners surely were unbeatable. Three months later they returned with the worst record of any New Zealand touring side, having lost seven matches, including all four internationals. The beefy New Zealand forwards were outscrummaged and outrun by a Springbok pack which contained the likes of Chris Koch, 'Okey' Geffin and Hennie Muller, and had it not been for the superhuman efforts of Bob Scott at fullback, the tourists would have returned with an even more depressing record. A player of the highest class, Scott maintained his great form throughout the series against the Lions in 1950, kicking the winning points in the crucial third test in Wellington after the All Blacks had lost Johnny Simpson through injury and Ron Elvidge had been badly shaken by a Jackie Matthews tackle.

In Australia the following year, a twenty-five-year-old winger from Wellington, Ron Jarden, made history by scoring 38 points for the All Blacks in the match against Central West, and at home a young full back received a mention in the newspapers when Waikato beat North Auckland 6–nil in the Ranfurly Shield. The six points came from two penalties kicked by a seventeen-year-old called Don Clarke. His incredible feats of goal-kicking soon brought him to the notice of the national selectors, and when the time came to pick the 1953 side to tour Britain his name was high on the list of possibles. But at the last minute Bob Scott made himself available to tour, and Clarke had to wait for another three years before the selectors gave him their nod of approval. The arrival of Clarke opened up a

Overleaf A fine study of the New Zealand flanker Ian Kirkpatrick, who in thirty appearances for his country has scored thirteen tries. Here he receives protection from hooker Ron Ulrich in the foreground, and behind from Keith Murdoch, a prop who took exception to the presence of a security guard in Cardiff during the 1972 visit and was sent home as a result of his actions

seam rich in points-scoring potential, but it closed for some considerable time to come the adventurous, exhilarating style of back play which had been in vogue since the war. Of his 207 international points, Clarke probably best remembers the six penalty goals he kicked to beat the 1959 Lions in the First Test in Dunedin, his 60-yard drop-goal in the second test against the Springboks in 1960, and his drop-goal from a mark which broke England at Christchurch in 1963. But in the winter of 1956, the outside world hadn't yet heard of 'Superboots' and it is certain that very few of the Springboks who had arrived in Waikato for the first game of their tour were over worried by the reputation of the local hero. Their record since 1949 had been a proud one – only three defeats in their fifteen internationals and a run of six successive wins in Australia immediately behind them. But they lost that day 14–10, with Clarke contributing a penalty, a conversion and a mammoth drop goal. It wasn't enough to get him into the side for the first test which the All Blacks won 10–6 or for the second which they lost 8–3, but he was brought in for the third, as was prop forward Kevin Skinner, who had come out of retirement, and back row forward Peter Jones, recalled after some time out of the international reckoning. All three played well enough in the All Blacks' 17–10 win to merit selection for the final test in Auckland. Early on Clarke took the steam out of the tourists with a 50-yard penalty goal; then Peter Jones, pouncing on a loose ball just inside the Springbok half, set off for the line in the manner of an Olympic sprinter, leaving his challengers far behind. The match over and the Springboks beaten in a test series for the first time since 1896, Jones made an historic broadcast to his eager public. Asked by the interviewer how he had felt after scoring, his reply was brief and very much to the point: 'Absolutely buggered,' he said.

That series brought to an end the international careers of several great All Blacks (and any possible broadcasting future for Peter Jones). Tiny White, Pat Vincent, Kevin Skinner, Bob Duff and Ron Jarden all went into retirement, and replacements had to be found as a matter of urgency – especially in the forwards. By the end of the following year two promising youngsters had emerged to fill the gaps – Colin Meads and Wilson Whineray. Whineray played for the All Blacks on seventy-seven occasions, captaining them in all but nine of these matches; Meads, whose last game in an All Blacks jersey was in 1971, won a record fifty-five caps and became one of the greatest lock forwards of all time. The tales of his strength are legion – how he would run up the mountainside with a sheep under either arm as part of his training routine; how he played in South Africa with a broken arm, and how he came back to play, against all medical advice, after a car accident had smashed vertebrae and ribs. 'Pine Tree' Meads was as rugged as the country in which he was raised, and together with brother Stan he formed the foundation of the fearsome King Country pack for many years. But his career was not without its share of controversy. He was involved in the incident which ended the playing career of one of the world's greatest scrum halves, Ken Catchpole; and again in 1966 when he laid out the little Welshman David Watkins. On his return home after the match, Meads was apparently asked by a schoolboy why he had punched the young David. 'Self defence,' was Goliath's straight-faced reply His most shameful moment, however, came a year later when the All Blacks were playing Scotland at Murrayfield, and with two minutes of the game remaining the referee Kevin Kelleher of Ireland sent him from the field. The memory remains horribly clear: 'As I walked off I was conscious of the close crowd booing me. I thought, "I'd like to get hold of one of you." Mostly though, I had this terrible feeling of shame. "That's the end," I thought. "That's finished everything".' (Alex Vesey: *Colin Meads – All Black*.) Like the dismissal of Cyril Brownlie forty-three years before, there was more than a suspicion of doubt about the decision, although human nature being what it is many considered that Meads had received his just deserts that day for previous indiscretions. Unquestionably there were blemishes on his career, but Meads played his rugby hard, granted no favours and looked for none, and the greatness he achieved in the game could not have been gained by constant recourse to foul play.

So the pattern for the 1960s was set. Meads, Whineray, Ken Gray, Kevin Tremain, Waka Nathan and Brian Lochore – these were some of the forwards who gave New Zealand domination over the rest of the world. Behind them were tip-top half backs in Ian Urban, Kevin Briscoe, Chris Laidlaw and Sid Going, and at the very back the men to kick the goals that mattered – Don Clarke, Mike Williment and Fergie McCormack. Winning rugby it was, adventurous it was not. One couldn't help but admire the awesome power and discipline in the All Blacks' play, but there were times when the outside backs were merely making up the numbers. But there were glorious exceptions – as when the 1963 side destroyed the Barbarians in their last match in Britain, and skipper Whineray galloped half the length of the field selling outrageous dummies as he went, to score a sensational try. And again in 1967 with Fred Allen as coach, when Chris Laidlaw and Earl Kirton were at their best, Fergie McCormack was playing like a 'souped up' version of Don Clarke, and the All Blacks forwards were at the height of their power, the British public saw some classical rugby. In between there were victories over Australia and South Africa. New Zealand were indeed the champions of the world.

The inevitable break-up began during an All Blacks tour to Australia in 1968, when the team which had powered through Britain struggled to beat Australia 19–18 – and then only after a controversial penalty try had been awarded to the tourists in the dying

seconds of the game. Chris Laidlaw, who captained the side that day, recognized that this was the end of an era: 'Fred Allen created a world record by smoking a cigarette for every New Zealand mistake, and probably sealed forever the doom of his much abused lungs. That match, more than any other factor, provoked his retirement as All Black coach.' As it turned out, Allen's sense of timing was impeccable, although victory over Wales in 1969 persuaded many that service on the machine could be delayed until after the 1970 tour to South Africa. At first it appeared that the optimists were right. In the build-up to the first international, the tourists coasted along winning all their games by resounding margins, and they remained unbeaten in all their provincial matches. But in the all-important matter of the tests they lost 3–1, which turned the tour into a catastrophic failure. The reasons given ranged from an excess of wine, women and hotel breaking, to a weak selection policy. (Twenty-seven of the thirty players were used in the four tests.) Whatever reasons, the famed All Black discipline had evaporated, and disturbing reports reached home that several of the players had little stomach for the fray. The two men who might have made a difference, Brian Lochore and Colin Meads, missed much of the tour because of injury. But the 1970 side were history-makers in one respect – they included four players of Maori or Polynesian blood – and it was the first time that New Zealand had been able to take a fully representative side to South Africa.

Defeat by the Springboks in South Africa was one thing, but to lose to the Lions in New Zealand was something else – something that had never happened before. In South Africa it had been evident that several of the All Black forwards, who had done so much to make New Zealand great, were not the force of old. In addition, the Lions, 1971 style, were different from their predecessors in that they were well prepared and, more important, they were determined to win, even if it meant abandoning their traditional running game. They took the All Blacks on at their own game, and beat them, and that was something that New Zealanders found very difficult to accept. Meads, who was still the best lock forward in the country, but by now way past his best, was made captain, and Lochore, against his better judgement, was hauled out of semi-retirement to play in the third test. The experiment failed, but it did highlight the problem that there was a very real lack of young talent waiting in the wings. Then there was the vexed question of the Maoris. The Maoris, who had played such a vital part in the New Zealand game, were in danger of losing their identity. The day before they played the Lions in Auckland, an article appeared in the newspaper suggesting that they should no longer play as a representative team. The article, ill-advised as it was, served only to make the Maoris play as if their lives and their very culture depended upon a successful result, and instead of being a festival of open rugby it was a shabby spectacle, second only to the game against Canterbury in its bitterness. Dark days indeed for New Zealand rugby. New players and new tactics had to be found, but both seemed to be in short supply and it was an unimaginative and insecure side which left for Britain the following year. Meads, whose international career had come to an end after the series against the Lions, remembers watching a newsreel of the party arriving at Heathrow. 'They came off the plane as if they were away on a social trip; they did not look like a team proud to be representing their country.' Matters were not helped by the attitude of the British press and public, who just could not resist the temptation to gloat over the events of the previous year. The Seventh All Blacks found that they were not being treated with the respect enjoyed by their predecessors, and possibly as a result they appeared surly and uncommunicative off the field, and something less than heroic on it. The sending home of Keith Murdoch after an extra

curricular *tour de force* against a security guard in Cardiff was the nadir. Yet they produced a remarkably good record despite losing five matches – more than any other All Blacks side in Europe. They were unbeaten in their international matches in Britain, and played their full part in an epic encounter with the Barbarians in Cardiff. In Ian Kirkpatrick, Peter Whiting, Sid Going, Bryan Williams, Joe Karam and Grant Batty, they had players of real merit, and mercifully all were able to display their talents in happier circumstances two years later when the All Blacks were invited to Ireland as part of the Irish Centenary celebrations. Under the captaincy of Andy Leslie, a fine number 8 and an excellent P.R.O., they successfully negotiated a final week of intense activity. On the Saturday they beat Ireland, in mid-week they beat a Welsh XV, and three days later they were unfortunate only to draw with a Barbarians side whose forwards had represented the Lions in the series against South Africa.

It had taken seventy-five years to build up to the side of 1967 (arguably the best ever to have represented New Zealand), and only three to descend into the trough of the early 1970s. During that time the emphasis had come increasingly to be upon winning, even at school level where the sterile techniques being taught to the senior sides were being drummed into six-year-olds, and the tiny tot winger, who had to spend his Saturday morning in the freezing cold on the off chance of receiving a pass, lost interest. The game was in danger of losing its appeal to the younger generations, who doubtless felt that winning was important, but considered the manner of victory to be of greater value. Andy Leslie and his team achieved both these aims in 1974, and in so doing brought renewed hope for the future of rugby in New Zealand.

During the Don Clarke era the running back went out of vogue in New Zealand, but in recent years the All Blacks have rediscovered the value of back play, and there is no more exciting talent in the country at the moment than that of the Auckland winger Bryan Williams. He first came to prominence during the tour to South Africa in 1970, and also caused the 1971 Lions considerable problems. Here he slips out of a John Dawes tackle during the First Test at Dunedin

7 SURVIVAL IN AUSTRALIA

The First Wallabies – the first Australian tour to Britain was in 1908, and under their new nickname the Wallabies played thirty-one matches in England and Wales, winning twenty-five and losing five. This piece of action took place during the first match of the tour against Devon, and despite the tragic death of the team mascot 'Bertie', the tourists won 24–3

The Master, 'Dally' Messenger, a legendary figure in Australian sporting history. He twice played for Australia against the All Blacks in 1907, before turning professional and touring Britain with the New Zealand League side. It was on this tour that Messenger received offers from various English soccer clubs for his services, but he refused and returned to Australia to assist in the establishment of the league game

T HE FIRST MENTION of a rugger match in Australia was in a report in the *Sydney Monitor* of 23 July 1829 which described the game as being a diversion for the British soldiers. There was little or no organized football, however, until the formation of the Sydney University Club in 1864 which was followed five years later by the establishment of the Wallaroo Club. This was the largest Australian club at that time, and it attracted members by advertising in the local newspaper. Initially there were only five replies, but gradually the membership increased and between 1876 and 1880 the club was invincible, winning the Sydney Championship five times.

The Wallaroos benefited greatly from the arrival of some Irish engineers, in particular two international players, Maurice Barlow and H. D. Walsh. The Australian game was also indebted to the Arnold brothers, Dick and Montague, who insisted that the laws were adhered to and that the spirit of the game was upheld, but they met with strong opposition in this regard, and it was principally the need for a uniform set of rules which led to the formation of the Southern Rugby Union in 1874 (renamed the New South Wales Rugby Union in 1892).

At this time the Rugby game was played only in New South Wales, and nine clubs were present at the formation of the Southern Union – Wallaroo, Newington College, Goulburn, Waratah, Balmain, North Shore, Sydney University, Camden College and King's School. The first President was J. J. Calvert, and W. H. Fletcher the first secretary. It was this body which continued to govern the game until the formation of the Australian Rugby Union in 1949.

There was a great deal of dissatisfaction at about this time concerning the rules. Dick Arnold, who had been educated at Rugby School, was naturally a devotee of the rules which had been drawn up at that establishment, but in 1877 a powerful movement headed by Sir Joseph Carruthers, then Secretary of the Sydney University Club,

Of all the Australian sides to tour Europe the most successful were the 1947 Wallabies. They lost only six of their thirty-five matches, winning three out of the five internationals. In this match they have become entangled with the students of Cambridge, and the third Wallaby from the right, preparing to join the action, is Nick Shehadie, one of the tour characters

pressed hard to change over to Victorian Rules (later Australian Rules) which had been started in Melbourne in 1858. Although many clubs decided to make the change to the Victorian game, Rugby was popular enough to withstand the competition, and by the early 1880s inter-state matches had been organized against Queensland and first contact had been made with New Zealand.

In 1882 sixteen New South Walians crossed the water for a short tour of New Zealand (the boat trip taking five days), but after the second game C. S. Raymond returned to Sydney, which left the minimum fifteen players to complete the remaining five matches. Despite this they gave a good account of themselves, winning four games and establishing a reputation for playing open football.

From the success of this tour sprang a series of fixtures between the countries. The very next year, in fact, a New Zealand side went to Australia and destroyed all opposition, including a New South Wales combination which was overwhelmed by 167 points to 17. After this the New Zealanders did at least leave behind two players, Harry Braddon a full back and a forward named Jim O'Donnell. The latter played for New South Wales against Queensland from 1884–6 and against the British tourists in 1888, while Braddon also played against the British side, and against Victoria and Queensland before becoming the third President of the N.S.W. Union.

The first official international played by Australia was in 1899 at the Sydney Cricket Ground when they beat a British side 13–3. One of the Australian heroes of that series, which Australia eventually lost 3–1, was S. A. Spragge, who scored 17 of his country's 23 points. He was an immensely talented runner and goalkicker, but a promising career was cut short when he died at the age of twenty-four.

Of all the New Zealand sides to have visited Australia, few were as popular as the 1903 team under the eccentric leadership of

The Three Thornetts – one of the most famous footballing families in Australia. Top left is Dick, while holding the ball in the picture on the right is brother John. Both played rugby union for Australia before Dick turned professional, playing with brother Ken (who is to be seen dismissing an opponent in the bottom left picture) in a league test in 1963. The picture to the right shows John playing for New South Wales against the 1966 Lions. In the background are two other Australian stalwarts: immediately behind John, partly obscured, is Tony Miller, second in the list of Australian cap winners, and to Miller's right, the one man ahead of him, is hooker Peter Johnson who won 42 caps from 1959–72

History was made at the Sydney Cricket Ground on 19 June 1965 when Australia beat South Africa for the first time. A record crowd of 46,000 watched the home side win 18–11 and here Jim Lenehan gets the ball away before being grounded by Tommy Bedford. Lenehan, who won 24 caps, still holds one record – a punt kicked during the 1958 Wallaby tour to Britain, which travelled an estimated distance of 120 yards

Jimmy Duncan, whose exploits with a cloth cap have been mentioned elsewhere. The tourists scored 276 points in ten matches, and the Maori winger Opai Asher was top try scorer with seventeen.

This tour was followed the next year by a visit from 'Darky' Bedell-Sivright's British side which won all fourteen of its matches. Making a second visit to the country was the Northampton forward Blair Swannell, who had been a member of the Rev. Mullineux's side five years earlier; he decided to settle in Australia and was chosen for the party which made a first tour to New Zealand in 1905.

The first international at Dunedin was, in effect, played against a New Zealand side of reserve strength – the All Blacks not yet having returned from their triumphant tour to Europe. The three points scored by Australia that day came from the Queensland winger Doug McLean, the founder of an extraordinary line of rugby players. He had three sons, all of whom went on to play for their country – Doug Junior and Jack who were both wingers, and Bill a forward. A generation later Jeff McLean, a grandson of the original Doug, made his debut for Australia against South Africa in 1971, and he was followed into the national side three years later by his brother Paul. When the Fifth Wallabies toured Britain in 1975-6 Paul scored 154 points, a record for an Australian on tour in the British Isles.

By 1907 rugby had reached the height of its popularity in New South Wales, and the visit of the All Blacks brought record crowds for the international matches. What's more there was a good deal of optimism amongst the home following prior to the first international, when New South Wales beat the tourists. The man of the match on that occasion was the local favourite, H. H. 'Dally' Messenger, one of the legendary figures in Australian sporting history. Unfortunately he suffered an injury towards the end of the game and was unable to take his place in the First Test, which New Zealand won 26–6. The second match also went to

the visitors, and in desperation the Australian selectors decided for the third encounter to field 'in toto' the New South Wales side which had earlier beaten the All Blacks. Their selection was justified: F. Wood scored a try which Messenger converted and the match ended in a draw.

Shortly after this the bubble burst, and Rugby Union was never again to enjoy the same sort of popularity in Australia. It was an injury to the New South Wales player Alick Burden which brought the situation to its inevitable conclusion. He had broken his shoulder whilst playing against Queensland and had been refused compensation for the loss of earnings by the N.S.W. Union. This was the opportunity for the 'anti union' men to make their move; a meeting was held at the sports store belonging to the famous cricketer Victor Trumper, and present were several influential rugby men including J. J. Giltinan, who had some knowledge of the new Rugby League code being played in England, and had been in contact with those who were attempting to establish the game in New Zealand. A constitution was drafted, a committee was elected and professional rugby was born in Australia.

Trumper it was who had the idea of inviting the newly formed New Zealand league side to stop off in Sydney en route to Britain, to play three demonstration matches. The Sydney Showground was hired for the occasion and the New Zealanders won all three matches which were played under the existing union rules. The tourists were guaranteed £250 each for the three matches; the Australians, who played under the name 'Pioneers', were each given ten shillings a match plus travelling expenses.

The exception was Dally Messenger, who had been persuaded by Giltinan and Trumper to turn professional; he was paid £150 a match, the theory behind such a generous offer being that Messenger had considerable influence in rugby playing circles, and his conversion to the league game would inevitably attract many other leading players.

In the past two decades Australia has produced two world class scrum halves; Ken Catchpole, who, until his career was brought to an abrupt end in 1968, was the greatest exponent of half back play in the world, and his successor in the national side, John Hipwell. Catchpole (left) played a leading part in Australia's first win over the Springboks in 1965, and although he appears to be constrained by Tommy Bedford, Greg Davis is on hand to help out. Below, a shot of Hipwell as he prepares to set his backs in motion

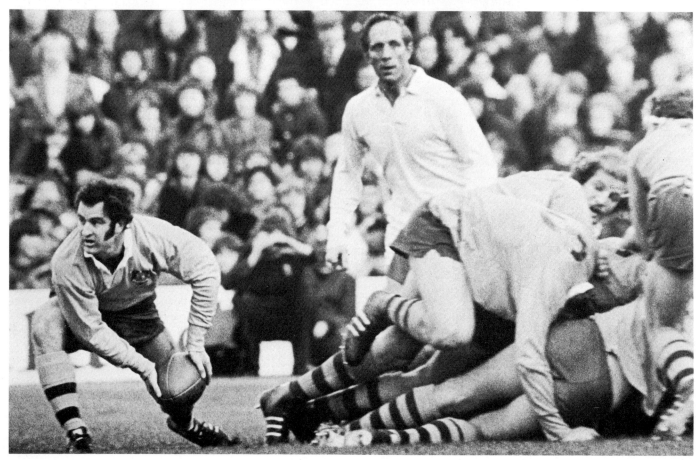

The three matches produced a profit of about £200, and it was therefore decided by Giltinan and his associates to invest all the money in the N.S.W. Rugby League.

Meanwhile Messenger had been invited to join the New Zealand party for their tour to Britain – an invitation which he was pleased to accept. He proved to be a sensation on the tour, and so impressive was his kicking that he was reputedly offered £2,000 to join the English soccer club Tottenham Hotspur, but he turned down the offer, preferring to return to Australia to help establish Rugby League. In memory of the great man, a portrait of him hangs at the Rugby League headquarters, inscribed simply 'The Master'.

The defection by so many top players had a marked effect on Rugby Union, and it was an under-strength team which left Australia in 1908 for a tour to Britain. Possibly with that in mind it was suggested that the side should be called the 'Rabbits', but this was rejected by the players, who chose the 'Wallabies' as their nickname. If their mascot was anything to go by they should have been called the 'Snakes', because they took with them a carpet snake who apparently answered to the name Bertie, and who had been smuggled into Britain wrapped round the body of one of the Australian players. Alas, the experience must have been too much for Bertie and he died before the first match of the tour against Devon. Somehow the Wallabies managed to overcome their grief, and the next day they won 24–3.

During the tour the Wallabies became Olympic Champions, an unexpected bonus for them. It came about because Cornwall, as the County Champions, had been nominated by the R.F.U. to represent Britain in the Olympics that year. Three weeks earlier they had lost to the Wallabies 18–5, and when the two sides met for a second time at the Olympic Stadium in Shepherds Bush, London, the Australians won again, this time by an even greater margin (32–3), and according to one report the Wallabies 'scored pretty much as they liked on a some-

what slippery ground in dull and rather dark weather'.

The tourists' international record must also have exceeded expectations – they beat England and lost narrowly to Wales. They had a powerfully built winger in Charles Russell, who scored twenty-four tries in twenty-six matches, and a superb goal kicker in Phil Carmichael; out of fifty-nine attempts at goal he converted fifty-six and finished up with 119 points on the tour.

On their return to Australia the union game was dealt another body blow when thirteen of the side went over to league, each one receiving a guarantee of £100. The decade following this was perhaps the most traumatic in the history of Rugby Union in Australia, with the upheaval of World War I and the disappearance of so many good players to the professional ranks.

Despite a short stopover by the Springboks in 1921, and a surprise defeat of the All Blacks by New South Wales in 1924, the Australian game was in a parlous state, and when an invitation came to tour Great Britain in 1927 it was declined on the grounds that suitable representatives could not be found. But New South Wales accepted the challenge and sent a side which was known as the 'Waratahs' from the emblem on the players' jerseys. During the tour they played five unofficial international matches against the Home Countries and France, winning three and losing two. The team was led by A. C. Wallace, who had played in the fabulous Scottish threequarter line of the mid-twenties, and under his influence the Waratahs played fast exciting football.

Two years later New Zealand sent a strong side to Australia for a tour which included three international matches. There was no earthly reason why the All Blacks should have considered defeat in any of the internationals, but they went home having lost all three. A crowd of 40,000 was at the Sydney ground for the First Test, in which Australia beat New Zealand for the first time since 1913. The Second Test was played

Conduct unbecoming? – the New South Wales Country XV get together for a set move designed to confuse England during their Australian tour in 1975. It also confused the law makers who could find nothing against the ruse except that it might have come under the heading of 'ungentlemanly conduct'. Awaiting the outcome of this particular manoeuvre are two bewildered Englishmen – Barry Nelmes and Roger Uttley

in Brisbane, the Australians winning again 17–9, and when the Australian skipper Sid King crossed over for the winning try in the Third Test, it was the first time that Australia had won three consecutive matches against New Zealand, and the first time that New Zealand had lost three consecutive matches against anybody.

In 1933, with South African rugby enjoying an extended run of good fortune, the Wallabies made a first visit to that country. In the Springbok line up were Bennie Osler, Danie Craven, Gerry Brand, Ferdie Bergh and 'Boy Louw'. Against that the Wallabies possessed several useful practitioners like Eddie Bonis, Aub Hodgson, Graham Cooke, Bob Loudon and W. H. 'Wild Bill' Cerutti, one of the toughest and most colourful characters in Australian rugby. He had originally been a soccer player but soon discovered that this was not quite physical enough, whereupon he switched to rugby which he played until he was nearly forty years old. Throughout his career he always insisted on wearing the no. 13 jersey.

The Springboks won the First Test 17–3, but a fortnight later, much to the South Africans' surprise, the Wallabies reversed the result with interest, winning 21–6. Captaining the Springboks that day was Bennie Osler, who for the first and last time in his career yielded to the press campaign for open rugby. The cumbersome Springbok forwards were thus called upon to match their speedy Australian counterparts, a task which proved beyond them, and by half time they were a well beaten side.

It was back to the old format for the next two tests in which South Africa made certain of winning the series, but the Wallabies came back to take the Fifth Test 15–4 and returned well pleased with their first visit to South Africa.

That final test at Bloemfontein marked the end of Osler's international career – a sad farewell perhaps, not only because he had finished with a defeat after so many years of glorious success, but with his departure

The style which set a tour record for Australian full back Paul McLean during the Wallabies tour to Britain in 1975–7. He scored 154 points more than any other Australian on tour in Britain. He is the latest member of a remarkable rugby playing family which was founded in 1905 when Doug McLean played for Australia against the All Blacks

many South Africans now looked forward to a more adventurous style of play along the lines demonstrated by the Wallabies.

Australia won the Bledisloe Cup for the first time in 1934. Three years earlier, Lord Bledisloe, who was then Governor General of New Zealand, had presented a trophy for the winners of the matches between Australia and New Zealand. Unfortunately, the first time that the two countries played for the prize, neither the cup nor Lord Bledisloe was present. Work on the trophy had not been completed and Lord Bledisloe had been forced to attend another engagement, so the New Zealanders, who won the match, proudly went away without the cup. Presumably the work had been finished by the time Australia won it three years later.

The 1947–8 Wallabies tour to Europe was one of the most successful of all Australian rugby tours. Eight years earlier a touring side had been selected and had actually arrived in Britain, but with the declaration of war they had to return without playing a game. Of that party only Bill McLean was in the 1947 side and he broke his leg in the first game against Combined Services, an injury which prevented him from taking any further part in the tour.

Another unfortunate was Charlie Eastes, a player of rare promise, who had gone with the Wallabies to New Zealand the previous year and had established a considerable reputation. Sadly for him, and for the Wallabies, he fractured an arm against Newport in the first part of the tour, but his early performances had been enough to attract the league scouts, and various offers were made to him, including one from the Los Angeles Rams who were anxious to acquire him for the American football circus. But Eastes resisted all offers and remained loyal to the union code.

The Wallabies won all but six of their thirty-five matches on the tour in Europe, three of the defeats coming from Wales, France and the Barbarians. This latter fixture was arranged at the last minute when it be-

came apparent that the tourists were running short of funds and would be unable to fulfil the matches which had been arranged in the United States and Canada. The Four Home Unions who were sympathetic to the Australians' plight agreed to stage an extra game at Cardiff Arms Park and asked the Barbarians to provide the opposition. The occasion proved to be so successful that it became a regular feature on the itineraries of every major touring side.

While the 1949 All Blacks were involved in their calamitous tour to South Africa, the Wallabies arrived in New Zealand for a short visit. It was a strong side with a formidable set of forwards; two in particular had very quickly made themselves known to New Zealand referees by their zealous play. One was Dave Brockhoff, a twenty-one-year-old forward who had been causing mayhem amongst the home backs, and had picked up a good many tries in the process.

The story is told that before the match against West Coast/Buller, the referee had entered the Australian changing room and asked 'Which one of you is Brockhoff?' Proudly Brockhoff stood up to signal his presence, whereupon the referee launched into a tirade on dirty play and issued a stern warning to the entire team. From all accounts the lecture didn't quite make the required impact upon Brockhoff, and the official found it necessary to send him to the touchline, not for the whole game but merely to cool off.

It was Brockhoff who was coach to the Australian side which played the two distasteful matches against England in Sydney and Brisbane in 1975, and it was the same man who came with the Fifth Wallabies to Britain as assistant manager a few months later. Articulate and fascinating in conversation, he was greatly respected by his players, and he played his full part in ensuring that the tour was a happy and successful one.

Another outstanding individual of the 1949 side was Nick Shehadie, the New South Wales lock forward who first played against New Zealand in 1947 and ended his international career on the tour to Britain ten years later. He became a highly successful businessman, but never altered his humorous approach to life, an approach reflected in the sign which hung outside his dry cleaning shop in Manly – 'Drop Your Tweeds at Nick's'.

On his tour to Britain during the 1957–8 season, Shehadie played against Wales and Ireland but did not take part in the game against England at Twickenham – a game which has lived in the memory only for its violence and for one piece of magic from Peter Jackson the English winger. As full time approached England were reduced to fourteen men but only eleven of them were effective members of the side, the other three suffering from concussion. The count on the scoreboard stood at 3 points each. In the twelfth minute of injury time the ball reached Jackson, stationed on the right wing; with a sidestep and a burst of acceleration he was past the converging defence, and having shrugged off one last, persistent defender, he went full tilt for the corner to score the winning try.

One of the few good things to emerge from the tour was the play of the nineteen-year-old Australian full back Jim Lenehan, who established himself as the number one choice – a position he held until his final international appearance against Ireland in 1967.

Of all the talented players to have represented Australia, however, very few have come anywhere near to matching the standards set by Ken Catchpole. As a scrum half he possessed the full range of skills, and many of the present day half backs, including Gareth Edwards, have based at least some part of their play upon Catchpole's style. He was made captain on his international debut against South Africa in 1961, a game which the Wallabies lost badly, but the following year he teamed up with a young fly half called Phil Hawthorne and that was the beginning of a partnership

which helped to steer Australia to some of her most memorable victories.

When John Thornett's team took on the Springboks in 1963 they lost the first international but came back to win successive tests – the Second and Third – a feat unequalled by any previous touring side in sixty-seven years and forty-seven internationals. In both matches Catchpole was the brains behind the operation, constantly directing the play and getting the maximum use out of the creative abilities of Hawthorne and the destructive talents of Greg Davis; it was the Catchpole/Hawthorne combination which conspired to beat Wales at Cardiff in 1966, and they were together again for the win over England on that same tour.

It was after this tour that the partnership broke up; Hawthorne joined St George's Rugby League Club for a fee of 30,000 dollars, and serious injury finished Catchpole's international career.

It happened in a match against the All Blacks in 1968 – Catchpole was caught in a ruck with one of his legs protruding from the mass of players, the other one trapped by the weight of bodies on top. It was at this point that Colin Meads entered the action, and in an effort to get at the ball Meads grabbed hold of Catchpole's leg and heaved. The pain was excruciating as the muscles tore, but more ominous was the numbness that followed. The injury was serious enough to prevent him from ever again wearing the Australian jersey, and so ended one of the most distinguished careers in international rugby.

Some time after the incident, Catchpole was asked whether he thought that Meads had acted with malice aforethought to which Catchpole replied, 'You'll have to ask him about that,' and indeed Meads is the only man who can truthfully answer the question. The All Black was certainly deeply hurt by some of the criticism he received as a result of the incident and he has always maintained that his sole aim was to get the ball. Suffice

The outstanding forward on the
Wallabies' last tour to Britain was
the No. 8 Mark Loane, who
despite injury proved himself to
be a very fine player. Here he is
in a race up field with the
Harlequin centre Tim Rutter
during the match against London
Counties at Twickenham

to say that when the two met five years later to play some festival rugby in Tonga, they did so on the best of terms.

Very few countries could have overcome the loss of such an outstanding performer as Catchpole as successfully as Australia. The man who replaced him was John Hipwell, who had for some time been Catchpole's understudy in the Australian team, although he was still a teenager. He had carefully modelled his game on that of his predecessor and was almost as good at it. A swift, accurate passer and a fine runner, he has been the mainstay of the Australian side since Catchpole's departure, but often the burden has proved too much, even for a man of his outstanding talent. Time without number he has been wooed by Rugby League suitors, but each time has refused, taking the view that no one needs to pay him money to play rugby.

Nevertheless there must have been times when he thought twice about refusing. It must be a desperately frustrating experience to be part of a good team one year, and the next find that the cream of the talent has been taken. Hipwell has seen many of Australia's most promising performers lured away to league – amongst them John Brass, Stephen Knight and Russell Fairfax.

It must be equally galling for the national selectors who work hard and cover many miles in their attempts to produce a strong side, only to discover all too quickly that their efforts have been in vain. Taking an optimistic view, however, the union game in Australia has been fortunate to be able to count upon so many loyal servants – men like Catchpole, Hipwell, John Thornett, one of a famous rugby playing family, and a most popular national captain, Peter Johnson, the leading Australian cap winner, and Tony Miller whose international career spanned fifteen years, and came to an end in 1967 when, at the age of thirty-seven, he played against the All Blacks. As long as the Australian game can produce and retain men of that calibre, it will survive and flourish.

8 THE HEROES AT THE MO'S

The first test match played at the
Newlands Ground in Cape Town
was against W. E. McLagan's
British side in 1891. The tourists
won the match 4–0 and with it
victory in the series

If I had my way with demonstrators,
I'd simmer them in oil;
I'd fill a pot with bitumen,
And bring them to the boil.

Anon

To begin with, the demonstrations at least had the merit of being different; the tight security, the coach trips between matches conducted in absolute secrecy, even the lunatic who chained himself to the coach steering wheel – all had a certain novelty value. But after several weeks, the restrictions imposed upon the 1969 Springboks in Britain became intolerable. In South Africa these serious-minded men were symbols of manhood; to many in the British Isles they represented repression. That they completed their itinerary and behaved impeccably throughout says a great deal for their self-control, but no one could pretend that it was a happy or successful tour.

From the outset the anti-apartheid section of the community was determined that the visit should not take place. Having failed in this aim the next step was to cause the maximum amount of disruption whilst the tour was in progress, and in this the demonstrators, some sincere in their principles, others merely professional hell raisers, were successful. The tour was a social flop and, more important from a South African viewpoint, the playing record was disastrous. They finished up with the poorest record of any South African side on tour in Britain, having failed to win a single international. Ironically, they returned home to a hero's welcome. But there was little to cheer – Springbok rugby had fallen behind the times, South African sportsmen faced ostracism. and above all the fear that sport and politics could not be kept apart was now confirmed beyond doubt.

Apartheid was not in the vocabulary of Canon. G. Ogilvie, who introduced the game of rugby to the young men of Cape Town. Nicknamed 'Gog' from the only legible part of his signature, Ogilvie had played the

Winchester code as a master at St Andrews College, Bradfield, and it was a variation of this code which he brought to the Diocesan College in Cape Town. By 1875 'Gog's Football' was being superseded by the Rugby code, and it was in this same year that Hamilton Rugby Club was founded, the first in South Africa. Western Province was the cradle of the game in those formative years, and after the establishment of Hamilton, there followed Villagers, Gardens, the University of Cape Town and the most famous of all, Stellenbosch University. Thence to the Eastern Cape, Western Transvaal, and Natal, and by the early 1890s the game was flourishing throughout South Africa.

In 1891 the visit of W. E. McLagan's British side was eagerly anticipated, the financial responsibility for which had been wholly undertaken by Cecil Rhodes who was then Prime Minister of Cape Colony. McLagan brought with him a gold cup which had been donated by Sir Donald Currie, founder of the Union Castle steamship line to South Africa, and it was Currie's wish that the trophy should be presented to the team which put up the best performance against the tourists. The cup went to Kimberley who lost by a try to nil, and immediately the Griqualand West Union handed it over to the South African Rugby Football Board, then three years old, so that it could be competed for on an interprovincial basis. Hence the birth of the Currie Cup.

There was little doubt that the British visit had a stimulating effect on South African rugby. The lessons taught by the tourists were swiftly absorbed, as the next British side discovered in 1896. Realizing the importance of forward strength the South Africans had unearthed some pretty impressive specimens, among them Barry Heatlie, regarded as being one of South Africa's finest forwards. He was also an inspiring captain and led the Springboks, playing for the first time in green jerseys, to

'When England met the South Africans at the Crystal Palace, the Springboks were handicapped by the illness of several good men. The match which was well fought in the most inclement weather and the slipperiest of grounds ended in a draw, each side securing a try.' This was a report on the international played on 8 December 1906 during the first Springbok tour to Britain under the captaincy of Paul Roos. The tourists played twenty-eight matches winning twenty-five, losing two, and drawing one – the international against England

THE DRAWN MATCH BETWEEN ENGLAND AND THE "SPRINGBOKS."

PHOTOGRAPHS BY RUSSELL, BY BOWDEN, AND BY ILLUSTRATIONS BUREAU.

THE ENGLISH TEAM AT THE CRYSTAL PALACE

SPRINGBOKS NEARLY OVER THE LINE: JACKSON CLAIMS A TRY.

AFTER THE HEEL OUT: SCRUM BREAKING UP

LINING OUT FOR A THROW IN.

JACKETT HURT TRYING TO PREVENT SPRINGBOKS FIRST TRY.

CARTWRIGHT KICKS OFF

HEELED OUT: A DASH FOR THE BALL. — P. ROOS. — A THROW IN: MARK YOUR MEN —

victory against the British side in Cape Town. Although the tourists won the rubber, the Springboks had got off the mark, and it was to be sixty-two years before they lost another series at home.

After the Boer War, Mark Morrison took a third British side to South Africa in 1903, but with one or two exceptions it was not a particularly strong team and the Springboks, with Heatlie still to the fore, and backs like Japie Krige and Bob Loubser emerging from obscurity, won the series. Krige, the 'artful dodger' in the centre and Bob Loubser were among the handful of players who drew un-qualified praise from the celebrated rugby supremo A. F. Markotter. For more than fifty years Markotter was the most influential man in the South African game. The zenith of his playing career came when he captained a Western Province Country XV against Morrison's tourists, but then an injury sus-tained on the cricket field of all places, pre-vented him from taking any more active part in the game. Thereafter he became coach to the Stellenbosch side and was a South African selector from 1921 to 1938. He made very few mistakes in his judgement of a player, but he demanded utter dedication from his protégés, and he could frequently be seen running on to the field to give some physical encouragement to those who were not giving of their best. But a kick in the pants from Markotter was a highly prized possession. 'Look, laddies,' he would say, 'I never kick a man down. I always kick him up, and I don't kick fools.' However, he did tend to suffer fools badly and on one occa-sion he approached a referee who had not enjoyed the best of afternoons: 'I know you did your best,' he said curtly, 'but for God's sake don't do it again.'

Having beaten a British side in South Africa, it was only natural that the Spring-boks should now wish to try their luck on an overseas tour, and in 1906 they arrived in Britain. Led by Paul Roos, they began in great style with fifteen consecutive wins. But then they met Scotland at Hampden Park in dreadful conditions, and lost their first international on foreign soil 6–0. The Springboks still had three internationals to play and of the three the scalp they coveted above all belonged to Wales, who had beaten Dave Gallaher's All Blacks the previous year. Wales that day fielded a back division as good as any that had previously repre-sented the Principality – Percy Bush and Dickie Owen were the half backs, Gwyn Nicholls, Rhys Gabe, Teddy Morgan and J. Williams made up the threequarter line. The Springboks' earlier experiences in Wales had taught them the value of sound scrummaging, and on the day the South African forwards proved to be the better unit. Steve Joubert scored an early try for the tourists, going through the enemy lines 'like a rat through a drainpipe', and before the end Loubser and J. W. E. Raaff had added two more. In the words of the chronicler A. G. Hales, when the fateful whistle sounded, 40,000 Celts walked away in gloomy silence wondering what in the name of all the saints was going to happen to the "Land of our Fathers". As a general rule they sing this and then wonder what is going to happen to the other folk.'

Before the outbreak of World War I, the Springboks managed one more visit to Britain. Included in the party were two sets of brothers, the Luyts, Richard, Freddie and John, and the Morkels, Jack and Gerhard. It was on this tour that Gerhard gained universal acclamation for his full back play. His fielding was faultless, his line and goal-kicking accurate and his defence sure. So sure in fact that many took exception to his methods. During the 1921 tour to Australia, Morkel was playing in Sydney and had to be smuggled out of the ground after he had laid low the local hero with a crunching tackle. It took a borrowed cap pulled well down over his eyes to get him past the crowd which was waiting outside.

By this time Morkel was thirty-four, and if he hadn't exactly appealed to the Australian crowds he was a great favourite in New

Bennie Osler, the 'Evil Genius' stands on the left of the picture along with Phil Mostert, an outstanding Springbok forward in the decade between 1921 and 1931. These were prosperous years for South African rugby, dictated to a great extent by the tactical brilliance of Osler. One critic wrote of him, *'He evolved a fly half game all his own, and his threequarters had to subordinate their individual merits and ability to the type of game he favoured in any match.'* His style produced countless imitators who possessed neither his skill nor his intelligence, and inevitably South African back play suffered as a result. He was, however, the greatest tactician and matchwinner in the South African game

Zealand, where he was irreverently referred to as 'uncle'. But 'uncle' still had a trick or two up his sleeve as he showed in the Second Test in Auckland, when he dropped a goal to ensure South Africa's victory. The week before the deciding test, the Springboks were staying in a seaside village and were using one of the local fields for working out. All week Morkel had been practising his drop goals and his accuracy was patently causing unrest amongst the natives. On the Thursday before the match he arrived at the ground for his final practice to find that the posts had disappeared. He set off at once in search of the groundsman and eventually found that individual red faced and apologetic. The villagers, it appeared, alarmed at what Morkel might do to the All Blacks, had removed the posts. In the event they had nothing to fear. The Wellington weather ran true to form, the wind raged, the rain poured, and the game ended in a scoreless draw.

The ten years between 1924 and 1933 were dominated by one man – Bennie Osler, the greatest tactician and match winner that South Africa has ever produced. Yet to many he was a curse; a player who stifled three-quarter play and devalued the running game. He was the first of the kicking fly halves, the pivot around whom the play revolved. There was no question that Osler was a genius at his art, but the pity was that his style was adopted by countless other players who lacked totally the same degree of skill which belonged to the master. His influence on the game gradually shifted the emphasis away from the backs, and the birth of Springbok forward power can be traced to this decade. There was no denying that it was an outstandingly successful period and South Africa was now launched upon an extended run of victories.

Osler made his international debut against the Lions in 1924, and early in the game he gave evidence of his abilities. With the tourists beginning to take control, he calmly dropped a goal to put the Springboks on their way to victory by 7 points to 3. But he

Left A scene from the international against Wales in Durban in 1964 which South Africa won 24–3. At half time the scores were level at 3–3, but then the Springbok forwards took control and here their No. 8 Doug Hopwood crosses for a try despite a tackle by Welsh centre John Dawes.

Right Hopwood's predecessor, Hennie Muller, leading the Springboks out at Murrayfield for the match against Scotland in 1952, the match which was to create a world points scoring record. The Springboks won 44–0, scoring nine tries, seven of which were converted by 'Okey' Geffin who is pictured following Muller on to the field

was not merely a scoring machine. His kicking both in attack and defence was devastatingly accurate, and it was this side of his play which often aroused the ire of the crowd. Danie Craven, who played in seven internationals as Osler's half back partner, recalls an occasion when Osler was receiving some 'stick' from the crowd for his excessive kicking. 'Daantjie,' he said to Craven, 'give me the ball again. I won't disappoint them.' So saying he once again kicked the ball into touch. As before there was booing. After the third touch kick the crowd became resigned to the inevitable and the reaction was less abrasive. 'That's better,' said Osler. 'They are beginning to mind their manners.'

Osler admitted that he was never completely happy playing outside Craven, the man who developed the dive pass and made it a useful weapon in the scrum half's armoury. He considered that too much time was wasted in the execution of the pass, and when it came it was too hard. Nevertheless, Craven was as much an innovator in the technique of passing as Osler was in the art of kicking, and it was the length and accuracy of his service in the 1937 series against the All Blacks which contributed greatly to the Springboks' victory. It was, however, during the 1931–2 tour to Britain that he established his reputation, his durability enabling him to cope with the heavy ground conditions. Craven's physique and versatility brought him the unique distinction of representing his country in four different positions – scrum half, centre, fly half and eighth man. His association with rugby did not end when he finished playing at the relatively young age of twenty-seven. He continued to have a profound influence on the game as a coach and administrator, and now as President of the South African Rugby Board, he is one of the leading figures in world rugby. A man passionately dedicated to breaking down the barriers that exist between black and white, he looks forward to the day when the Springboks will once again be able to participate universally in

Over the years the matches between the Springboks and the All Blacks have produced some desperately close struggles and this international at Port Elizabeth in 1960 was one of them. With the series standing level at 1–1 everything depended upon the result of the Fourth Test, and it was this try by Martin Pelser which gave South Africa the match and the series

competitive rugby.

The 'Osler Era', of course, contained many other great players besides Osler and Craven. There was for instance the Western Province forward Phil Mostert who gained the ultimate accolade from that pugnacious Irishman J. D. Clinch: 'He is the hardest to bring down, and I do not believe that he can be knocked out.' Then there was Gerry Brand who created history in the match against England at Twickenham in 1932 when he dropped a goal from his own twenty-five. It was estimated that the ball travelled ninety yards before falling to earth well over the dead ball line. He was five years later in the Springbok side which toured Australia and New Zealand and succeeded in scoring 190 points during the tour.

This was perhaps the greatest of Springbok sides, containing as it did Brand, Craven, D. O. Williams, Philip Nel, Ferdie Bergh and the Louw brothers, Fanie and 'Boy'. With the All Blacks and the Springboks level at one victory apiece, there was a record crowd of 60,000 at Eden Park for the deciding match. Before the kick off a telegram arrived from Paul Roos, the Springbok captain during the 1906 tour of Britain. His exhortations consisted of three words: 'Scrum, scrum, scrum.' It was sound advice. Whenever possible the South African skipper Nel called for a scrum instead of a lineout, and the All Blacks who had been concentrating on their lineout play in practice, were scrummaged into the ground. With the forwards in control and Craven firing out his bullet-like passes, the South African wingers L. Babrow and Williams made the most of the opportunities given to them. Babrow scored two tries, Williams one, and the Springboks had won a series against the All Blacks for the first time.

Many of the stars of that campaign were back on parade when the Lions toured South Africa in 1938, but the war saw to it that an entirely new side had to be found for the visit of Fred Allen's All Blacks in 1949. The visitors lacked nothing in confidence;

the New Zealand Army team (Kiwis) had just completed a thoroughly successful tour to Britain and France, and mindful of the Springboks scrummaging in the 1937 series the All Blacks had brought with them some huge forwards. This was the one bit of thinking they got right. They had, however, reckoned without the careful planning of Danie Craven, the Springbok coach, Aaron (Okey) Geffin, the goalkicking prop, and the destructive talents of a young No. 8 called Hennie Muller. Throughout the series Muller chased, harried and spoiled, and at the end of the tour his play brought forth some bitter invective from the New Zealand critics. The South Africans, who played with a 3–4–1 scrum formation, had for many years been employing their eighth man as a tight loose forward, and there was no doubt that Muller was an outstanding exponent of this sort of play. Extraordinarily fast for a big man (he was an even time sprinter), he was invariably first to the break down. Having got there his all round football skills enabled him to make effective use of the possession he had gained. He regarded his display in the first international against the 'Forty Niners' as his best, and there were few who would disagree with this assessment. For the record, Geffin kicked five penalty goals out of five attempts, and the Springboks won 15–11. Throughout the series Geffin continued to kick goals, Muller went on flattening the opposition, and South Africa won the series 4–0.

The Springboks were without a serious rival at this time. The tour to Britain in 1951–2 was wonderfully successful, with thirty wins out of thirty-one matches, the only defeat being sustained against London Counties. Their points for total of course, received a considerable boost with the record 44–0 victory over the Scots at Murrayfield. They scored nine tries in all, six of them coming from the forwards, among whom Muller and Chris Koch were outstanding. The hardest of the internationals on that tour was against Wales at Cardiff. The

The Springbok scrum half and captain Dawie de Villiers preparing to kick during the First Test against the Lions at Pretoria in 1968. Shielding de Villiers from possible hindrance is Jan Ellis, and the Lion lying helpless on his back is Bob Taylor of Northampton. South Africa won the match 25–20

Above The Springbok centre Mannetjies Roux caught in the act of scoring against the 1968 Lions in the Fourth Test in Johannesburg which South Africa won 19–6

Top right The two scrum halves, Gareth Edwards of Wales and South Africa's de Villiers, shake hands and exchange jerseys after the international at Cardiff Arms Park in 1970 which ended in a 6–6 draw

Right A commonplace occurrence during the 1970 tour as demonstrators invade the field before the international against Scotland at Murrayfield

Welsh forwards were in superb form, and behind them was a potentially brilliant outside half, Cliff Morgan. But Morgan was as yet inexperienced in this grade of football and he was bottled up by Muller and his back row colleagues Stephen Fry and 'Basie' Van Wyk. The Springboks won 6–3.

South Africa saw a different side to Morgan during the thrilling series against the Lions three years later. It was his individual spark which put the Lions one up in the series after the First Test, and throughout the tour he was a constant menace to South African defences. The Springboks squared the account in the Second Test at Cape Town, when Tom Van Vollenhoven scored a hat trick of tries, but at the end of the series, which finished level at 2–2, it was obvious that cracks were beginning to appear in the Springbok machine. There was concern amongst South African experts that the forwards were not the force of old. If the Lions had been able to secure so much possession in South Africa what, they wondered, would the All Blacks do when the Springboks toured New Zealand the following year? Not only did the Springboks lose that series 3–1, they lost a two match series against France in 1958, their first at home since 1896.

These setbacks convinced the Springbok selectors that they would have to revert to the solid type of forward play upon which they had built their reputation. Thus when the All Blacks made a third visit to South Africa in 1960, they were totally unprepared for the onslaught. Avril Malan at lock forward was captain and he had with him in the forwards Johann Claassen, a magnificent lineout jumper, Piet du Toit, an obdurate scrummager, Chris Koch and at No. 8 Doug Hopwood, a worthy successor to Hennie Muller. In the back division were two strong running centres. Ian Kirkpatrick and John Gainsford, and the neatest of fly halves in Keith Oxlee. With the series depending upon the final test at the Boet Erasmus Stadium, the Springboks triumphed 8–3 in

The Currie Cup which has been in existence for eighty-five years continues to be a great crowd puller, and in this match in 1975 Northern Transvaal, on their way to becoming champions for the third year running, have the beating of Western Province. The picture shows the Northern Transvaal winger Pierre Spies being tackled by the Western Province full back Dawie Snyman

Overleaf Rising Damp – the Welsh and Springbok packs sweat it out during the 1970 match at the Arms Park, Cardiff. The game was drawn 6–6 and it preserved the Springboks' remarkable record against Wales. Wales, in fact, is the only one of the International Board countries never to have beaten South Africa

what Danie Craven described as one of the most bitterly contested forward struggles he had seen in his long association with test rugby.

It was against this background that the fifth Springboks arrived in Britain later that year; a side of machine-like efficiency with players in reserve like Frik du Preez, then a flanker but later to become a second row forward to rank with the best. Their object was to win matches, and as one critic put it, this became 'a magnificent obsession'. The records show that they succeeded in their narrow aim with just one defeat in thirty-four games, and that in the last match of the tour to a Barbarians side which abandoned for the day their traditional running style. The tourists took their defeat well, and it was generally considered that Rugby had benefited as a result of this reverse in their fortunes, although the Springboks were not unnaturally sceptical about the manner of the Barbarians victory.

It was impossible not to be impressed by the cold efficiency of the tourists, but they had failed to win many friends, and were criticized as being an unsociable bunch. Interestingly enough, thirteen years later Hannes Marais, who captained the Springboks against the '1974 Lions', wrote: 'We found the Lions extremely unsociable. We were at great pains during the series to get to the various receptions on time and to try to mix with them. Unfortunately we were given the cold shoulder.' Is unsociability then tied up in some inextricable way with dedication and success? Maybe it is the case that victory makes players less approachable, but is it not also true that continued prosperity for the guests tends to bring the worst out of the hosts? At any rate it is perhaps worth recording that when Avril Malan brought the Springboks back to Britain for a short tour in 1965, they failed to win any of their five matches but were described as being 'extremely popular socially', and were praised for being 'good losers'.

In that same year they lost three inter-

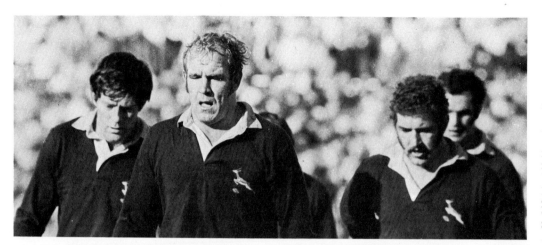

Some outstanding Springbok forwards: Hannes Marais (left) leads his men from the field after a test defeat by the 1974 Lions. On his right is Jan Ellis, who formed such a magnificent back row partnership with Tommy Bedford, seen below about to pass the ball to the third member of the back row triumvirate, Piet Greyling. On Bedford's right is South Africa's leading cap winner, Frik du Preez

nationals to New Zealand and two to Australia, where doubtless they were also hailed as 'fair old cobbers'. Although they beat the Lions in 1968 for the second time in six years, France in the same year and Australia in 1969, it was clear that South African rugby was losing ground. By this time many of the stalwarts of the Springbok pack had retired – men like Claassen, Hugo Van Zyl, Piet du Toit and Martin Pelser, who had gone over to the Rugby League code, and there were no ready replacements.

The full force of anti-apartheid feeling first hit the Springboks during the 1969 tour to Britain. The opening game against Oxford University in the stark surroundings of Twickenham was watched by three thousand paying spectators and twice as many policemen. The tourists submitted feebly by 6 points to 3. This was to be the pattern throughout the tour, and it was little wonder that the Springboks returned to their homeland with such an execrable record. Diversions apart, the tourists lacked the necessary playing strength; the loose forward trio of Jan Ellis, Piet Greyling and Tommy Bedford were notable exceptions, while Frik du Preez ploughed a lone furrow amongst the tight forwards. Dawie de Villiers, who came with the reputation of being the number one scrum half in the world, failed to justify that ranking, no doubt because as captain he had matters other than rugby on his mind. A minister of the Dutch Reformed Church, he was considered a suitable leader in all quarters, but he had the misfortune to be in control of poor sides. He had captained the Springboks in the losing series against New Zealand four years previously, and with the All Blacks due to visit South Africa in 1970 there were many who felt that a change in leadership would be beneficial.

This was the series that the All Blacks could not lose and the Springboks had to win. Prior to the tour New Zealand had insisted that Maoris be included otherwise the visit would be cancelled. The South African Government yielded and for the first time the All Blacks arrived in the Republic with a fully representative side. It was the first multi-racial team to compete in South Africa, and how well they began. In the opening ten matches they scored 276 points and the crowds warmed to the sensational running of the teenage Maori winger Bryan Williams. Despite this, South Africa won the First Test. The All Blacks recovered their poise sufficiently to win the Second, although the game will remain engraved on several medical cards. By the Third Test, the tourists, their selection policy in shreds, and many of their players softened by the good life, were easy prey for the Springboks who won the final two matches and the series.

Apart from this and two successful series against France, the 1970s have brought little else of cheer to South Africa. Beaten at home by England and again by the Lions, they have been denied competition at the highest level and this has inevitably led to a decline in standards. It was a bitter blow to Danie Craven when the proposed tour to New Zealand in 1973 was called off because the Government would not agree to the selection of the team on a multi-racial basis. There have, however, been slight concessions in recent years, and in 1972 England played matches against the Cape Coloureds and an African XV, as did the Lions in 1974. Perhaps this can be seen as a chink in the armour of apartheid, and in time it will lead to further concessions which in turn will enable South African sportsmen and women to compete freely all over the world.

Overleaf Hopes that the 1976 All Blacks might become the first New Zealand side to win a test series in South Africa, were temporarily raised by their display in the Second Test at Bloemfontein which they won 15–9. The All Black hero on that occasion was centre Joe Morgan, who is seen putting the finishing touch to a dazzling run. This win squared the series at 1–1, but the Springboks came back to win the remaining two tests at Newlands and at Ellis Park to take the series 3–1

9 L+S RUGBYM+N

The first international football match in France – the match between Stade Français and Rosslyn Park at Levallois-Perret. Although the French club lost heavily, French critics were encouraged by the performance and thereafter there was regular contact between the two countries

A lineout in the international between France and New Zealand at Colombes Stadium in 1925. The All Blacks won 37–8, but once again the French were undismayed, recognizing that it was no disgrace to be beaten by the 'Champions of the World'

LTHOUGH THE PULSE of French rugby beats strongest in the South, the game has always enjoyed an enthusiastic following throughout the entire country. British students are thought to have introduced a form of the game to the port of Le Havre early in the 1870s, and some ten years later Parisians, out for a promenade in the Bois de Boulogne, would amuse themselves by watching Britons engaged in this curious sport. The Club Championship was actually started in Paris – the first final being played in 1892 between Racing Club de France and Stade Français. The records show that Racing Club won, but their claim to the title 'Champions of France' was slightly pretentious, because the competition at this time was limited to teams from the capital. Gradually it embraced the provinces and, apart from Stade Français who won the title eight times before 1910, the most successful team was Bordeaux, seven times Champions before World War I.

In 1892, with twenty clubs now established in France, the London side Rosslyn Park arrived in Paris to play Stade Français, and comfortably won the encounter, but the French critics were undismayed, one of them boasting, 'Is it not surprising that, after such limited practice, the French could challenge the masters of the game and make them play hard to win?' According to Olympic records, it was France who were soon to become masters of the world.

It was 1900, and Paris was hosting the Olympic Games. At this time rugby was one of the recognized events, although none of the International Board countries was much interested in the competition, regarding it as a parade ground for emergent countries. The final was held at Vincennes between Germany and France, who successfully reversed the result of the Franco-Prussian War beating Germany by 27–16 or 25–16 or 27–17 depending on which paper you read the following day. In the 1920 Olympics in Antwerp there were two teams entered for the event – France and the United States,

and victory went to the Americans by 8 points to nil. It was the United States who won again four years later when the Games returned to Paris. The headline in the *New York Herald* the following day read:

YANK RUGGERS DEFEAT FRENCH – TAKE 17 TO 3 GAME BEFORE 30,000 SPECTATORS

The report continued: 'Playing unbeatable football under murky skies, in a stormy atmosphere and before an excited and antagonistic crowd, the American Rugby team raised the Stars and Stripes over Colombes Stadium yesterday afternoon. The Americans played better football than they had ever played before, using the French style of group playing to the bewilderment of their opponents and smashing through the French lines time after time with well guarded individual plays which left the Frenchmen scattered the length of the field.' At the end of the game there was more than a hint of suspicion amongst the French following that the Americans had co-opted a number of gridiron players for the afternoon, but some research into the matter has shown that the players were all 'bona fide' rugby men from Stanford University.

Although the Fédération Français de Rugby did not come into being until 1920, the French XV had been sampling the delights of international football since the visit of Dave Gallaher's All Blacks in 1906. The game was played at Parc des Princes, and the tourists, beaten only once during their stay in Britain, won 38–8. Far from being regarded as a failure, the French were delighted with their performance – after all were they not now on a similar footing to Cardiff, the only other side to score eight points against Gallaher's men? It was left to Dr Jacques Duffourcq, who played for France on that occasion, to put the result into perspective. He described the game as being 'a series of black avalanches'. Three months later, when France lost her second inter-

France on the attack against
England at Twickenham in 1973.
Above, scrum half Astre gets the
ball away to his backs, and in
another movement, right, the
French threequarters seem to
have found a bit of room for
themselves as they stretch the
English cover. The match,
however, was won by England
14–6

national, this time to England, he remembered it as being 'a series of white avalanches'.

There followed matches against Wales in 1908 (lost 36–4), Ireland in 1909 (lost 19–8), and Scotland in 1910 (lost 27–0). Between 1906 and 1914, in fact, France played 28 matches, losing 27 and winning 1. To Scotland fell the dubious distinction of being the first side to lose to the Tricolours, going down 16–15 at Stade Colombes in February 1911. With less than an hour to go until the kick off, France were still a man short, owing to the fact that their wing threequarter Charles Vareilles hadn't appeared. In desperation the selectors turned to the French sprinter André Franquenelle, who had travelled with the party, but only as a spectator. As the teams were about to take the field Vareilles turned up, but he was too late. Franquenelle played and acquitted himself well enough to merit selection on two more occasions. For Vareilles, it was the end of his international career.

The Scots experience in Paris two years later served to put a further strain on the 'Auld Alliance'. This time Scotland won 21–3, but the manner of their victory and the performance of the referee, Mr W. Baxter from England, incurred the wrath of the patriotic and volatile crowd. Unfortunately Baxter's ignorance of the French language contributed very largely to his downfall. Mistaking the crowd's jeering for applause, he smiled and bowed in acknowledgement, an action which found even less favour with the spectators who, thinking that he was mocking them, became more incensed, and Baxter was indeed fortunate to escape from the ground with his life. The following year there was no match between the countries.

The bitter memories of that encounter dimmed during the next five years as war raged throughout Europe, and in 1920 the Scots returned to Paris. In the French side that day was one of the great personalities of French rugby, M. F. Lubin-Lubrère. He had returned home from the war with seventeen bullets in his body and blind in one eye. The surgeons extracted the bullets but could do nothing to restore his sight, and thereafter it was a relatively simple task for opponents to immobilize him by clapping a hand over his good eye. But when he ran out at Parc des Princes for the Scottish encounter, he found himself standing next to a sympathetic opponent – that other Cyclops, Jock Wemyss, who had also lost the sight of an eye during the war!

It was the game against Ireland later that season which brought joy to the Gallic rugby fraternity. That was the day when France first won a match on foreign soil. They scored five tries in their 15–7 win, and at the end of the game their winger Adolphe Jaureguy was led from the field weeping with joy. Throughout the next decade, a string of French defeats was punctuated by the occasional surprise – in 1922, for instance, when France played England at Twickenham in the presence of King George V, and with two minutes to go were ahead 11–6. That they were in such a position was quite remarkable. Jaureguy had been unable to take time off from his work in a tax office, and was therefore unable to take part, while the top French threequarter of the day, François Bordes, had been forced to withdraw on the morning of the match because of an injury. Into their places had come a couple of teenagers – R. Ramis and A. Laffond. With the wind behind them, England were quickly six points ahead, thanks to two penalty goals by H. L. V. Day, who was playing in borrowed boots. Then France struck back, and following a fine break by the new cap Ramis, R. Got scored a try. Minutes later, France had scored again and miraculously they got a third try when René Lasserre went over near the posts. This one was converted by the French captain René Crabos, and France led by five points. In the remaining two minutes joy turned to despair when England scored a try which the 'accursed Monsieur Day' goaled to level the scores. For all that, the French had come desperately close to gaining their first win at Twickenham, and from now on the other countries would have to take them seriously.

When France beat England in Paris five years later, and again at Colombes in 1931, it seemed that they had caught up with the giants of the rugby world. After twenty-five years of toil they were stronger than they had ever been. Unfortunately there was a worm in the apple. A disease was running through the French game which was causing apprehension across the Channel, and fearful of it spreading, the Home Unions severed relations with France. The game against England on 6 April 1931 was to be their last Championship appearance for sixteen years.

Between 1920 and 1931 French rugby had come of age. With the encouragement of several international victories the game had caught the imagination, and leading players like Crabos, Juareguy, Lasserre and Phillipe Struxiano were national heroes. But while the internationals had gone some way to arousing public interest, it was the Club Championship which was the real French passion – particularly in the South. A Championship game between Toulouse and Bordeaux would engender far greater emotion than an international in Paris which was far removed from the heart of the game. It was a day when shops would close, extra police would be drafted in to cope with the crowds and there was a carnival atmosphere. Unfortunately there was also all the atmosphere of the bull ring. When the protagonists entered the arena it was blood the throng were after, and in most cases it was blood they got. 'Victory at all costs,' became the motto, and it led to the most appalling violence from players and spectators alike. Brutality was not the only abuse – top players could quite easily be 'bought' by clubs who held out houses, jobs and cash bonuses as bait. It was common knowledge that some players actually lived off their rugby earnings. But just as victory brought fame and wealth, so did defeat bring igno-

miny, and there were reports of players attempting to commit suicide after a bad run in the Championship. Hard as the Fédération tried to prevent such shameful practices they had, by the late 1920s, got out of control. Several influential clubs sickened by this 'shamateurism' cut themselves free from the Fédération and formed the French Amateur Rugby Union, an action which doubtless persuaded the Home Unions to follow suit and break off their rugby ties with France. In their letter to the French Fédération they made it quite plain why such an action was deemed necessary, 'because of the unsatisfactory state of the game in France, the unions will be unable to arrange or fulfil fixtures with France or with French clubs at home or away, until we are satisfied that the control and conduct of the game has been placed on a satisfactory basis in all essentials.'

France remained persona non grata until after the outbreak of World War II by which time her rugby was in a chaotic mess. To begin with, very little attention had been paid to the consequences of the separation. After all, the Club Championship was still thriving, and on the international front, Germany, Italy and Rumania were still eager to provide opposition. Unfortunately, without regular exposure to top class opposition, standards dropped alarmingly. By this time many Frenchmen were of the opinion that if the suspension of the Club Championship was the price of peaceful co-existence with Britain, then it was a price they would have to pay. In 1939, the International Board with thoughts probably distracted by more serious events in Europe at that time, agreed that Anglo-French relations should be renewed, and as an act of faith the French Fédération voted for the suspension of the Club Championship. Although the war prevented any matches from being played in the International Championship, a British XV played France at Parc des Princes on 25 February 1940 and won by 36 points to 3 – a fair measure of the French decline.

French forwards very much to
the fore in this sequence: above,
in the 1976 match against
England at Parc des Princes;
below, as Elie Cester wrestles the
ball away from Japan in 1973,
and right, in the dramatic game
against Wales at the Arms Park
in 1976, where prop forward
Gilbert Cholley prepares to feed
his scrum half and captain,
Jacques Fouroux

Incredibly, the lessons learned during the desolate 1930s were quickly forgotten. Back came the Club Championship in 1943, and by the end of the decade all the old abuses, violence, poaching of players and financial rewards, had reappeared. Once again France found herself in danger of excommunication. The International Board, meeting in Edinburgh in 1952, ruled that unless the Championship was abolished, relations with France would again be broken off. By some miracle of diplomacy, the French Fédération managed to convince the I.B. that they could keep their house in order and at the same time retain their beloved championship. During the next ten years France was to enjoy the adoration and admiration of the rugby public. Their abandoned, improvised style was, at its best, the most thrilling form of entertainment – 'Champagne Rugby' of the finest vintage.

In 1951 France was fortunate in having considerable assets – at scrum half Gérard Dufau, and the legendary back row trio of Guy Basquet, Jean Matheu and 'Monsieur Rugby', Jean Prat. That season they were joined by a young forward who was destined to have a profound influence on the French game – Lucien Mias. As a tactician and leader he had no peer, and when he decided to retire from the game in 1954 to concentrate on his medical studies, it was a sad loss to his country. He was persuaded to make an international comeback four years later, however, and it was he who assumed control of the side during their triumphant tour to South Africa in 1958.

By the mid-fifties, the strife of the pre-war years forgotten, the French considered that they had a team which was the equal of any in the world, and in 1954 they were given the opportunity to prove it. Bob Stuart's All Blacks had just completed a tour to Britain, and of their 28 games had lost only two. Long French memories went back to 1906, when Dave Gallaher's All Blacks had routed France 38–8, and again to 1925 when Cliff Porter's side won 30–6. Now the All Blacks were back in Paris, confident of another victory, but this was to be the Tricolours' day, although how they won remains a mystery. New Zealand took ball from the lineout, ball from the scrum and ball from the ruck – they ran it through their forwards, they ran

Left A day to remember in French rugby was the first win over New Zealand. It took place on 27 February 1954 against Bob Stuart's All Blacks, who had just completed a successful tour to Britain. It took this one score by Jean Prat to decide the issue in favour of France

Right The fête of the Championship. Championship matches are the life blood of the game in France; they are occasions for pageantry and passion, highlighting the best and the worst elements in sport

it through their backs – they employed short passes, long passes and medium passes, but it all came to nought against the French defence. Just before half time France took a short break from their defensive duties to make a sortie upfield; the ball went to Jean Prat and with three opponents clamped to him he plunged over the line for the only score of the match.

There was very little in the 1957 season of encouragement to the French. They had just lost all four Championship matches, and had struggled to beat Rumania before 93,000 spectators in Bucharest. With the tour to South Africa ahead, very few Frenchmen were optimistic about the coming campaign, one fan writing, 'with a wretched spoon we must now help ourselves to a compound of rose leaves, shamrock, thistles and leeks. For the glory of the greatest of games, may we digest it.' The witch's brew seemed to work, because the following season the French sprang from their traps with a 39–0 win over Rumania and a 19–0 victory against Australia. There followed a first win over Wales in Cardiff, and the defeat of Ireland, and France finished the Five Nations Tourna-

ment in third place. Now the French public awaited the announcement of the party for the South African adventure. When it came there were few who took issue with the selections – it looked a competent side which would not let France down. There was Michel Vannier at full back, always more highly rated abroad than he was in his homeland. He was terribly injured during the tour and returned home on crutches, his playing career apparently over. But back he came after a year's absence and played in the national side until 1961. In the three-quarter line there was the 'careless rapture' of Jean Dupuy and the attacking genius of Roger Martine; at scrum half, little Pierre Danos, who once averred that there are two kinds of rugby players – those who play pianos and those who shift them. He was, without any a question, a player. There was never any doubt about the ability of the French backs, the real problem concerned the forwards – would they be strong enough and willing enough to stand up to the frightening strength of the Springboks? Although Michel Celaya had been appointed tour captain, an injury to him meant that

Mias came back to lead the side. Here was a natural leader – a man who led by example, a 'bulldozer with a brain'. He was fortunate in having with him men of character like François Moncla, Bernard Mommejat, Robert Vigier and Alfred Rocques, 'The Rock'. It was Rocques who did more than anyone to destroy the reputation of the Springbok scrummaging. The extraordinary thing about him was that he was thirty-three years old before he won his first cap. Up until the age of twenty-six he had played soccer for the local side, much to the disappointment of the town barber who had been prophesying a great rugby future for Rocques ever since his mother had brought him into the shop as a small boy to have his hair cut. By the time he left for South Africa Rocques already had the reputation of being an extremely tough forward.

Such durability was of crucial importance to the tourists. Within three weeks of the tour starting, a third of the side had been injured and yet, against all the odds, they managed to hold the Springboks to a 3–3 draw in the first test. The injury problem was still acute prior to the Second Test in Johannesburg. Pierre Lacaze, who was replacing the injured Vannier, took the field pumped with pain killer; Dupuy had a thigh injury, and skipper Mias was feeling several degrees below par. Conditions were perfect for open rugby, but neither side was prepared to make the mistake which could lose the game. The Springboks feared the French backs, the French feared the Springbok forwards. It was the Springboks in fact who were more adventurous, and there were several near things on the French line, one of them beautifully described by Alex Potter and Georges Duthen: 'When Lochner passed to Skene there was only one Frenchman who could do anything about it. And he, surely, was too far away. Well, the French had done their best. There was a try against them, and the only thing to do was . . . but stay! Here comes that Frenchman Pierre Barthe in white headgear and running

Michel Crauste – a magnificent back row forward, who shared in some memorable French triumphs, and who learned much from the teachings of Mias

Top 'The bulldozer with a brain', Lucien Mias, was an inspiring captain whose leadership brought France to the forefront of world rugby in the 1950s

Above 'Monsieur Drop', Pierre Albaladejo practising his deadly art

Above Another great forward of the 1950s, François Moncla, was captain in this match against Wales in Cardiff, which France won 16–8

Right Lucien Mias's greatest triumph came with victory in South Africa in 1958, a feat which could not have been achieved without the strength of men like Alfred Rocques 'The Rock', who is seen here leading his tired but happy colleagues from the field at the end of the match as though a satanic fork was within an inch of his buttocks. A great oblique sprint . . . he reaches Skene who has transmitted to Kaminer. He reaches Kaminer who has transmitted to Prinsloo. Surely it is too late. But no. With all his remaining energy he plunges . . . And he brings Prinsloo down almost on the French line. We breathe again.' (Potter and Duthen: *The Rise of French Rugby*.) The Springboks did eventually score the only try of the game, but lost to a penalty from Lacaze and a drop goal from Martine. France had won the series.

Before the party had left for South Africa, M. René Crabos, President of the French Fédération, had said to the players, 'We don't ask for miracles, we simply ask that you should distinguish yourselves by your conduct, that you should do your best in your matches, and if you can score a little win here and there . . .' Now it was an emotional moment for him as he stood on the airport tarmac awaiting the arrival home of Mias and his men.

One more goal remained for France – an outright win in the Five Nations Tournament. They achieved this the very next season when they became the 1959 Champions. In 1960 they shared top place with England, but then in the next two glorious years France were again outright winners. It was now clear that French Rugby was exceptionally strong, with a staggering depth of talent. This was obvious from the way that selectors would pick players, and if they were not immediately successful, they could be replaced by players who were every bit as talented. The selectors did, however, make some fairly impressive errors in judgement. There was, for instance, the case of Pierre Albaladejo ('Monsieur Drop') who came into the side as a twenty-one-year-old in 1954. He was discarded after one game and had to wait until 1960 before he made a second appearance, but then went on to gain 24 selections. No French team during these halcyon years was complete without Michel Crauste. 'He was,' wrote Denis

Lalanne, the French critic, 'the Cerdan of Rugby, as much for his terrifying rage in battle as for his extreme kindness to his neighbour.' When his wife's ill health forced him to leave Paris for warmer climes, he made for Lourdes where Jean Prat was enthroned, but his real mentor was Mias, whose leadership and attitude towards the game greatly influenced Crauste. There were signs of the Mias touch in Crauste's captaincy in 1964, when he led the French to victory over the Springboks in South Africa. Nicknamed 'Attila', he was no innocent on the field, but he took his share of knocks in return. This was especially the case during the 1961 tour to New Zealand where he was singled out for some particularly harsh treatment, and not always from his opponents on the field. During a game at Timaru one infuriated matron could contain herself no longer, and rushing on to the pitch she delivered 'un coup de parapluie' to the astounded Crauste. But there was another side to the man. When Guy Boniface, a

The Brothers – André (left) and Guy Boniface, two wonderfully talented threequarters, played together in the French side until 1966. When Guy was tragically killed in a car accident two years later, it seemed that André would have nothing more to do with the game. Today, however, he has found new interest in the sport through his work as a commentator

Guy Camberabero getting down
to business as he drops a goal
against Ireland at Lansdowne
Road in 1967. Ireland's Barry
Bresnihan attempts to ward off
danger, but it is already too late

brilliantly talented centre and the darling of the French crowds was killed in a car accident in 1968, it seemed that his equally talented brother André would cut himself off completely from the game which had given them both so much joy. The story is told that he could not even bear to watch a match on television until a very old friend arrived at his house on the day that France were playing Scotland. 'It was Michel Crauste,' Boniface recalls, 'with his honest open eyes and his overwhelming calm. He was holding his small son by the hand. He turned on the television for me, and we watched the game like two brothers.' Today, Boniface is a rugby commentator.

The 1960s brought two more Championship successes to France in 1967 and 1968. Those were the days of that beautifully balanced full back Pierre Villepreux, of Jo Maso, and of two of the finest forwards to play for France, Benoit Dauga and Walter Spaghero. Unfortunately for France the two were engaged in a long standing feud which prevented them from affording each other even the basic civilities, and when they played together in the national side the team performance was inevitably impaired. One can't help wondering how the two would have reacted to a leader like Mias. Strangely enough, when Dauga was injured and was lying paralysed in a hospital bed, his international rugby career finished, it is told that Spanghero travelled half way across France to visit his old rival.

Apart from a lack of leadership, France suffered from some weirdly inconsistent selection policies, which brought wholesale changes after almost every match, be it a victory or a defeat. True, it underlined the remarkable depth of talent available, but it did little to inspire confidence amongst the players. There have been signs of late, however, that changes are taking place, not only in matters of selection, but also in regard to tactics. There is now a far more disciplined approach to forward play, more akin to the British style. They have a pack of

forwards who stick very much to the principles laid down by a famous club coach, 'that forwards should be like mourners at a funeral – up front with the family and not behind with the friends.' The recent success of Béziers in the Club Championship has convinced the French that consistency at international level can only be achieved by organized forward play. The transition is still taking place, but with a fine new breed of players like J. C. Skrela, J. P. Rives, J. F. Gourdon and F. Sangali, France need have few worries about the future.

As far as the Club Championship is concerned, it continues to thrive although not without the occasional ripple of discontent. There is still concern about rough play, about the number of foreign players who have been lured to the South by something more than the heat and a passionate love of French culture, and about Club directors who appear to have interests over and above the game itself. The International Board, while frequently stating its displeasure with the state of affairs, has realized that the problems are well nigh insoluble. The French for their part take the philosophical view that, like the weather, such problems will always be with us.

Left Perhaps the most exciting of all French threequarters in recent years, Jo Maso was always more highly rated abroad than he was in his country; but he was nevertheless a beautifully balanced centre and won seventeen caps between 1967 and 1973

Right Benoit Dauga, the most capped Frenchman and one of the greatest forwards ever produced by the country. Behind him, partially strangled, is another outstanding French forward, Walter Spanghero. Their mutual dislike of each other prevented France from reaping the full benefits of having two such fine forwards in the side

The new attitude in the French side is typified by players like J. P. Romeu who is seen passing the ball in the 1976 match against Wales. Behind him is the flaxen haired J. P. Rives, and it is upon talents such as these that the future of French rugby rests

10 THE LIONS' TALE

WHILST IT MAY not have been part of nature's plan that a Welshman should pack down in a scrummage side by side with an Irishman, or that a Scotsman should pass the ball to an Englishman, it is to the eternal credit of three cricketers that this unlikely fusion came to pass as early as it did. In 1877 Alfred Shaw and Arthur Shrewsbury had taken part in a successful cricket tour to Australia, and together with A. E. Stoddart they conceived the idea of taking a British rugby team to the Antipodes. They submitted the plan to the Rugby Football Union, who refused to give their patronage to the venture, but offered no serious objection provided that there was no breach of the amateur code.

The preparations completed, the team, consisting mainly of Englishmen, a few Scotsmen and a lone representative from the Isle of Man, left England on 8 March 1888 for Australia and New Zealand. During the nine months that they were away they played fifty-four matches, nineteen of them under Australian Rules, and it was significant that the only two defeats suffered by the tourists came from New Zealand sides. The hardships encountered by those pioneers on their travels were many and varied, and tragedy struck when the captain R. L. Seddon was drowned in a sculling accident, but at least a start had been made, and there was ample proof that the touring instinct amongst rugby men was strong enough to repeat the exercise.

Three years later W. E. McLagan's side left for a first tour to South Africa. After a record-breaking voyage on the *Dunottar Castle* (they arrived in Cape Town sixteen days after leaving Southampton) travel became rather less luxurious. A nine-hour trip in a 'coach and ten' was not uncommon, and as often as not players would take the field exhausted after long, uncomfortable journeys. The playing conditions too were alien to the visitors, and the Scottish winger Paul Clauss described the ground as being 'absolutely destitute of grass – hard and covered with a reddish dust so that with the bright sun overhead there was a considerable glare.' Despite the conditions they returned with the most successful record of any British side, winning every one of their nineteen matches, including the three internationals. They scored 223 points and conceded one, the value of a try at that time. Top try scorer was the Blackheath centre R. L. Aston who at 6ft 3ins and 210lbs took some stopping, and it was fitting that he should score the first try for a British side in an international overseas when he crossed the line in the First Test at Port Elizabeth. He went on to score thirty tries, a record which has never been threatened by any other British player on tour.

The first two touring sides from Britain had been Anglo-Scottish in composition, but in 1896 it was the Irish who joined forces with the English for the return to South Africa. A gregarious bunch of fellows, the party included the Dublin Wanderers forward T. J. Crean who had been a member of the Irish XV which had won the International Championship in 1894 and again just prior to the departure for South Africa. Although his presence failed to prevent a first international defeat for a British side, they won the series 3–1. At the end of the tour Crean remained in South Africa with his club and country colleague Robert Johnston, and when the Boer War broke out in 1899 both joined the Imperial Light Horse, both became captains and both won the Victoria Cross. It was during a Boer attack at Tygerskloof that Crean won his medal. Despite being wounded himself, he rallied his men, showing great courage in the process, and it was only when he was wounded for a second time that he was brought to his knees with the words, 'By Christ, I'm kilt entoirely.' Happily, second sight was not one of his numerous gifts and he lived to tell the tale of his 'death' many times over.

It is quite wrong to imagine that the chief problem facing representative teams from the British Isles and Ireland lies in finding a

Above W. E. McLagan, the Scotsman who captained the first British team to South Africa in 1891. The team returned with the best record of any British side, having won all nineteen matches, including the three internationals

Right Captains both – R. Cove-Smith, who led the 1924 Lions to South Africa passing the time of day with Captain Strong aboard the *Edinburgh Castle* en route to South Africa. In direct contrast to the 1891 tour, Cove-Smith's party returned with the worst record of any Lions side, having lost nine of their twenty-one matches, including all four internationals

suitable blend amongst players from four countries each with its own traditions and each producing players who come from vastly dissimilar backgrounds. But with one or two painful exceptions this has never been an obstacle either on or off the field. The one recurring burden throughout the years has been the non-availability of the best players either because of pressure of business or because an individual's financial situation will not allow him to sacrifice four or five months' wages. This was the case when the Rev. M. Mullineux took a team to Australia in 1899, and again four years later when a British side lost a series in South Africa for the first time. D. R. (Darky) Bedell-Sivright, the belligerent Scottish forward, had the same problem with his team in Australia and New Zealand in 1904. Only four of the thirteen forwards had been capped, and it was little wonder that the brilliant Welsh backs, Tommy Vile, Percy Bush, Teddy Morgan and Willie Llewellyn had few opportunities to show their class.

The 1910 team to South Africa was closer to being representative of the strength of British rugby than any of its predecessors. Led by the Irish front row forward Dr Tom Smyth, it contained the game's outstanding personality of the period, C. H. (Cherry) Pillman. Apart from being the top points scorer on tour, he played with distinction in the international matches both as a loose forward and as a fly half. Pillman had studied the New Zealand tactic of playing seven forwards and one 'rover', a man whose job it was to harry the opposition and to set up attacks for his backs. He had seen the All Blacks captain Dave Gallaher play this type of game to great effect some years earlier and had been sold on the idea. Now he took it to South Africa where it was immediately acclaimed, and Pillman became the star attraction. Oddly enough it was as a fly half that he enjoyed his finest hour. It was the Second Test at Port Elizabeth; the tourists had already lost six games including the first international, and were expected to do no better on this occasion, but Pillman, who had been injured, was now restored to the side and was down to play in the fly half position. If ever there was an inspired piece of selection this was it, because Pillman took it upon himself to recover British prestige. He was everywhere; back on his own line to make a try-saving tackle; up in attack to break through the Springbok defence. Down 3–0 at half time, the tourists hit back with two tries, the second after Pillman had swivelled and swerved his way past a line of Springbok defenders enabling M. E. Neale to ground the ball. Many years after the event the South African captain W. A. Millar wrote, 'If ever a man can be said to have won an international through his own unorthodox and single-handed efforts, it can be said of the inspired black-haired Pillman I played against on the Crusaders ground that day.' Unfortunately neither Pillman nor the other members of the side could maintain the momentum for the deciding test at Cape Town, and the series

One of the most spectacular tries in the history of Lions tours was scored by the Welsh winger Ken Jones after full back Lewis Jones had begun the move close to his own line. It was during the Fourth Test at Auckland in 1950, which the Lions lost 11–8

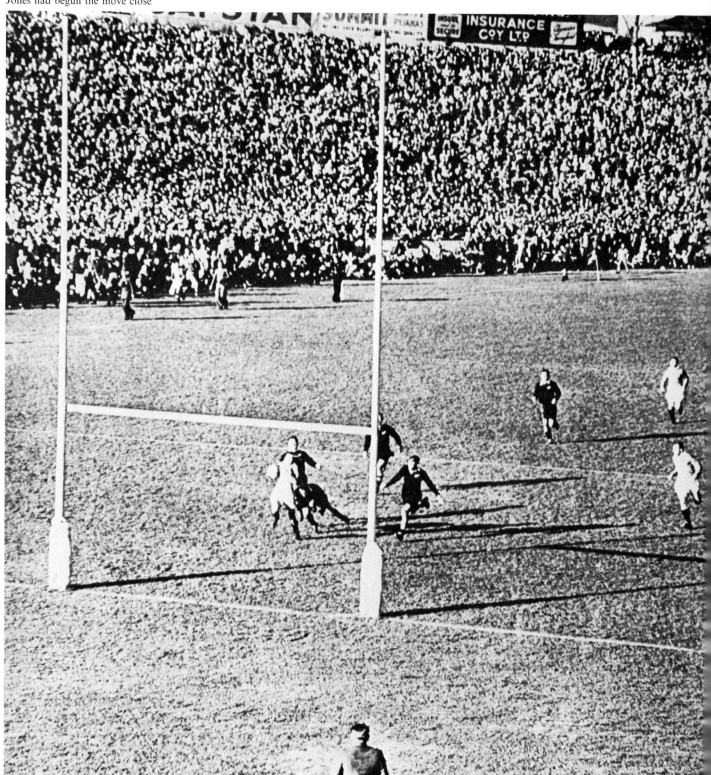

The 1930 Lions began well in the test series against New Zealand. They won the first international 6–3 and lost the second narrowly 13–10. In a scene from that match in Christchurch, the New Zealander Bert Cooke (No. 5) tackles A. L. Novis, who has just received a pass from fly half Roger Spong (on ground). On the extreme left of the picture is the great New Zealand threequarter Mark Nicholls

was lost.

There were enough world class players in Britain in the mid-1920s to field a couple of fifteens, and yet when Dr Cove-Smith's side returned from the trip to South Africa in 1924 it was with the poorest record of any British team. Once again many of the top players had been forced to decline the invitation to tour. In addition the Scottish full back Dan Drysdale, although brilliant in his general play, was unable to get his goal-kicking right, and he failed in all attempts at goal during the tour. In the end the kicking was entrusted to Tom Voyce, and doubtless to his own enormous surprise he finished up as top scorer with 37 points. Even the lighter side was touched by disaster. On the boat going out to South Africa, Jammy Clinch, who was taking seriously his job as entertainments officer, had written, produced and was starring in a revue. He had, into the bargain, acquired some very attractive young ladies to assist him, but in his attempts to impress his audience, he had been over ambitious with a high kick, and had slipped on the floor badly jarring his spine. This was the first of many injuries suffered by the tourists which inevitably contributed towards the poor results, but injuries are an accepted part of touring, and there was not sufficient depth in the reserve strength to offer resistance to the Springboks.

Writing about the tour afterwards the Welshman Rowe Harding was in no doubt that failure was due to the absence of top class players, and looking ahead to the 1930 tour to the Antipodes, he urged the governing bodies to make money available to those who could not afford to finance the trip out of their own pockets. 'Each man is expected to supply himself with a wardrobe which cannot cost less than £50, in addition to a sum of £70 for incidental expenses. This means that only men of means and leisure can represent British Rugby while it is well known that a good many of our best players have neither means nor leisure. People will say that no solution is possible without breaking the existing rules relating to amateurism. In that case by all means break and amend the rules. Until that is done we had much better abandon these teams abroad; they do no good to British rugby, and they do a great deal of harm to British national popularity.'

Had Harding written these words forty years later, he would have been preaching to the converted, but British rugby was not ready for such radicalism in the late 1920s, and the side which left for Australia and New Zealand in 1930 contained the mix as before – one or two players of outstanding quality, and several more who fell far short of international standard. Yet the Lions (so named during the previous tour because of the Lion motif on the team tie) had made a highly creditable start. The England fly half Roger Spong had been delighting the crowds with his elusive running, and among the forwards George Beamish of Ireland and the Welshman Ivor Jones had been showing excellent form. Jones it was who set up the try in the First Test at Dunedin which gave the Lions victory, but thereafter it was the same old story as New Zealand forward power proved to be too much for the individual brilliance of the British backs, and the All Blacks took the series 3–1.

Throughout the tour there was a marked bitterness between officials of the New Zealand Rugby Union and the Lions manager Mr James Baxter. The trouble started during the very first game of the tour against Wanganui, when the local players disappeared into their changing room at half time as was the New Zealand custom. Baxter took exception to this, pointing out that it was a violation of the laws which state that 'no player may leave the field with the referee's permission which should only be granted in exceptional circumstances'. Later in the tour he criticized the New Zealand scrum formation of seven forwards and one 'rover', the tactic so effectively employed by England's 'Cherry' Pillman in South Africa twenty years earlier. In the eyes of many New Zealanders Baxter had now gone too far, and he received some fairly cool treatment for the remainder of the tour. But he must have comforted himself in his loneliest moments with the knowledge that he had the law on his side, and shortly after the Lions returned home the International Board made changes in the scrummaging laws which forced New Zealanders to abandon their 2–3–2 forma-

The Greatest Test – the title given, with some justification, to the first international between South Africa and the Lions at Johannesburg in 1955. The Lions won 23–22 with the result in doubt until the very last kick of the match. It was the genius of Cliff Morgan which put the Lions on the road to victory, and in the sequence on the left he evades Basie Van Wyk to score one of the tourists' five tries.

On the right are two great moments from the 1959 Lions tour to New Zealand. Top, Bev Risman dives past Don Clarke for the winning try in the Fourth Test at Auckland, and bottom, Tony O' Reilly touches down for one of his seventeen tour tries in the First Test at Dunedin. Behind O'Reilly is Don Clarke who was to have a profound influence on the result of that match by kicking six penalties

tion.

Despite the warnings of men like Rowe Harding, the majority opinion in Britain favoured the view that rugby should be played first and foremost for fun, and that the principles and ideals which had guided its founders should be strictly adhered to. There was nothing extraordinary therefore about the official approach made to Douglas Prentice as the 1930 Lions were about to set sail. 'Look here Doug, we think you'd better skipper this side.' It was all very amateurish and delightfully informal, but unfortunately it did not tend to win many matches, especially against the organization and dedication of the All Blacks and the Springboks.

The 1938 Lions in South Africa suffered all the failings and hardships of their predecessors – not enough strength in depth and injuries to key players. They were particularly unlucky in that they lost the services of their number one place kicker, Vivian Jenkins, who was injured in the first international, but once again there was no adequate cover, and another series was lost.

Perhaps World War II did something to harden the British attitude. At any rate by the time the 1950 side left for the Antipodes an official tours committee had been formed, and as if to herald a new age the team turned out in their now famous red jerseys, white shorts and blue stockings with green tops. Although they returned from New Zealand without an international win, here at last was a team worthy of British rugby. All four tests had been keenly contested and in every case the result could have gone either way. For once the All Blacks had been made to feel the weight of the Lions forwards, and in the backs the tackling of Jack Matthews and the running of Bleddyn Williams, Ken Jones and Jack Kyle was a constant source of concern to the opposition. Of the many superlative tries scored by the tourists, they held back the best for the final match of the tour when Ken Jones sprinted fifty yards following a move which had started inside

their own twenty-five. But it was Kyle who most impressed the New Zealand public, and in his book *Haka*, Winston McCarthy wrote, 'Kyle's football always had a touch of genius about it whether he was shuffling past a player, grubber kicking or fooling the opposition into a false sense of security.'

When the Lions went on trek to South Africa five years later it was another fly half, a Welshman named Cliff Morgan, who tormented opposing defences with his darting runs and precise kicking. The First Test in Johannesburg, considered by many to be the greatest international match ever played, was watched by a world record crowd of 95,000. In the matches leading up to the Test the Lions forwards had shown themselves to be stronger than their predecessors, whilst the back division was unquestionably the finest ever to have visited South Africa. Yet within minutes of the second half starting, the Lions appeared to be in a hopeless mess. They were trailing 11 points to 8, and their excellent forward Reg Higgins was being led injured from the field. But how the seven Lions forwards fought. And inspired by a superb Cliff Morgan try, the tourists found themselves leading 23–11. Shaken by

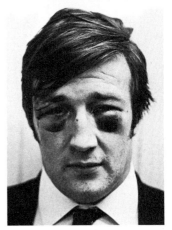

The Lions at Bay – Injuries have always been one of the major problems on Lions tours. Top, Richard Sharp is carried from the field during the match against Northern Transvaal in 1962. He received a broken cheekbone as the result of a tackle by the Springbok centre Mannetjies Roux. Above, the aftermath of the 1971 'Battle of Canterbury' in which the Lions lost the services of their Scottish prop forward Sandy Carmichael, who sustained broken bones in both cheeks in the bitter encounter at Lancaster Park

The Lions at Play
Top, Dewi Bebb of Wales sets off
for the All Blacks line pursued by
R. E. Rangi during the Second
Test at Wellington in 1966. New
Zealand won 16–12. Bottom, the
1971 superstar Barry John
weaves his way past All Black
hooker Tanie Norton in the First
Test at Dunedin which the Lions
won 9–3

this turn of events, the Springboks regrouped and set about the Lions. Jeff Butterfield, who scored the Lions opening try, well remembers the atmosphere: 'The Springboks were giants in green and too many of them. They interpassed among the forwards and continually crashed towards our line. It seemed never ending.'

During that interminable second half, the Springboks closed the gap to four points, and with the game moving into injury time Theunis Briers went over for his second try. South Africa were just one point behind now with the conversion to come. The kick was not a difficult one in normal circumstances, but for J. H. Van der Schyff, who had been called upon to attempt the conversion, the circumstances were anything but normal, and to the indescribable relief of the fourteen Lions standing weakly behind their goal line the ball went wide of the posts. Almost immediately the final whistle went, and Morgan glanced round to see the mighty Welsh lock forward Rhys Williams collapsed on the ground in utter exhaustion: 'His enormous frame lying like a mortal coil on the frost brown Ellis Park revealed the price of victory.'

Although the series was shared with two wins apiece, the Lions had come close to achieving the dream of a win in the Southern Hemisphere, and it was with renewed hope that Ronnie Dawson took his 1959 side to Australia and New Zealand. He certainly had forwards of the right proportions to compete with the All Blacks, and the backs looked every bit as good as the 1955 vintage. How could it be otherwise with players like Tony O'Reilly, Peter Jackson, David Hewitt and Ken Scotland? Off the field, Dawson's men proved to be equally entertaining, and from the sang-froid of the Englishman David Marques to the bluntness of the Welsh steel worker Ray Prosser the team spirit was quite outstanding. Marques, who wore a pinstripe suit and a bowler hat everywhere except on the pitch and in bed, refused to let anybody or anything upset him. During the tour there

This was the try which put the Lions on their way to victory in the 1971 First Test at Dunedin. Ian (Mighty Mouse) McLaughlan forces his way past Sid Going (No. 9) and Fergie McCormack, charges down a defensive kick by Alan Sutherland, and falls on the ball for his only try of the tour

Lift Off, as Gareth Edwards deals forcibly with the challenge of All Blacks fly half Bob Burgess during the Third Test in Wellington. Mike Gibson in the background seems to have some sympathy with Burgess's plight

was considerable controversy caused by the fact that many of the New Zealand players were wearing protective shoulder pads in the form of a harness under their jerseys. Following complaints about this practice from Alf Wilson, the Lions manager, it was agreed that no player could wear one without first having obtained a medical certificate. This ruling proved to be only a minor hindrance to the dedicated hypochondriac, and in one provincial match no fewer than thirteen of the local opposition turned out wearing their protective clothing. Despite this the Lions won fairly easily, and after the match Marques was engaged in conversation with one of the home team. 'We were terrible,' complained the New Zealander. 'Not at all,' replied Marques generously. 'I thought you did jolly well – considering that you only had two fit men.'

Then there was Prosser, the prop from Pontypool who had been born with ears so big that it was apparently eighteen months before his mother knew whether he was going to walk or fly. But Prosser was very definitely earthbound, a forthright character who once rebuked a miserly colleague, 'Brother, you'm got short arms an' deep pockets.' His repartee with the intellectual twins O'Reilly and Andy Mulligan was irresistible: 'The trouble with you varsity blokes,' he would say, 'is that you keep on usin' all em big words like "corrugated" and "marmalade".' Mulligan and O'Reilly for their part were in constant demand to appear on radio and television with their double act, and there was more than a hint of a suspicion that they had given an unscheduled performance in downtown Auckland on the eve of the Fourth Test. But the next day they combined just as brilliantly on the field for Mulligan to put O'Reilly over for his seventeenth try of the tour, a record for a Lion in New Zealand. By that time, however, the All Blacks, ably assisted by Don Clarke, had already won the series. It was Clarke who had kicked six penalties to the Lions four tries to win the First Test, and it

was the same man who had fallen across the line to score the winning try in the Second. The Third went comfortably to New Zealand, but it was a measure of the Lions spirit that they came back with a courageous display to win the final match 9–6, and it was a measure of their popularity that 63,000 turned out to watch them.

The 1950s had been prosperous years for the Lions, although victory in a series still evaded them. This seemed to bring massive withdrawal symptoms during the next decade. Generally speaking there was a

The Scarlet Runners – on the left the Welsh full back J. P. R. Williams, seen here in typical action for the 1974 Lions in South Africa; and right, the Welsh No. 8 Mervyn Davies in action during the same tour

dearth of good backs, and the forwards, although of sufficient ballast, lacked the technique to cope with the scrummaging of the Springboks and the rucking of the All Blacks. Of the twelve internationals played in South Africa and New Zealand during these years, the Lions failed to win one. Again injury played an important part in the overall results, and when François Roux, the South African winger, launched himself at the unfortunate Richard Sharp in a provincial match, breaking the Englishman's jaw in the process, the 1962 Lions lost their

most potent attacking force.

The 1966 venture 'down under' was not blessed with good fortune. The captaincy had been given to the Scottish lock forward Mike Campbell-Lamerton, but there was strong feeling, especially in Wales, that the honour should have been given to the Welsh No. 8 Alan Pask, and subsequent events showed that the Welshman might have been the better choice. The Australian part of the tour exceeded all expectations, with the Lions triumphant in both internationals, the second by a record margin of 31–0. By this

A controversial end to the 1974 Lions tour in South Africa. Having won the first three internationals, the Lions required victory in the final match at Ellis Park to achieve a clean sweep in the series. With the score standing at 13–13, Fergus Slattery made a final assault on the Springbok line and crossed, but was not awarded the try. Slattery claimed that he had touched down, Peter Cronje, the Springbok centre who tackled him, claimed that he did not. The evidence from this photograph appears to support the Springbok point of view, but try or no try, the game ended in a draw and the Lions finished their tour unbeaten

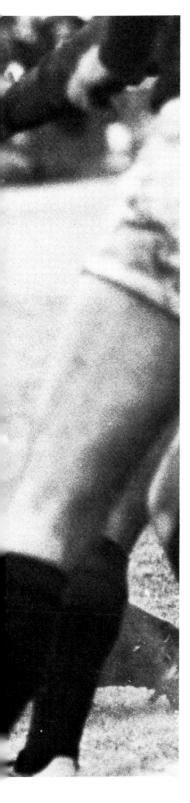

time it was clear that they had some very useful backs in Mike Gibson, David Watkins and Dewi Bebb, but it was felt by the Lions management that the All Blacks could only be beaten by dominating their forwards. It was a grave miscomputation because New Zealand forward play was then second to none, and by the time this had been painfully driven home the Lions had lost all four internationals. The tour over, Wilson Whineray, the former All Blacks captain, wrote: 'The Lions greatest strength was in their backs, and unquestionably the outstanding back was Mike Gibson.' There were to be better days ahead for Gibson and for the Lions.

Before that, however, the Lions were called upon to fulfil a tour to South Africa. Under the captaincy of Tom Kiernan they were a happy, lively group who devised a swift and effective method of dismantling hotels, but were not quite so efficient when it came to taking the Springboks apart, and they also failed to win a test. Indeed, had it not been for Kiernan the record would have been considerably worse. He scored seventeen points in the First Test, six in the Second and six in the Third, but he was unable to save the series.

It was now more than seventy years since a British side had last won a series, and it was obvious that the days had long since gone when one piece of individual genius could win matches of this importance. The Welsh had realized this when they sent out a strong side to New Zealand in 1969 and suffered humiliating defeats in both internationals. Having previously dabbled in coaching, they now adopted it wholeheartedly and the other home countries were forced to follow suit, otherwise they would have been left hopelessly far behind. When the time came to select the Lions for New Zealand in 1971, therefore, each of the four home countries was pursuing a similar policy. A strong manager was chosen in Dr Douglas Smith who had toured Australia and New Zealand as a player with the 1950

Lions. He had with him an outstanding captain in the London Welshman John Dawes, and a coach of proven ability in Carwyn James, whose only misfortune as a player had been that his career had run concurrently with that of Cliff Morgan.

Between them, these three men saw to it that this was the best prepared side ever to leave on an overseas tour. Despite a morale shattering defeat in the very first match against Queensland, which the good Dr Smith attributed to circadian dysrhythma, the 1971 Lions became the first British side to win a series against New Zealand. The records tumbled – Barry John, the tour superstar, scored 180 points, a record for any Lions player, and a record for any individual touring Briton; John Bevan, the Cardiff winger, equalled Tony O'Reilly's record of seventeen tries, and the side went through New Zealand without losing a provincial match. What made this side different from its predecessors was that, for the first time this century, the British forwards were more than a match for their opponents. Experienced campaigners like Bill McBride and Delme Thomas brought the best out of raw recruits like Gordon Brown and Derek Quinnell, and although never quite able to equal the All Blacks in the rucks, the Lions' tight play was superior to anything they had previously produced. For this much of the credit went to the Irishman Ray McLoughlin who, along with his front row colleague Sandy Carmichael, was injured in the fifth match against Canterbury and thereafter took no further part in the tour. But his theories about forward play proved of immense value to Carwyn James, and to the two men who had to step in as front line props, Ian (Mighty Mouse) McLaughlan and Sean Lynch, nicknamed 'The Fire Brigade' after his attempts to put out a nonexistent fire in a Napier hotel. These two men had begun the tour as reserves, but now they rose magnificently to the occasion, and it was McLaughlan's try in the First Test at Dunedin which put the Lions on their historic way.

It was during this crucial First Test that Barry John gave his finest performance. His tactical kicking gradually enabled the Lions to emerge from the total eclipse they had suffered during the opening quarter when the All Blacks had mounted one ferocious attack after another. As each attack faltered on the rock-like defence of Dawes and Mike Gibson, John repeatedly drove the All Blacks further and further back into their own territory until at last their spirit was broken. It was dour ten-man rugby which had the critics complaining that this was no way for the British to play the game, but after years of defeat the moment of victory, when it came with the drawn game at Eden Park, was long overdue and as a result was all the more welcome. A new age in British rugby had arrived, with a breed of forwards like McLaughlan, Brown, Fergus Slattery and Mervyn Davies, all possessing a physical and mental hardness which demanded an opponent's respect, and backs in the mould of Gareth Edwards and J. P. R. Williams, who allied to their immense skill a fierce determination to win.

The breakthrough had been achieved, and the way was now clear for the Lions to complete the 'double' in the Southern Hemisphere when they went to South Africa in 1974. Not only did they win the series, but Willie John McBride's team went unbeaten through the tour and provided the climax to the great Irishman's career. For the team there was any amount of records; they scored 107 tries; Andy Irvine's total of 156 points was the highest by a Lion in South Africa; Alan Old's 37 points in the game against South-West Districts was the highest individual score by a Lion in any country, and the Lions' total of 97 points in that match surpassed the previous highest score by a Lions side. With their 26–9 win in the Third Test at Port Elizabeth, the Lions became the first side this century to win a four-match series in South Africa, and for the Fourth Test at Ellis Park 75,000 people paid

a record £326,250.

These are the bare facts, and when the final whistle sounded in the last match the 1974 Lions had finished up with the best record of any British side since 1889. There was no doubting the fact that they possessed a highly efficient set of backs and a magnificently drilled pack, and from many observers they earned the title 'the greatest Lions', but it must be remembered that the Springboks were some way short of top international class, and for a great number of people the memory of Robin Thompson's side nineteen years earlier remained untarnished.

Since R. L. Seddon and his team had pioneered the way to Australia and New Zealand in 1888, and W. E. McLagan's side had won the first international against South Africa three years later, the wheel had turned full circle; the masters, who had spent so many of the intervening years as pupils, were once again masters. For those who believe that sport is all about winning, then the two most recent Lions sides have reached the pinnacle, but there remains a wisp of cloud on the horizon. In the mad haste to become superefficient, there is a fear that the flair has gone out of British rugby, and coaching is taking much of the blame. Good coaching, of course, will always allow for individual expression within a disciplined framework, but it might be worth noting the words of Colin Meads who has played against enough British teams to know what he is talking about. 'I see Britain as being in a unique position in world rugby, but I wonder if the British themselves appreciate it. New strength in the forwards has not automatically cancelled out brilliance in the backs. So why not use the new to exploit the traditional? That seems to make a lot of rugby sense to me.'

11 THE WORLD OVAL

The Rugby game spread in the early years through British businessmen and the armed forces. Above, as early as 1874 the British colony at Yokohama were playing the game in Japan and, much to the amusement of the locals, they are here seen giving a demonstration of the art.

Below, a match played by the Fifty-Ninth Regiment at Khelat-I-Gilzai provides the troops with some relaxation during the Afghan War

The brave old British game, my boys –
The dear old British game;
Tho' we're far apart, we are one at heart,
While we play at the grand old game.
The Otago R.F.U. Annual

THE BRITISH GENIUS for thinking up so many pleasant ways of wasting time is surely to be commended; it is only a charlatan who would disagree with the philosophy of a healthy mind in a healthy body. He would argue, of course, that such a philosophy has severely hampered mankind's progress, and that billions of 'work years' have been lost through devotion to the great god sport. What he has probably failed to appreciate is that sport in general and rugby in particular has played an important part in the advancement of many nations. Take Fiji for instance.

It is a little over a hundred years since the natives stopped putting their opponents in a pot and eating them; but in 1874 peace came to Fiji when the last king, Ratu Seru Cakobau, weary of the intertribal conflicts, ceded his country to Queen Victoria. Within ten years rugby was being played by the National Constabulary, and by 1905 the Fijians themselves had taken it up. It was a game which greatly appealed to the superbly built, fun loving islanders – they adopted it as their national sport, and nowadays more than 10,000 people actively take an interest in it.

Then there was the legendary tale of how the game reached Brazil; a theatrical group from Bristol was touring South America at the turn of the century, and while they were in Rio de Janiero they spent the afternoons playing rugby on Copacabana Beach.

Rugby first came to the Argentine with the arrival of British engineers who were building railways across the pampas, and although it remains secondary to soccer as a national sport, its growth during the last twenty years has been quite astonishing. In 1927 a British team of Lions strength toured the country, and then nine years later a predominantly English side repeated the visit. At that time the game was played mainly by expatriated Britons, but as an increasing number of homebred players became integrated into the athletics clubs so the game became more popular.

The Argentinians owe a great deal to the South African coach Izaac Van Heerden who assisted the national side in the mid-1960s and did his job so well that when Argentina toured South Africa in 1966 they beat the Junior Springboks. Then followed visits by Wales, Scotland and Ireland and each country in turn received a severe mauling from the 'Pumas'.

In amongst the predominantly Latin names still appears the odd 'Morgan' and 'Harris Smith', and any side from the home country can be assured of a warm reception. For a start, the team will probably be billeted in the Hurlingham Club not far from the centre of Buenos Aires, and will receive frequent calls from old colonials anxious to hear news of the old country. The attitude towards rugby in the Argentine is not exactly the one envisaged by the game's founders – there is a well organized league system with promotion and relegation and, as in France, winning is of extreme importance. Each club has its own coach, and while the top players may not enjoy quite the same public adulation as their soccer brethren, they are well enough known to adorn the pages of the national glossies. The other doubt expressed by the International Board concerns the Argentinian temperament which is infinitely more volatile than that of the French. In front of their own crowds and with their own referees they get away with acts of brutality which have never been part of the rugby game, and to some extent this has accounted for their recent successes against visiting sides. It would be a great pity if this was going to prevent the Argentinians from gaining international recognition, because there is enough natural talent in this country to enable them to play a significant role in world rugby.

Rumania has always maintained close cultural links with France – before the last war many of the young intelligentsia went to Paris University to study, and it was there that the athletically minded joined Paris University Club (P.U.C.), where rugby enjoyed a special status. So the seed was sown in Bucharest, at first amongst the bourgeoisie; but then under the influence of Communism, it spread throughout the Popular Republic. In 1954 Swansea accepted an invitation to take a side to Bucharest and play against Locomatavia, the Rumanian club champions; the following year Locomatavia returned the visit playing not only against Swansea but also against Bristol, Cardiff and Harlequins. Playing the full strength of these club sides, the Rumanians beat Swansea and Bristol, drew with Harlequins and lost to Cardiff by a three point margin.

Nevertheless, the rugby world was not quite prepared for the events of 1957 when the full representative might of France went to Bucharest to play a first international against Rumania. Curiosity more than anything else brought out a world record crowd of more than 95,000 for the event, and although France had finished at the foot of the Five Nations Championship that season, they saw little prospect of defeat in this match.

The play was broadcast on French radio and there is a beautifully descriptive account, which appears in Potter and Duthen's book *The Rise of French Rugby*, of how the game's progress was received in a French café in Montmartre:

'When the half-time score was announced (Rumania 9 France 6) the café keeper, an ex-hooker, went along the streets collecting fans who, thinking France would win in a trot, had not bothered to give ear. They poured in, most of them in working clothes, and several wearing Basque berets.

'In the forty-seventh minute Rumania were leading 12–6. In the fifty-fourth minute it was Rumania 15 France 6, and one of the

On 16 October 1976 the Pumas of Argentina were just one kick away from causing a major upset in world rugby. With seconds to go they were leading Wales, the champions of Europe, by two points at the Arms Park. Then Wales were awarded a penalty which Phil Bennett goaled to give his side victory by 20 points to 19. But the Pumas had shown by their performance that afternoon that they were capable of holding their own in the highest company, and that they had some very distinguished players; men like Alejandro Travaglini, who is seen on the right having received the ball from Hugo Porta, another skilled performer. The man who has worked the base of the Argentinian scrum for the last eight years – Adolfo Etchegaray, below, seems unaware of the fact that the Welsh flanker Trevor Evans is lying in wait for him

beret wearers said, "This is a veritable calamity, recalling the greatest rugby upset of all time. I refer to the victory of those gladiators, exponents of American football, who, converted into rugby players for the Olympic Games Tournament of 1924, defeated the might of France by 17 points to 3 and thus gave the United States . . ."

'Another beret wearer: "Silence! Who wants tales of history when history is being made?"

'Sixty-fifth minute: Rumania 15 France 9; seventieth minute: Rumania 15 France 12; seventy-fifth minute: Rumania 15 France 15.

'The man who had dug into history: "Our honour may be saved."

'Seventy-seventh minute: a forty-yard penalty kick by the French full back Michel Vannier. He took a drop kick. The radio speaker at top speed: "It looks good, it looks good. It looks good, and now it is descending and it still looks good, and could give France a miraculous win; and now the ball hits the bar and falls . . . on the right side, for France."

'Final score – Rumania 15 France 18.

' "Landlord! Fill them up!".'

The result of that match had to some extent prepared the French for their first defeat by Rumania, which came in 1960. The following year the match was drawn, and then in 1962 when France were Five Nations Champions, Rumania won again, 3–0.

Unfortunately the Rumanians became preoccupied with winning and seldom did they risk playing the open attractive football which came naturally to them. Attendances and standards dropped, but in recent years the International Board have encouraged visits to and from Rumania, and it is to be hoped that, with its horizons broadened, the Rumanian game will shake off its obsession with results, and this will lead to a return to the style which two decades ago brought the country to the forefront of the rugby world.

Organized rugby has been played in Japan for something like eighty years. It was

Edward Clarke, the son of a Yokohama baker who, having won his place in the Cambridge University side, returned to the University of Keio and taught the game to his students in 1897. The British colonies at Yokohama and Kobe had been playing rugby for some time before that date – there are photographic records of a game being played at Yokohama as early as 1874.

By the end of the century an increasing number of Japanese were taking an interest in the game, and in 1900 Keio University played its first match against Yokohama Country Athletic Club, a club which had been formed by the British residents in Yokohama. The match became an annual fixture, and in the same year another annual match was organized between Keio and a team from the Kobe Country Club. It was eleven years before any other Japanese sides registered interest, but in 1911 Kyoto College and the University of Doshisha were formed and began playing regular fixtures against Keio.

Between 1911 and 1923 there was a tremendous upsurge in interest, and in that latter year His Royal Highness the Prince of Wales played in a match whilst on a visit to Japan. In 1926 the Japanese Rugby Federation was established, and there followed regular contact with many countries.

In 1927, the University of Waseda, the national champions, undertook a first tour to Australia; having made the journey by cargo boat, they played five matches losing them all. Three years later, a Japanese side left for a tour to Canada. Seven games were played of which six were won and one drawn, and in the years ahead Japan played hosts to the Canadians, the Australians and the New Zealand Universities. Regular contact with these countries brought a considerable improvement in Japanese rugby standards, and the New Zealanders were held to a draw by the combined universities of Japan.

The outbreak of World War II prevented a continuation of that improvement, but two weeks after the Japanese surrender a

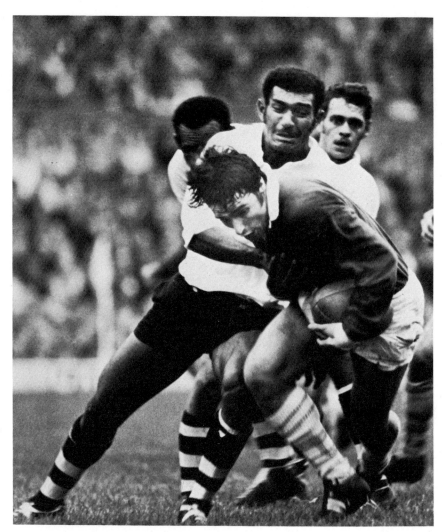

number of players got together to resurrect the game. It required a good deal more than their enthusiasm, however, to restore the game to its pre-war standards. This was the age of the professional sportsman, and the sport which had caught the public imagination in Japan was baseball. The majority of young athletes with ambition were drawn to this game by the money and stardom which it offered, and as a consequence rugby was one of the sports which suffered.

The only answer was to import sides from overseas to promote the game, and throughout the 1950s Japan threw open her doors to rugby tourists. The universities of Oxford

Three teams always assured of a
warm welcome in Britain – on
the left the Fijians in action
against London Counties during
their tour in 1970; right, Talilotu
Ngaluafe of Tonga passes out to
his wing in the 1974 match
against England Under 23s at
Twickenham, and below the
Japanese tourists in full cry for
the Welsh line at Cardiff Arms
Park in 1973

and Cambridge led the way and then in 1958 came the hardest test which had yet faced Nippon – a visit from the New Zealand Under-23 side. The tourists had little difficulty in winning all their games, which was hardly surprising when you consider that the team included forwards like Wilson Whineray, Colin Meads and Kel Tremain, while Pat Walsh, Terry Lineen and Ross Brown were numbered amongst the backs.

It did not take the Japanese long to absorb the various lessons taught by their overseas visitors, and soon afterwards they produced one of the biggest upsets in history when they went to New Zealand and downed the Junior All Blacks. This win did much to stimulate the rebirth of rugby in Japan and now, some twenty years later, there are reckoned to be more than 2000 clubs in existence. In 1969 was held the first of the Asiatic Tournaments, and in this event the Japanese have shown themselves to be far and away the strongest rugby playing country in that part of the world.

They have been greatly assisted on occasions by top class players from other countries whose work has taken them East. One name which comes to mind is the former Blackheath and England scrum half Simon Clarke who, at 5ft 6ins and 10 stone, in his boots, was, by all accounts, invited to turn out for his new club as a second row forward. It is this lack of height which has proved to be the major obstacle to Japan's progress against the world rugby powers. 'They are,' observed Clarke some years ago, 'just not big enough to play power forward rugby like the All Blacks or Springboks. In any case their natural inclination is to run the ball all the time from any position. Kicking is almost a last resort, and because of that they are not very good at it. But if a team came to Britain they would be a great success.'

How right he was – although the side which toured Wales and France in 1973 failed to win many matches, the European crowds loved their running and handling skills and admired their courage and discipline. In the summer of 1975 Wales returned the visit and ran up some mammoth scores; once again the lack of height and weight in the forwards had proved too great a handicap, but surely it is not above the inventive Japanese mind to come up with an effective cross between a fly weight and a Sumo wrestler.

There is alternatively the remedy offered by the Welsh bard Max Boyce, in a song he dedicated to these popular tourists in 1973:

Western Mail say we too small,
We can get no ball at all;
But we eat bamboo shoots to grow,
Fit platform boots to second row.

Two major problems have hampered the game's progress in Canada; the climate, which makes it impossible to continue playing throughout the winter without a break, and the enormous distances which have to be covered. In the late 1860s English students attending McGill University started the game in Quebec Province, but it was in British Columbia where rugby made the greatest advance. In the 1880s, a New Zealander, A. St.-G. Hammersley, migrated to Vancouver and his enthusiasm made so many converts that by the end of the decade the British Columbia Union had been formed.

With the advent of air transport and the hard work of an Englishman called Robert Spray, there was increased communication between the provinces, and in 1965 the Canadian Rugby Union was established.

Canada has always been a popular place for touring rugby practitioners and many international sides have stopped off on the way to, or back from, a major tour. One of the most popular sides to tour Canada was the Barbarians in 1957, a team of Lions' strength which preached the rugby gospel both on and off the field. At one stage during the tour they were invited to appear on a television magazine programme. The programme producer, an American, had decided that he would present the group to the

In 1947 the Wallabies began a magnificent tradition by playing the last match of their tour against the Barbarians. Ever since that day major touring sides have rung the curtain down with a game against the cream of British talent which has led to some of the greatest moments in the history of the sport. This picture shows the Welsh and British Lions winger J. J. Williams rounding the Australian scrum half Rod Hauser to score for the Barbarians in the 1976 match in Cardiff

Nation as 'a team of rugby missionaries from Britain come to teach us about the ball game called rugby'. Moreover he intended that it should be a mini epic – carpenters were called in and a set was rigged with shop fronts in which were placed half a dozen beautiful models. The plan was that, at a given signal, the Barbarians had to wave at the cameras while the commentator said his piece: 'Ladies and gentlemen of Canada, meet the Barbs. These are Barbarians from England come to teach us about the ball game rugby football. Here they are window shopping in the streets of Toronto.' At which point the Irishman Tom Reid put his arm through what should have been the shop window and embraced one of the girls. But the commentator was equal to

the occasion, and in an inspired moment he ad-libbed, 'Barbarians – they sure are Barbarians.'

The idea of the Barbarians, the most exclusive rugby club in the world, was moved at an oyster supper in Bradford in October 1890, some six months after W. P. Carpmael had taken a touring side to Yorkshire and the Midlands. It is not exactly clear who thought up the name 'Barbarians', but in the words of O. L. Owen it was decided to give the club a name 'dignified by the famous victory of Arminius over Varus and his legions somewhere in Germany about 2000 years ago'.

The first tour was in the 1890–1 season to the North of England, where the Barbarians beat Hartlepool Rovers and drew with

Of all the games between the Barbarians and touring sides none, surely, produced a finer spectacle than the encounter with the All Blacks in 1973, a match which brought the greatest try ever seen at the Arms Park. The action leading up to the try was thrillingly described by N.Z.B.C. radio commentator Bob Irvine . . .

'The ball is bouncing over the Barbarians twenty-five, bad one for Bennett going back for it and picking it up – up there with him is Scown

. . . He's got past Scown, he's cutting up the middle again, he's feeding it on the left now to John Williams who's taken by Brian Williams . . .

on now to Quinnell . . .

from Quinnell to Gareth Edwards . . .

. . . Back it comes on the left again to Pullin and further out to John Dawes – up to the half way line he comes – oh, this is extra action stuff!

. . . Back it goes on the right to David,

Edwards is going for the corner . . .

and Edwards has the second . . .

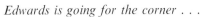

Bradford, but the third match against Swinton was cancelled because of the frost. Even in those early days the Barbarians style was exciting to watch and an extract appears in the 'History of Hartlepool Rovers' relating to that first match: 'The feature of the season was, however, a visit from the Barbarians comprising players drawn from English, Scottish and Welsh clubs including A. E. Stoddart, R. L. Aston, Gregor McGregor and S. M. J. Woods, and after a well-contested game the visitors won by three goals and one try to one goal and one try. It was a splendid exposition and one of the best matches I have seen (and, as an object lesson, it ought to have been witnessed by all other players, and probably some of them learned how happily the rules could be put into operation), and as long as the Barbarians and the Rovers can meet and show the same skill, the games will be a delight to watch.'

It was not long before the Barbarians extended the sphere of their operations into the West Country and Wales, and by the beginning of the new century the Easter tour to the Principality was one of the highlights of the season. The tourists' adopted clubhouse on these occasions became the Esplanade Hotel at Penarth, which survived generations of abuse until quite recently when it was demolished, not by rugbymen, but in the name of progress.

As the years passed the Barbarians were called upon to fulfil an increasing number of engagements, and in 1934 they were the guest side at the Middlesex Sevens; the side, containing 'five knowledgeable Scotsmen, one Englishman and one Welshman', beat Richmond in the final.

In the 1947–8 season the Wallabies were touring Britain and had recorded three international victories against Scotland. Ireland and England, but as the tour drew to its close it was clear that the tourists were running short of funds. It was therefore decided to play an extra match so that money could be raised to pay for the return trip to Australia via the United States and Canada, and what greater draw could there be than a match against a Barbarians side containing all the big names of the day?

The game was played at Cardiff Arms Park, the Barbarians won 9–6 and that was the start of a magnificent tradition. Since that day there have been countless thrilling and emotional moments as touring sides played their final match against the pride of British rugby; in 1963 there was an encounter against the All Blacks when Wilson Whineray's men played the game of their lives and Whineray capped the afternoon by scoring a try; that same day when the All Black prop Ian Clarke, playing for the Barbarians, dropped a goal to the astonishment of his brother Don; the crunching tackle by Haydn Mainwairing on Avril Malan, the Springbok captain, in 1961; the gallant fight back by Brian Lochore's All Blacks in 1967, and the 'game of the century' against the All Blacks in 1972 when Gareth Edwards put the finishing touch to a move which had been started by Phil Bennett just inches from his own line.

These are magical moments in sport of which the participants and the administrators who have given so much time and devotion to the club can rightly feel proud – men like the late Brigadier Glyn Hughes and Jock Wemyss, wonderful characters both, who typified the Barbarian spirit and established the reputation of the club world wide.

It has never been the Barbarians' aim to be a domestic substitute for the Lions; rather it has been their philosophy that rugby is an exercise in skilled endeavour and comradeship to be played purely for enjoyment on the field and for the cementing of friendships off it. Throughout the years the Barbarians have remained true to the doctrine of the club motto that 'Rugby is a game for gentlemen of all classes but never for a bad sportsman of any class.'

RESULTS

INTERNATIONAL MATCHES

England v. Scotland
England v. Ireland
England v. Wales
England v. France
England v. New Zealand
England v. South Africa
England v. Australia
Scotland v. Ireland
Scotland v. Wales
Scotland v. France
Scotland v. New Zealand
Scotland v. South Africa
Scotland v. Australia
Ireland v. Wales
Ireland v. France
Ireland v. New Zealand
Ireland v. South Africa
Ireland v. Australia
Wales v. France
Wales v. New Zealand
Wales v. South Africa
Wales v. Australia
France v. South Africa
France v. New Zealand
France v. Australia
New Zealand v. South Africa
New Zealand v. Australia
South Africa v. Australia

GRAND SLAM WINNERS

TRIPLE CROWN WINNERS

INTERNATIONAL CHAMPIONSHIP WINNERS

INTERNATIONAL TOURS

British Isles to Australia and New Zealand
British Isles to South Africa
New Zealand to British Isles and France
New Zealand to South Africa
South Africa to British Isles and France
South Africa to Australia and New Zealand
Australia to British Isles and France
Australia to South Africa
England to Australia and New Zealand
England to South Africa
England to Fiji and New Zealand
England to Australia
Ireland to South Africa
Ireland to Australia
Ireland to New Zealand
Wales to South Africa
Wales to Australia, New Zealand and Fiji
France to South Africa
France to Australia and New Zealand
Scotland to South Africa
Scotland to Australia
Scotland to New Zealand

INTERNATIONAL RECORDS

Australia
British Isles
England
France
Ireland
New Zealand
Scotland
South Africa
Wales

ENGLISH COUNTY CHAMPIONSHIPS

RUGBY FOOTBALL UNION CLUB COMPETITION

SCOTTISH CLUB CHAMPIONS

FRENCH CHAMPIONSHIPS

CURRIE CUP (South Africa)

RANFURLY SHIELD (New Zealand)

UNIVERSITY MATCH (Oxford and Cambridge)

INTERNATIONAL MATCHES

ENGLAND v. SCOTLAND
Played 92
England won 43
Scotland won 35
Drawn 14

1871 Raeburn Place (Edinburgh)
Scotland 1G 1T to 1T
1872 The Oval (London)
England 2G 2T to 1G
1873 Glasgow
Drawn no score
1874 The Oval
England 1G to 1T
1875 Raeburn Place
Drawn no score
1876 The Oval
England 1G 1T to 0
1877 Raeburn Place
Scotland 1G to 0
1878 The Oval
Drawn no score
1879 Raeburn Place
Drawn 1G each
1880 Manchester
England 2G 3T to 1G
1881 Raeburn Place
Drawn 1G 1T each
1882 Manchester
Scotland 2T to 0
1883 Raeburn Place
England 2T to 1T
1884 Blackheath (London)
England 1G to 1T
1885 No Match
1886 Raeburn Place
Drawn no score
1887 Manchester
Drawn 1T each
1888 No Match
1889 No Match
1890 Raeburn Place
England 1G 1T to 0
1891 Richmond (London)
Scotland 3G (9) to 1G (3)
1892 Raeburn Place
England 1G (5) to 0
1893 Leeds
Scotland 2DG (8) to 0
1894 Raeburn Place
Scotland 2T (6) to 0
1895 Richmond
Scotland 1PG 1T (6) to 1PG (3)
1896 Glasgow
Scotland 1G 2T (11) to 0
1897 Manchester
England 1G 1DG 1T (12) to 1T (3)
1898 Powderhall (Edinburgh)
Drawn 1T (3) each
1899 Blackheath
Scotland 1G (5) to 0
1900 Inverleith (Edinburgh)
Drawn no score
1901 Blackheath
Scotland 3G 1T (18) to 1T (3)

1902 Inverleith
England 2T (6) to 1T (3)
1903 Richmond
Scotland 1DG 2T (10) to 2T (6)
1904 Inverleith
Scotland 2T (6) to 1T (3)
1905 Richmond
Scotland 1G 1T (8) to 0
1906 Inverleith
England 3T (9) to 1T (3)
1907 Blackheath
Scotland 1G 1T (8) to 1T (3)
1908 Inverleith
Scotland 1G 2DG 1T (16) to 2G (10)
1909 Richmond
Scotland 3G 1T (18) to 1G 1T (8)
1910 Inverleith
England 1G 3T (14) to 1G (5)
1911 Twickenham
England 2G 1T (13) to 1G 1T (8)
1912 Inverleith
Scotland 1G 1T (8) to 1T (3)
1913 Twickenham
England 1T (3) to 0
1914 Inverleith
England 2G 2T (16) to 1G 1DG 2T (15)
1920 Twickenham
England 2G 1T (13) to 1DG (4)
1921 Inverleith
England 3G 1T (18) to 0
1922 Twickenham
England 1G 2T (11) to 1G (5)
1923 Inverleith
England 1G 1T (8) to 2T (6)
1924 Twickenham
England 3G 1DG (19) to 0
1925 Murrayfield
Scotland 2G 1DG (14) to 1G 1PG 1T (11)
1926 Twickenham
Scotland 2G 1DG 1T (17) to 3T (9)
1927 Murrayfield
Scotland 1G 1DG 4T (21) to 2G 1PG (13)
1928 Twickenham
England 2T (6) to 0
1929 Murrayfield
Scotland 4T (12) to 2T (6)
1930 Twickenham
Drawn no score
1931 Murrayfield
Scotland 5G 1T (28) to 2G 1PG 2T (19)
1932 Twickenham
England 2G 2T (16) to 1T (3)
1933 Murrayfield
Scotland 1T (3) to 0
1934 Twickenham
England 2T (6) to 1T (3)
1935 Murrayfield
Scotland 2G (10) to 1DG 1T (7)
1936 Twickenham
England 3T (9) to 1G 1PG (8)
1937 Murrayfield
England 2T (6) to 1PG (3)
1938 Twickenham
Scotland 2PG 5T (21) to 1DG 3PG 1T (16)
1939 Murrayfield
England 3PG (9) to 2T (6)
1947 Twickenham
England 4G 1DG (24) to 1G (5)
1948 Murrayfield
Scotland 2T (6) to 1PG (3)
1949 Twickenham
England 2G 3T (19) to 1PG (3)
1950 Murrayfield
Scotland 2G 1T (13) to 1G 1PG 1T (11)
1951 Twickenham
England 1G (5) to 1T (3)
1952 Murrayfield
England 2G 1DG 2T (19) to 1T (3)

1953 Twickenham
England 4G 2T (26) to 1G 1T (8)
1954 Murrayfield
England 2G 1T (13) to 1T (3)
1955 Twickenham
England 1PG 2T (9) to 1PG 1T (6)
1956 Murrayfield
England 1G 2PG (11) to 1PG 1T (6)
1957 Twickenham
England 2G 1PG 1T (16) to 1PG (3)
1958 Murrayfield
Drawn 1PG (3) each
1959 Twickenham
Drawn 1PG (3) each
1960 Murrayfield
England 3G 1DG 1PG (21) to 3PG 1T (12)
1961 Twickenham
England 1PG 1T (6) to 0
1962 Murrayfield
Drawn 1PG (3) each
1963 Twickenham
England 2G (10) to 1G 1DG (8)
1964 Murrayfield
Scotland 3G (15) to 1PG 1T (6)
1965 Twickenham
Drawn England 1T (3) Scotland 1DG (3)
1966 Murrayfield
Scotland 1PG 1T (6) to 1DG (3)
1967 Twickenham
England 3G 2PG 1DG 1T (27) to 1G 2PG 1T (14)
1968 Murrayfield
England 1G 1PG (8) to 1PG 1DG (6)
1969 Twickenham
England 1G 1T (8) to 1PG (3)
1970 Murrayfield
Scotland 1G 2PG 1T (14) to 1G (5)
1971 Twickenham
Scotland 2G 1DG 1T (16) to 3PG 2T (15)
*1971 Murrayfield
Scotland 4G 1PG 1T (26) to 1PG 1DG (6)
1972 Murrayfield
Scotland 4PG 1DG 2T (23) to 3PG (9)
1973 Twickenham
England 2G 2T (20) to 1G 1PG 1T (13)
1974 Murrayfield
Scotland 1G 2PG 1T (16) to 1DG 1PG 2T (14)
1975 Twickenham
England 1PG 1T (7) to 2PG (6)
1976 Murrayfield
Scotland 2G 2PG 1T (22) to 1G 2PG (12)
*Non-championship match

ENGLAND v. IRELAND
Played 88
England won 49
Ireland won 31
Drawn 8

1875 The Oval (London)
England 2G 1T to 0
1876 Dublin
England 1G 1T to 0
1877 The Oval
England 2G 2T to 0
1878 Dublin
England 2G 1T to 0
1879 The Oval
England 3G 2T to 0
1880 Dublin
England 1G 1T to 0
1881 Manchester
England 2G 2T to 0

1882 Dublin
Drawn 2T each
1883 Manchester
England 1G 3T to 1T
1884 Dublin
England 1G to 0
1885 Manchester
England 2T to 1T
1886 Dublin
England 1T to 0
1887 Dublin
Ireland 2G to 0
1888 No Match
1889 No Match
1890 Blackheath (London)
England 3T to 0
1891 Dublin
England 2G 3T (9) to 0
1892 Manchester
England 1G 1T (7) to 0
1893 Dublin
England 2T (4) to 0
1894 Blackheath
Ireland 1DG 1T (7) to 1G (5)
1895 Dublin
England 2T (6) to 1T (3)
1896 Leeds
Ireland 2G (10) to 1DG (4)
1897 Dublin
Ireland 1DG 3T (13) to 2PG 1T (9)
1898 Richmond (London)
Ireland 1PG 2T (9) to 1PG 1T (6)
1899 Dublin
Ireland 1PG 1T (6) to 0
1900 Richmond
England 1G 1DG 2T (15) to 1DG (4)
1901 Dublin
Ireland 2G (10) to 1PG 1T (6)
1902 Leicester
England 2T (6) to 1T (3)
1903 Dublin
Ireland 1PG 1T (6) to 0
1904 Blackheath
England 2G 3T (19) to 0
1905 Cork
Ireland 1G 4T (17) to 1T (3)
1906 Leicester
Ireland 2G 2T (16) to 2T (6)
1907 Dublin
Ireland 1G 1GM 3T (17) to 1PG 2T (9)
1908 Richmond
England 2G 1T (13) to 1PG (3)
1909 Dublin
England 1G 2T (11) to 1G (5)
1910 Twickenham
Drawn no score
1911 Dublin
Ireland 1T (3) to 0
1912 Twickenham
England 5T (15) to 0
1913 Dublin
England 1PG 4T (15) to 1DG (4)
1914 Twickenham
England 1G 4T (17) to 1G 1DG 1T (12)
1920 Dublin
England 1G 3T (14) to 1G 1PG 1T (11)
1921 Twickenham
England 1G 1DG 2T (15) to 0
1922 Dublin
England 4T (12) to 1T (3)
1923 Leicester
England 2G 1DG 3T (23) to 1G (5)
1924 Belfast
England 1G 3T (14) to 1T (3)
1925 Twickenham
Drawn 2T (6) each
1926 Dublin
Ireland 2G 1PG 2T (19) to 3G (15)

1927 Twickenham
England 1G 1T (8) to 1PG 1T (6)
1928 Dublin
England 1DG 1T (7) to 2T (6)
1929 Twickenham
Ireland 2T (6) to 1G (5)
1930 Dublin
Ireland 1DG (4) to 1T (3)
1931 Dublin
Ireland 1PG 1T (6) to 1G (5)
1932 Dublin
England 1G 2PG (11) to 1G 1PG (8)
1933 Twickenham
England 1G 4T (17) to 1PG 1T (6)
1934 Dublin
England 2G 1T (13) to 1T (3)
1935 Twickenham
England 1G 3PG (14) to 1T (3)
1936 Dublin
Ireland 2T (6) to 1T (3)
1937 Twickenham
England 1PG 2T (9) to 1G 1T (8)
1938 Dublin
England 6G 1PG 1T (36) to 1G 3T (14)
1939 Twickenham
Ireland 1G (5) to 0
1947 Dublin
Ireland 2G 1PG 3T (22) to 0
1948 Twickenham
Ireland 1G 2T (11) to 2G (10)
1949 Dublin
Ireland 1G 2PG 1T (14) to 1G (5)
1950 Twickenham
England 1T (3) to 0
1951 Dublin
Ireland 1PG (3) to 0
1952 Twickenham
England 1T (3) to 0
1953 Dublin
Drawn 2PG 1T (9) each
1954 Twickenham
England 1G 1PG 2T (14) to 1PG (3)
1955 Dublin
Drawn Ireland 1PG 1T (6) England 2T (6)
1956 Twickenham
England 1 G 3PG 2T (20) to 0
1957 Dublin
England 1PG 1T (6) to 0
1958 Twickenham
England 1PG 1T (6) to 0
1959 Dublin
England 1PG (3) to 0
1960 Twickenham
England 1G 1DG (8) to 1G (5)
1961 Dublin
Ireland 1G 2PG (11) to 1G 1T (8)
1962 Twickenham
England 2G 1PG 1T (16) to 0
1963 Dublin
Drawn no score
1964 Twickenham
Ireland 3G 1T (18) to 1G (5)
1965 Dublin
Ireland 1G (5) to 0
1966 Twickenham
Drawn 1PG 1T (6) each
1967 Dublin
England 1G 1PG (8) to 1PG (3)
1968 Twickenham
Drawn England 2PG 1DG (9) Ireland 3PG (9)
1969 Dublin
Ireland 1G 2PG 1DG 1T (17) to 4PG 1T (15)
1970 Twickenham
England 2DG 1T (9) to 1PG (3)
1971 Dublin
England 3PG (9) to 2T (6)
1972 Twickenham
Ireland 1G 1DG 1PG 1T (16) to 1G 2PG (12)

1973 Dublin
Ireland 2G 1PG 1DG (18) to 1G 1PG (9)
1974 Twickenham
Ireland 2G 1PG 1DG 2T (26) to 1G 5PG (21)
1975 Dublin
Ireland 2G (12) to 1G 1DG (9)
1976 Twickenham
Ireland 2PG 1DG 1T (13) to 4PG (12)

ENGLAND v. **WALES**
Played 81
England won 33
Wales won 37
Drawn 11

1881 Blackheath (London)
England 7G 1DG 6T to 0
1882 No Match
1883 Swansea
England 2G 4T to 0
1884 Leeds
England 1G 2T to 1G
1885 Swansea
England 1G 4T to 1G 1T
1886 Blackheath
England 1GM 2T to 1G
1887 Llanelli
Drawn no score
1888 No Match
1889 No Match
1890 Dewsbury
Wales 1T to 0
1891 Newport
England 2G 1T (7) to 1G (3)
1892 Blackheath
England 3G 1T (17) to 0
1893 Cardiff
Wales 1G 1PG 2T (14) to 1G 3T (11)
1894 Birkenhead
England 4G 1GM (24) to 1T (3)
1895 Swansea
England 1G 3T (14) to 2T (6)
1896 Blackheath
England 2G 5T (25) to 0
1897 Newport
Wales 1G 2T (11) to 0
1898 Blackheath
England 1G 3T (14) to 1DG 1T (7)
1899 Swansea
Wales 4G 2T (26) to 1T (3)
1900 Gloucester
Wales 2G 1PG (13) to 1T (3)
1901 Cardiff
Wales 2G 1T (13) to 0
1902 Blackheath
Wales 1PG 2T (9) to 1G 1T (8)
1903 Swansea
Wales 3G 2T (21) to 1G (5)
1904 Leicester
Drawn England 1G 1PG 2T (14)
Wales 2G 1GM (14)
1905 Cardiff
Wales 2G 5T (25) to 0
1906 Richmond (London)
Wales 2G 2T (16) to 1T (3)
1907 Swansea
Wales 2G 4T (22) to 0
1908 Bristol
Wales 3G 1DG 1PG 2T (28) to 3G 1T (18)
1909 Cardiff
Wales 1G 1T (8) to 0
1910 Twickenham
England 1G 1PG 1T (11) to 2T (6)

1911 Swansea
Wales 1PG 4T (15) to 1G 2T (11)
1912 Twickenham
England 1G 1T (8) to 0
1913 Cardiff
England 1G 1DG 1T (12) to 0
1914 Twickenham
England 2G (10) to 1G 1DG (9)
1920 Swansea
Wales 1G 2DG 1PG 1T (19) to 1G (5)
1921 Twickenham
England 1G 1DG 3T (18) to 1T (3)
1922 Cardiff
Wales 2G 6T (28) to 2T (6)
1923 Twickenham
England 1DG 1T (7) to 1T (3)
1924 Swansea
England 1G 4T (17) to 3T (9)
1925 Twickenham
England 1PG 3T (12) to 2T (6)
1926 Cardiff
Drawn 1T (3) each
1927 Twickenham
England 1G 1PG 1GM (11) to 1PG 2T (9)
1928 Swansea
England 2G (10) to 1G 1T (8)
1929 Twickenham
England 1G 1T (8) to 1T (3)
1930 Cardiff
England 1G 1PG 1T (11) to 1T (3)
1931 Twickenham
Drawn England 1G 2PG (11)
Wales 1G 1GM 1T (11)
1932 Swansea
Wales 1G 1DG 1PG (12) to 1G (5)
1933 Twickenham
Wales 1DG 1T (7) to 1T (3)
1934 Cardiff
England 3T (9) to 0
1935 Twickenham
Drawn England 1PG (3) Wales 1T (3)
1936 Swansea
Drawn no score
1937 Twickenham
England 1DG (4) to 1T (3)
1938 Cardiff
Wales 1G 2PG 1T (14) to 1G 1T (8)
1939 Twickenham
England 1T (3) to 0
1947 Cardiff
England 1G 1DG (9) to 2T (6)
1948 Twickenham
Drawn England 1PG (3) Wales 1T (3)
1949 Cardiff
Wales 3T (9) to 1DG (3)
1960 Twickenham
Wales 1G 1PG 1T (11) to 1G (5)
1951 Swansea
Wales 4G 1T (23) to 1G (5)
1952 Twickenham
Wales 1G 1T (8) to 2T (6)
1953 Cardiff
England 1G 1PG (8) to 1PG (3)
1954 Twickenham
England 3T (9) to 1PG 1T (6)
1955 Cardiff
Wales 1PG (3) to 0
1956 Twickenham
Wales 1G 1T (8) to 1PG (3)
1957 Cardiff
England 1PG (3) to 0
1958 Twickenham
Drawn England 1T (3) Wales 1PG (3)
1959 Cardiff
Wales 1G (5) to 0
1960 Twickenham
England 1G 2PG 1T (14) to 2PG (6)

1961 Cardiff
Wales 2T (6) to 1T (3)
1962 Twickenham
Drawn no score
1963 Cardiff
England 2G 1DG (13) to 1PG 1T (6)
1964 Twickenham
Drawn 2T (6) each
1965 Cardiff
Wales 1G 1DG 2T (14) to 1PG (3)
1966 Twickenham
Wales 1G 2PG (11) to 1PG 1T (6)
1967 Cardiff
Wales 5G 2PG 1DG (34) to 4PG 3T (21)
1968 Twickenham
Drawn England 1G 1PG 1T (11)
Wales 1G 1DG 1T (11)
1969 Cardiff
Wales 3G 2PG 1DG 2T (30) to 3PG (9)
1970 Twickenham
Wales 1G 1DG 3T (17) to 2G 1PG (13)
1971 Cardiff
Wales 2G 2DG 1PG 1T (22) to 1PG 1T (6)
1972 Twickenham
Wales 1G 2PG (12) to 1PG (3)
1973 Cardiff
Wales 1G 1PG 4T (25) to 2PG 1DG (9)
1974 Twickenham
England 1G 2PG 1T (16) to 1G 2PG (12)
1975 Cardiff
Wales 1G 2PG 2T (20) to 1T (4)
1976 Twickenham
Wales 3G 1PG (21) to 3PG (9)

ENGLAND _v._ FRANCE
Played 51
England won 29
France won 16
Drawn 6

1906 Paris
England 4G 5T (35) to 1G 1T (8)
1907 Richmond (London)
England 5G 1DG 4T (41) to 2G 1PG (13)
1908 Paris
England 2G 3T (19) to 0
1909 Leicester
England 2G 4T (22) to 0
1910 Paris
England 1G 2T (11) to 1T (3)
1911 Twickenham
England 5G 2PG 2T (37) to 0
1912 Paris
England 1G 1DG 3T (18) to 1G 1T (8)
1913 Twickenham
England 1G 5T (20) to 0
1914 Paris
England 6G 3T (39) to 2G 1T (13)
1920 Twickenham
England 1G 1PG (8) to 1T (3)
1921 Paris
England 2G (10) to 2PG (6)
1922 Twickenham
Drawn England 1G 2PG (11)
France 1G 2T (11)
1923 Paris
England 1G 1DG 1T (12) to 1PG (3)
1924 Twickenham
England 2G 3T (19) to 1DG 1T (7)
1925 Paris
England 2G 1GM (13) to 1G 2T (11)
1926 Twickenham
England 1G 2T (11) to 0

1927 Paris
France 1T (3) to 0
1928 Twickenham
England 3G 1T (18) to 1G 1T (8)
1929 Paris
England 2G 2T (16) to 2T (6)
1930 Twickenham
England 1G 2T (11) to 1G (5)
1931 Paris
France 2DG 2T (14) to 2G 1T (13)
1947 Twickenham
England 2T (6) to 1PG (3)
1948 Paris
France 1G 1DG 2T (15) to 0
1949 Twickenham
England 1G 1DG (8) to 1DG (3)
1950 Paris
France 2T (6) to 1T (3)
1951 Twickenham
France 1G 1PG 1T (11) to 1T (3)
1952 Paris
England 2PG (6) to 1T (3)
1953 Twickenham
England 1G 2T (11) to 0
1954 Paris
France 1G 1DG 1T (11) to 1T (3)
1955 Twickenham
France 2G 2DG (16) to 2PG 1T (9)
1956 Paris
France 1G 2PG 1T (14) to 2PG 1T (9)
1957 Twickenham
England 3T (9) to 1G (5)
1958 Paris
England 1G 1PG 2T (14) to 0
1959 Twickenham
Drawn 1PG (3) each
1960 Paris
Drawn France 1PG (3) England 1T (3)
1961 Twickenham
Drawn 1G (5) each
1962 Paris
France 2G 1T (13) to 0
1963 Twickenham
England 2PG (6) to 1G (5)
1964 Paris
England 1PG 1T (6) to 1T (3)
1965 Twickenham
England 2PG 1T (9) to 1PG 1T (6)
1966 Paris
France 2G 1T (13) to 0
1967 Twickenham
France 2G 1DG 1PG (16) to 3PG 1DG (12)
1968 Paris
France 1G 2DG 1PG (14) to 1DG 2PG (9)
1969 Twickenham
England 2G 3PG 1T (22) to 1G 1DG (8)
1970 Paris
France 4G 2DG 1PG 2T (35) to 2G 1PG (13)
1971 Twickenham
Drawn England 1G 3PG (14)
France 1G 1PG 1DG 1T (14)
1972 Paris
France 5G 1PG 1T (37) to 1G 2PG (12)
1973 Twickenham
England 2PG 2T (14) to 1G (6)
1974 Paris
Drawn 1G 1PG 1DG (12) each
1975 Twickenham
France 4G 1PG (27) to 4PG 2T (20)
1976 Paris
France 3G 3T (30) to 1G 1PG (9)

ENGLAND _v._ NEW ZEALAND
Played 10
England won 2
New Zealand won 8
Drawn 0

1905 Crystal Palace (London)
New Zealand 5T (15) to 0
1925 Twickenham
New Zealand 1G 1PG 3T (17)
to 1G 1PG 1T (11)
1936 Twickenham
England 1DG 3T (13) to 0
1954 Twickenham
New Zealand 1G (5) to 0
1963 _1_ Auckland
New Zealand 3G 1DG 1PG (21)
to 1G 2PG (11)
_2_ Christchurch
New Zealand 1GM 2T (9) to 1PG 1T (6)
New Zealand won series 2-0
1964 Twickenham
New Zealand 1G 2PG 1T (14) to 0
1967 Twickenham
New Zealand 4G 1T (23)
to 1G 1PG 1T (11)
1973 Twickenham
New Zealand 1G 1DG (9) to 0
1973 Auckland
England 2G 1T (16) to 1G 1T (10)

ENGLAND _v._ SOUTH AFRICA
Played 7
England won 2
South Africa won 4
Drawn 1

1906 Crystal Palace (London)
Drawn 1T (3) each
1913 Twickenham
South Africa 2PG 1T (9) to 1T (3)
1932 Twickenham
South Africa 1DG 1T (7) to 0
1952 Twickenham
South Africa 1G 1PG (8) to 1T (3)
1961 Twickenham
South Africa 1G (5) to 0
1969 Twickenham
England 1G 1PG 1T (11) to 1G 1PG (8)
1972 Johannesburg
England 1G 4PG (18) to 3PG (9)

ENGLAND _v._ AUSTRALIA
Played 9
England won 3
Australia won 6
Drawn 0

1909 Blackheath (London)
Australia 3T (9) to 1T (3)
1948 Twickenham
Australia 1G 2T (11) to 0
1958 Twickenham
England 1PG 2T (9) to 1DG 1PG (6)
1963 Sydney
Australia 3G 1T (18) to 3T (9)

1967 Twickenham
Australia 1G 3DG 2PG 1T (23)
to 1G 2PG (11)
1973 Twickenham
England 1G 2PG 2T (20) to 1PG (3)
1975 *1* Sydney
Australia 2PG 2DG 1T (16) to 1G 1PG (9)
2 Brisbane
Australia 2G 2PG 3T (30) to 2G 3PG (21)
Australia won series 2–0
1976 Twickenham
England 1G 3PG 2T (23) to 2PG (6)

SCOTLAND *v.* IRELAND
Played 86
Scotland won 44
Ireland won 39
Drawn 3

1877 Belfast
Scotland 6G 2T to 0
1878 No Match
1879 Belfast
Scotland 2G 1T to 0
1880 Glasgow
Scotland 3G 2T to 0
1881 Belfast
Ireland 1G to 1T
1882 Glasgow
Scotland 2T to 0
1883 Belfast
Scotland 1G 1T to 0
1884 Raeburn Place (Edinburgh)
Scotland 2G 2T to 1T
1885 Raeburn Place
Scotland 1G 2T to 0
1886 Raeburn Place
Scotland 4G 2T to 0
1887 Belfast
Scotland 2G 2T to 0
1888 Raeburn Place
Scotland 1G to 0
1889 Belfast
Scotland 1DG to 0
1890 Raeburn Place
Scotland 1DG 1T to 0
1891 Belfast
Scotland 4G 2T (14) to 0
1892 Raeburn Place
Scotland 1T (2) to 0
1893 Belfast
Drawn no score
1894 Dublin
Ireland 1G (5) to 0
1895 Raeburn Place
Scotland 2T (6) to 0
1896 Dublin
Drawn no score
1897 Powderhall (Edinburgh)
Scotland 1G 1PG (8) to 1T (3)
1898 Belfast
Scotland 1G 1T (8) to 0
1899 Inverleith (Edinburgh)
Ireland 3T (9) to 1PG (3)
1900 Dublin
Drawn no score
1901 Inverleith (Edinburgh)
Scotland 3T (9) to 1G (5)
1902 Belfast
Ireland 1G (5) to 0
1903 Inverleith
Scotland 1T (3) to 0
1904 Dublin
Scotland 2G 3T (19) to 1T (3)

1905 Inverleith
Ireland 1G 2T (11) to 1G (5)
1906 Dublin
Scotland 2G 1GM (13) to 2T (6)
1907 Inverleith
Scotland 3G (15) to 1PG (3)
1908 Dublin
Ireland 2G 2T (16) to 1G 1PG 1T (11)
1909 Inverleith
Scotland 3T (9) to 1PG (3)
1910 Belfast
Scotland 1G 3T (14) to 0
1911 Inverleith
Ireland 2G 2T (16) to 1 DG 2T (10)
1912 Dublin
Ireland 1DG 1PG 1T (10) to 1G 1T (8)
1913 Inverleith
Scotland 4G 3T (29) to 2G 1DG (14)
1914 Dublin
Ireland 2T (6) to 0
1920 Inverleith
Scotland 2G 1PG 2T (19) to 0
1921 Dublin
Ireland 3T (9) to 1G 1T (8)
1922 Inverleith
Scotland 2T (6) to 1T (3)
1923 Dublin
Scotland 2G 1T (13) to 1T (3)
1924 Inverleith
Scotland 2G 1T (13) to 1G 1T (8)
1925 Dublin
Scotland 2G 1DG (14) to 1G 1PG (8)
1926 Murrayfield
Ireland 1T (3) to 0
1927 Dublin
Ireland 2T (6) to 0
1928 Murrayfield
Ireland 2G 1T (13) to 1G (5)
1929 Dublin
Scotland 2G 2T (16) to 1DG 1T (7)
1930 Murrayfield
Ireland 1G 3T (14) to 1G 2T (11)
1931 Dublin
Ireland 1G 1T (8) to 1G (5)
1932 Murrayfield
Ireland 4G (20) to 1G 1T (8)
1933 Dublin
Scotland 2DG (8) to 2T (6)
1934 Murrayfield
Scotland 2G 1PG 1T (16) to 3T (9)
1935 Dublin
Ireland 4T (12) to 1G (5)
1936 Murrayfield
Ireland 1DG 2T (10) to 1DG (4)
1937 Dublin
Ireland 1G 2T (11) to 1DG (4)
1938 Murrayfield
Scotland 2G 1DG 1PG 2T (23) to 1G 3T (14)
1939 Dublin
Ireland 1PG 1GM 2T (12) to 1T (3)
1947 Murrayfield
Ireland 1T (3) to 0
1948 Dublin
Ireland 2T (6) to 0
1949 Murrayfield
Ireland 2G 1PG (13) to 1PG (3)
1950 Dublin
Ireland 3G 2PG (21) to 0
1951 Murrayfield
Ireland 1DG 1T (6) to 1G (5)
1952 Dublin
Ireland 1PG 3T (12) to 1G 1PG (8)
1953 Murrayfield
Ireland 4G 2T (26) to 1G 1PG (8)
1954 Belfast
Ireland 2T (6) to 0
1955 Murrayfield
Scotland 2PG 1DG 1T (12) to 1PG (3)

1956 Dublin
Ireland 1G 3T (14) to 2G (10)
1957 Murrayfield
Ireland 1G (5) to 1PG (3)
1958 Dublin
Ireland 2PG 2T (12) to 2T (6)
1959 Murrayfield
Ireland 1G 1PG (8) to 1PG (3)
1960 Dublin
Scotland 1DG 1T (6) to 1G (5)
1961 Murrayfield
Scotland 2G 1PG 1T (16) to 1G 1T (8)
1962 Dublin
Scotland 1G 1DG 2PG 2T (20) to 1PG 1T (6)
1963 Murrayfield
Scotland 1PG (3) to 0
1964 Dublin
Scotland 2PG (6) to 1PG (3)
1965 Murrayfield
Ireland 2G 1DG 1T (16) to 1DG 1PG (6)
1966 Dublin
Scotland 1G 2T (11) to 1PG (3)
1967 Murrayfield
Ireland 1G (5) to 1PG (3)
1968 Dublin
Ireland 1G 1PG 2T (14) to 2PG (6)
1969 Murrayfield
Ireland 2G 2T (16) to 0
1970 Dublin
Ireland 2G 2T (16) to 1G 1DG 1T (11)
1971 Murrayfield
Ireland 1G 2PG 2T (17) to 1G (5)
1972 No Match
1973 Murrayfield
Scotland 2PG 3DG 1T (19) to 2PG 2T (14)
1974 Dublin
Ireland 1G 1PG (9) to 2PG (6)
1975 Murrayfield
Scotland 2PG 2DG 2T (20)
to 1G 1PG 1T (13)
1976 Dublin
Scotland 4PG 1DG (15) to 2PG (6)

SCOTLAND *v.* WALES
Played 80
Scotland won 34
Wales won 44
Drawn 2

1883 Raeburn Place (Edinburgh)
Scotland 3G to 1G
1884 Newport
Scotland 1DG 1T to O
1885 Glasgow
Drawn no score
1886 Cardiff
Scotland 2G 1T to 0
1887 Raeburn Place
Scotland 4G 8T to 0
1888 Newport
Wales 1T to 0
1889 Raeburn Place
Scotland 2T to 0
1890 Cardiff
Scotland 1G 2T to 1T
1891 Raeburn Place
Scotland 1G 2DG 5T (14) to 0
1892 Swansea
Scotland 1G 1T (7) to 1T (2)
1893 Raeburn Place
Wales 1PG 3T (9) to 0
1894 Newport
Wales 1DG 1T (7) to 0

1895 Raeburn Place
Scotland 1G (5) to 1DG (4)
1896 Cardiff
Wales 2T (6) to 0
1897 No Match
1898 No Match
1899 Inverleith (Edinburgh)
Scotland 1GM 2DG 3T (21) to 2G (10)
1900 Swansea
Wales 4T (12) to 1T (3)
1901 Inverleith
Scotland 3G 1T (18) to 1G 1T (8)
1902 Cardiff
Wales 1G 3T (14) to 1G (5)
1903 Inverleith
Scotland 1PG 1T (6) to 0
1904 Swansea
Wales 3G 1PG 1T (21) to 1T (3)
1905 Inverleith
Wales 2T (6) to 1T (3)
1906 Cardiff
Wales 3T (9) to 1PG (3)
1907 Inverleith
Scotland 2T (6) to 1PG (3)
1908 Swansea
Wales 2T (6) to 1G (5)
1909 Inverleith
Wales 1G (5) to 1PG (3)
1910 Cardiff
Wales 1G 3T (14) to 0
1911 Inverleith
Wales 2G 1DG 6T (32) to 1DG 2T (10)
1912 Swansea
Wales 2G 2DG 1T (21) to 2T (6)
1913 Inverleith
Wales 1G 1T (8) to 0
1914 Cardiff
Wales 2G 2DG 1PG 1T (24) to 1G (5)
1920 Inverleith
Scotland 2PG 1T (9) to 1G (5)
1921 Swansea
Scotland 1G 1PG 2T (14) to 2DG (8)
1922 Inverleith
Drawn Scotland 1PG 2T (9) Wales 1G 1DG (9)
1923 Cardiff
Scotland 1G 2T (11) to 1G 1PG (8)
1924 Inverleith
Scotland 4G 1PG 4T (35) to 2G (10)
1925 Swansea
Scotland 1G 1DG 5T (24) to 1G 1PG 2T (14)
1926 Murrayfield
Scotland 1G 1PG (8) to 1G (5)
1927 Cardiff
Scotland 1G (5) to 0
1928 Murrayfield
Wales 2G 1T (13) to 0
1929 Swansea
Wales 1G 3T (14) to 1DG 1PG (7)
1930 Murrayfield
Scotland 1G 1DG 1T (12) to 1G 1DG (9)
1931 Cardiff
Wales 2G 1T (13) to 1G 1T (8)
1932 Murrayfield
Wales 1PG 1T (6) to 0
1933 Swansea
Scotland 1G 1PG 1T (11) to 1T (3)
1934 Murrayfield
Wales 2G 1T (13) to 1PG 1T (6)
1935 Cardiff
Wales 1DG 2T (10) to 2T (6)
1936 Murrayfield
Wales 2G 1T (13) to 1T (3)
1937 Swansea
Scotland 2G 1T (13) to 2T (6)
1938 Murrayfield
Scotland 1G 1PG (8) to 2T (6)
1939 Cardiff
Wales 1G 1PG 1T (11) to 1PG (3)

1947 Murrayfield
Wales 2G 1PG 3T (22) to 1G 1PG (8)
1948 Cardiff
Wales 1G 1PG 2T (14) to 0
1949 Murrayfield
Scotland 2T (6) to 1G (5)
1950 Swansea
Wales 1DG 1PG 2T (12) to 0
1951 Murrayfield
Scotland 2G 1DG 1PG 1T (19) to 0
1952 Cardiff
Wales 1G 2PG (11) to 0
1953 Murrayfield
Wales 1PG 3T (12) to 0
1954 Swansea
Wales 1PG 4T (15) to 1T (3)
1955 Murrayfield
Scotland 1G 1DG 1PG 1T (14) to 1G 1T (8)
1956 Cardiff
Wales 3T (9) to 1PG (3)
1957 Murrayfield
Scotland 1DG 1PG 1T (9) to 1PG 1T (6)
1958 Cardiff
Wales 1G 1T (8) to 1PG (3)
1959 Murrayfield
Scotland 1PG 1T (6) to 1G (5)
1960 Cardiff
Wales 1G 1PG (8) to 0
1961 Murrayfield
Scotland 1T (3) to 0
1962 Cardiff
Scotland 1G 1T (8) to 1DG (3)
1963 Murrayfield
Wales 1DG 1PG (6) to 0
1964 Cardiff
Wales 1G 1PG 1T (11) to 1T (3)
1965 Murrayfield
Wales 1G 2PG 1T (14) to 2DG 2 PG (12)
1966 Cardiff
Wales 1G 1T (8) to 1PG (3)
1967 Murrayfield
Scotland 1G 1DG 1T (11) to 1G (5)
1968 Cardiff
Wales 1G (5) to 0
1969 Murrayfield
Wales 1G 2PG 2T (17) to 1PG (3)
1970 Cardiff
Wales 3G 1T (18) to 1DG 1PG 1T (9)
1971 Murrayfield
Wales 2G 1PG 2T (19) to 4PG 2T (18)
1972 Cardiff
Wales 3G 3PG 2T (35) to 1G 2PG (12)
1973 Murrayfield
Scotland 1G 1T (10) to 3PG (9)
1974 Cardiff
Wales 1G (6) to 0
1975 Murrayfield
Scotland 3PG 1DG (13) to 2PG 1T (10)
1976 Cardiff
Wales 2G 3PG 1DG 1T (28) to 1G (6)

SCOTLAND v. FRANCE
Played 46
Scotland won 23
France won 21
Drawn 2

1910 Inverleith (Edinburgh)
Scotland 3G 4T (27) to 0
1911 Paris
France 2G 2T (16) to 1G 1DG 2T (15)
1912 Inverleith
Scotland 5G 1PG 1T (31) to 1T (3)

1913 Paris
Scotland 3G 2T (21) to 1T (3)
1914 No Match
1920 Paris
Scotland 1G (5) to 0
1921 Inverleith
France 1T (3) to 0
1922 Paris
Drawn 1T (3) each
1923 Inverleith
Scotland 2G 2T (16) to 1GM (3)
1924 Paris
France 4T (12) to 1DG 1PG 1T (10)
1925 Paris
Scotland 2G 5T (25) to 1DG (4)
1926 Paris
Scotland 1G 1PG 4T (20) to 1PG 1T (6)
1927 Murrayfield
Scotland 4G 1PG (23) to 2T (6)
1928 Paris
Scotland 5T (15) to 2T (6)
1929 Murrayfield
Scotland 1PG 1T (6) to 1T (3)
1930 Paris
France 1DG 1T (7) to 1T (3)
1931 Murrayfield
Scotland 2PG (6) to 1DG (4)
1947 Paris
France 1G 1T (8) to 1PG (3)
1948 Murrayfield
Scotland 2PG 1T (9) to 1G 1PG (8)
1949 Paris
Scotland 1G 1T (8) to 0
1950 Murrayfield
Scotland 1G 1T (8) to 1G (5)
1951 Paris
France 1G 2PG 1T (14) to 2PG 2T (12)
1952 Murrayfield
France 2G 1PG (13) to 1G 2PG (11)
1953 Paris
France 1G 1DG 1PG (11) to 1G (5)
1954 Murrayfield
France 1T (3) to 0
1955 Paris
France 1PG 4T (15) to 0
1956 Murrayfield
Scotland 2PG 2T (12) to 0
1957 Paris
Scotland 1DG 1PG (6) to 0
1958 Murrayfield
Scotland 1G 1PG 1T (11) to 2PG 1T (9)
1959 Paris
France 2DG 1T (9) to 0
1960 Murrayfield
France 2G 1T (13) to 1G 1PG 1T (11)
1961 Paris
France 1G 1DG 1PG (11) to 0
1962 Murrayfield
France 1G 2PG (11) to 1PG (3)
1963 Paris
Scotland 1G 1DG 1PG (11) to 1DG 1PG (6)
1964 Murrayfield
Scotland 2G (10) to 0
1965 Paris
France 2G 2T (16) to 1G 1T (8)
1966 Murrayfield
Drawn Scotland 1T (3) France 1PG (3)
1967 Paris
Scotland 2PG 1DG (9) to 1G 1T (8)
1968 Murrayfield
France 1G 1T (8) to 1PG 1T (6)
1969 Paris
Scotland 1PG 1T (6) to 1PG (3)
1970 Murrayfield
France 1G 1DG 1T (11) to 2PG 1T (9)
1971 Paris
France 2G 1PG (13) to 1G 1PG (8)

1972 Murrayfield
Scotland 1G 1PG 1DG 2T (20) to 1G 1PG (9)
1973 Paris
France 3PG 1DG 1T (16) to 2PG 1DG 1T (13)
1974 Murrayfield
Scotland 1G 3PG 1T (19) to 1PG 1DG (6)
1975 Paris
France 1PG 1DG 1T (10) to 3PG (9)
1976 Murrayfield
France 3PG 1T (13) to 1PG 1DG (6)

SCOTLAND v. NEW ZEALAND
Played 7
Scotland won 0
New Zealand won 6
Drawn 1

1905 Inverleith (Edinburgh)
New Zealand 4T (12) to 1DG 1T (7)
1935 Murrayfield
New Zealand 3G 1T (18) to 1G 1T (8)
1954 Murrayfield
New Zealand 1PG (3) to 0
1964 Murrayfield
Drawn no score
1967 Murrayfield
New Zealand 1G 2PG 1T (14) to 1DG (3)
1972 Murrayfield
New Zealand 1G 2T (14) to 1DG 2PG (9)
1975 Auckland
New Zealand 4G (24) to 0

SCOTLAND v. SOUTH AFRICA
Played 8
Scotland won 3
South Africa won 5
Drawn 0

1906 Glasgow
Scotland 2T (6) to 0
1912 Inverleith
South Africa 2G 2T (16) to 0
1932 Murrayfield
South Africa 2T (6) to 1T (3)
1951 Murrayfield
South Africa 7G 1DG 2T (44) to 0
1960 Port Elizabeth
South Africa 3G 1T (18) to 2G (10)
1961 Murrayfield
South Africa 2PG 2T (12) to 1G (5)
1965 Murrayfield
Scotland 1G 1DG (8) to 1G (5)
1969 Murrayfield
Scotland 1PG 1T (6) to 1PG (3)

SCOTLAND v. AUSTRALIA
Played 6
Scotland won 4
Australia won 2
Drawn 0

1947 Murrayfield
Australia 2G 2T (16) to 1DG 1PG (7)

1958 Murrayfield
Scotland 2PG 2T (12) to 1G 1T (8)
1966 Murrayfield
Scotland 1G 1PG 1T (11) to 1G (5)
1968 Murrayfield
Scotland 2PG 1T (9) to 1PG (3)
1970 Sydney
Australia 1G 1PG 5T (23) to 1PG (3)
1975 Murrayfield
Scotland 1G 1T (10) to 1PG (3)

IRELAND v. WALES
Played 78
Ireland won 26
Wales won 47
Drawn 5

1882 Dublin
Wales 2G 2T to 0
1883 No Match
1884 Cardiff
Wales 1DG 2T to 0
1885 No Match
1886 No Match
1887 Birkenhead
Wales 1DG 1T to 3T
1888 Dublin
Ireland 1G 1DG 1T to 0
1889 Swansea
Ireland 2T to 0
1890 Dublin
Drawn 1G each
1891 Llanelli
Wales 1G 1DG (6) to 1DG 1T (4)
1892 Dublin
Ireland 1G 2T (9) to 0
1893 Llanelli
Wales 1T (2) to 0
1894 Belfast
Ireland 1PG (3) to 0
1895 Cardiff
Wales 1G (5) to 1T (3)
1896 Dublin
Ireland 1G 1T (8) to 1DG (4)
1897 No Match
1898 Limerick
Wales 1G 1PG 1T (11) to 1PG (3)
1899 Cardiff
Ireland 1T (3) to 0
1900 Belfast
Wales 1T (3) to 0
1901 Swansea
Wales 2G (10) to 3T (9)
1902 Dublin
Wales 1G 1DG 2T (15) to 0
1903 Cardiff
Wales 6T (18) to 0
1904 Belfast
Ireland 1G 3T (14) to 4T (12)
1905 Swansea
Wales 2G (10) to 1T (3)
1906 Belfast
Ireland 1G 2T (11) to 2T (6)
1907 Cardiff
Wales 2G 1DG 1PG 4T (29) to 0
1908 Belfast
Wales 1G 2T (11) to 1G (5)
1909 Swansea
Wales 3G 1T (18) to 1G (5)
1910 Dublin
Wales 1DG 5T (19) to 1T (3)
1911 Cardiff
Wales 2G 1PG 1T (16) to 0

1912 Belfast
Ireland 1G 1DG 1T (12) to 1G (5)
1913 Swansea
Wales 2G 1PG 1T (16) to 2G 1PG (13)
1914 Belfast
Wales 1G 2T (11) to 1T (3)
1920 Cardiff
Wales 3G 1DG 3T (28) to 1DG (4)
1921 Belfast
Wales 1PG 1T (6) to 0
1922 Swansea
Wales 1G 2T (11) to 1G (5)
1923 Dublin
Ireland 1G (5) to 1DG (4)
1924 Cardiff
Ireland 2G 1T (13) to 1DG 2T (10)
1925 Belfast
Ireland 2G 1PG 2T (19) to 1T (3)
1926 Swansea
Wales 1G 2T (11) to 1G 1PG (8)
1927 Dublin
Ireland 2G 1PG 2T (19) to 1G 1DG (9)
1928 Cardiff
Ireland 2G 1T (13) to 2G (10)
1929 Belfast
Drawn 1G (5) each
1930 Swansea
Wales 1PG 3T (12) to 1DG 1PG (7)
1931 Belfast
Wales 1G 1DG 2T (15) to 1T (3)
1932 Cardiff
Ireland 4T (12) to 1DG 2T (10)
1933 Belfast
Ireland 1DG 1PG 1T (10) to 1G (5)
1934 Swansea
Wales 2G 1T (13) to 0
1935 Belfast
Ireland 2PG 1T (9) to 1PG (3)
1936 Cardiff
Wales 1PG (3) to 0
1937 Belfast
Ireland 1G (5) to 1PG (3)
1938 Swansea
Wales 1G 1PG 1T (11) to 1G (5)
1939 Belfast
Wales 1DG 1T (7) to 0
1947 Swansea
Wales 1PG 1T (6) to 0
1948 Belfast
Ireland 2T (6) to 1T (3)
1949 Swansea
Ireland 1G (5) to 0
1950 Belfast
Wales 2T (6) to 1PG (3)
1951 Cardiff
Drawn Wales 1PG (3) Ireland 1T (3)
1952 Dublin
Wales 1G 1PG 2T (14) to 1PG (3)
1953 Swansea
Wales 1G (5) to 1T (3)
1954 Dublin
Wales 1DG 3PG (12) to 2PG 1T (9)
1955 Cardiff
Wales 3G 1PG 1T (21) to 1PG (3)
1956 Dublin
Ireland 1G 1DG 1PG (11) to 1PG (3)
1957 Cardiff
Wales 2PG (6) to 1G (5)
1958 Dublin
Wales 3T (9) to 1PG 1T (6)
1959 Cardiff
Wales 1G 1T (8) to 1PG 1T (6)
1960 Dublin
Wales 2G (10) to 2PG 1T (9)
1961 Cardiff
Wales 2PG 1T (9) to 0
1962 Dublin
Drawn Ireland 1DG (3) Wales 1PG (3)

1963 Cardiff
Ireland 1G 1DG 2PG (14) to 1DG 1T (6)
1964 Dublin
Wales 3G (15) to 2PG (6)
1965 Cardiff
Wales 1G 1DG 1PG 1T (14) to 1G 1PG (8)
1966 Dublin
Ireland 1DG 1PG 1T (9) to 1PG 1T (6)
1967 Cardiff
Ireland 1T (3) to 0
1968 Dublin
Ireland 1PG 1DG 1T (9) to IPG 1DG (6)
1969 Cardiff
Wales 3G 1DG 1PG 1T (24) to 1G 2PG (11)
1970 Dublin
Ireland 1G 1DG 1PG 1T (14) to 0
1971 Cardiff
Wales 1G 2PG 1DG 3T (23) to 3PG (9)
1972 No Match
1973 Cardiff
Wales 1G 2PG 1T (16) to 1G 2PG (12)
1974 Dublin
Drawn Ireland 3PG (9) Wales 1G 1PG (9)
1975 Cardiff
Wales 3G 2PG 2T (32) to 1T (4)
1976 Dublin
Wales 3G 4PG 1T (34) to 3PG (9)

IRELAND v. FRANCE
Played 49
Ireland won 24
France won 22
Drawn 3

1909 Dublin
Ireland 2G 1PG 2T (19) to 1G 1T (8)
1910 Paris
Ireland 1G 1T (8) to 1T (3)
1911 Cork
Ireland 3G 1DG 2T (25) to 1G (5)
1912 Paris
Ireland 1G 2T (11) to 2T (6)
1913 Cork
Ireland 3G 3T (24) to 0
1914 Paris
Ireland 1G 1T (8) to 2T (6)
1920 Dublin
France 5T (15) to 1DG 1T (7)
1921 Paris
France 4G (20) to 2G (10)
1922 Dublin
Ireland 1G 1PG (8) to 1T (3)
1923 Paris
France 1G 3T (14) to 1G 1T (8)
1924 Dublin
Ireland 2T (6) to 0
1925 Paris
Ireland 1PG 2T (9) to 1T (3)
1926 Belfast
Ireland 1G 1PG 1T (11) to 0
1927 Paris
Ireland 1G 1PG (8) to 1T (3)
1928 Belfast
Ireland 4T (12) to 1G 1T (8)
1929 Paris
Ireland 2T (6) to 0
1930 Belfast
France 1G (5) to 0
1931 Paris
France 1T (3) to 0
1947 Dublin
France 4T (12) to 1G 1PG (8)

1948 Paris
Ireland 2G 1T (13) to 2T (6)
1949 Dublin
France 2G 2PG (16) to 3PG (9)
1950 Paris
Drawn France 1DG (3) Ireland 1PG (3)
1951 Dublin
Ireland 1PG 2T (9) to 1G 1T (8)
1952 Paris
Ireland 1G 1PG 1T (11) to 1G 1PG (8)
1953 Belfast
Ireland 2G 2T (16) to 1DG (3)
1954 Paris
France 1G 1T (8) to 0
1955 Dublin
France 1G (5) to 1PG (3)
1956 Paris
France 1G 2DG 1T (14) to 1G 1PG (8)
1957 Dublin
Ireland 1G 1PG 1T (11) to 2PG (6)
1958 Paris
France 1G 1DG 1PG (11) to 2PG (6)
1959 Dublin
Ireland 1DG 1PG 1T (9) to 1G (5)
1960 Paris
France 1G 3DG 3T (23) to 2T (6)
1961 Dublin
France 2DG 2PG 1T (15) to 1PG (3)
1962 Paris
France 1G 2T (11) to 0
1963 Dublin
France 3G 2DG 1T (24) to 1G (5)
1964 Paris
France 3G 1DG 3T (27) to 1DG 1T (6)
1965 Dublin
Drawn 1T (3) each
1966 Paris
France 1G 1PG 1T (11) to 1DG 1PG (6)
1967 Dublin
France 1G 2DG (11) to 1PG 1T (6)
1968 Paris
France 2G 1PG 1DG (16) to 2PG (6)
1969 Dublin
Ireland 1G 1DG 3PG (17) to 2PG 1T (9)
1970 Paris
France 1G 1DG (8) to 0
1971 Dublin
Drawn Ireland 2PG 1T (9) France 2PG 1DG (9)
1972 Paris
Ireland 2PG 2T (14) to 1G 1PG (9)
*1972 Dublin
Ireland 3G 2PG (24) to 1G 2T (14)
1973 Dublin
Ireland 2PG (6) to 1T (4)
1974 Paris
France 1G 1PG (9) to 2PG (6)
1975 Dublin
Ireland 2G 1PG 1DG 1T (25) to 1PG 1DG (6)
1976 Paris
France 2G 2PG 2T (26) to 1PG (3)
*Non-championship match

IRELAND v. NEW ZEALAND
Played 7
Ireland won 0
New Zealand won 6
Drawn 1

1905 Dublin
New Zealand 3G (15) to 0
1924 Dublin
New Zealand 1PG 1T (6) to 0

1935 Dublin
New Zealand 1G 2PG 2T (17) to 2PG 1T (9)
1954 Dublin
New Zealand 1G 1DG 1PG 1T (14) to 1PG (3)
1963 Dublin
New Zealand 1PG 1T (6) to 1G (5)
1973 Dublin
Drawn Ireland 2PG 1T (10)
New Zealand 1G 1T (10)
1974 Dublin
New Zealand 1G 3PG (15) to 2PG (6)

IRELAND v. SOUTH AFRICA
Played 8
Ireland won 1
South Africa won 6
Drawn 1

1906 Belfast
South Africa 1PG 4T (15) to 1PG 3T (12)
1912 Dublin
South Africa 4G 6T (38) to 0
1931 Dublin
South Africa 1G 1T (8) to 1PG (3)
1951 Dublin
South Africa 1G 1DG 3T (17) to 1G (5)
1960 Dublin
South Africa 1G 1T (8) to 1PG (3)
1961 Cape Town
South Africa 3G 1PG 2T (24) to 1G 1PG (8)
1965 Dublin
Ireland 2PG 1T (9) to 1PG 1T (6)
1970 Dublin
Drawn 1G 1PG (8) each

IRELAND v. AUSTRALIA
Played 6
Ireland won 4
Australia won 2
Drawn 0

1947 Dublin
Australia 2G 2T (16) to 1PG (3)
1958 Dublin
Ireland 1PG 2T (9) to 2T (6)
1967 Dublin
Ireland 2DG 1PG 2T (15) to 1G 1DG (8)
1967 Sydney
Ireland 1G 1DG 1T (11) to 1G (5)
1968 Dublin
Ireland 2G (10) to 1T (3)
1976 Dublin
Australia 1G 2PG 2T (20) to 2PG 1T (10)

WALES v. FRANCE
Played 49
Wales won 33
France won 13
Drawn 3

1908 Cardiff
Wales 3G 1PG 6T (36) to 1DG (4)
1909 Paris
Wales 7G 4T (47) to 1G (5)

1910 Swansea
Wales 8G 1PG 2T (49) to 1G 2PG 1T (14)
1911 Paris
Wales 3G (15) to 0
1912 Newport
Wales 1G 3T (14) to 1G 1T (8)
1913 Paris
Wales 1G 2T (11) to 1G 1T (8)
1914 Swansea
Wales 5G 2T (31) to 0
1920 Paris
Wales 2T (6) to 1G (5)
1921 Cardiff
Wales 2PG 2T (12) to 1DG (4)
1922 Paris
Wales 1G 2T (11) to 1T (3)
1923 Swansea
Wales 2G 1PG 1T (16) to 1G 1T (8)
1924 Paris
Wales 1DG 2T (10) to 2T (6)
1925 Cardiff
Wales 1G 2T (11) to 1G (5)
1926 Paris
Wales 1DG 1T (7) to 1G (5)
1927 Swansea
Wales 2G 5T (25) to 1DG 1T (7)
1928 Paris
France 1G 1T (8) to 1T (3)
1929 Cardiff
Wales 1G 1T (8) to 1T (3)
1930 Paris
Wales 2DG 1T (11) to 0
1931 Swansea
Wales 5G 1DG 2T (35) to 1T (3)
1947 Paris
Wales 1PG (3) to 0
1948 Swansea
France 1G 2T (11) to 1PG (3)
1949 Paris
France 1G (5) to 1T (3)
1950 Cardiff
Wales 3G 1PG 1T (21) to 0
1951 Paris
France 1G 1PG (8) to 1T (3)
1952 Swansea
Wales 1DG 2PG (9) to 1G (5)
1953 Paris
Wales 2T (6) to 1PG (3)
1954 Cardiff
Wales 2G 3PG (19) to 2G 1PG (13)
1955 Paris
Wales 2G 2PG (16) to 1G 1DG 1PG (11)
1956 Cardiff
Wales 1G (5) to 1T (3)
1957 Paris
Wales 2G 1PG 2T (19) to 2G 1T (13)
1958 Cardiff
France 2G 2DG (16) to 1PG 1T (6)
1959 Paris
France 1G 1PG 1T (11) to 1PG (3)
1960 Cardiff
France 2G 2T (16) to 1G 1PG (8)
1961 Paris
France 1G 1T (8) to 2T (6)
1962 Cardiff
Wales 1PG (3) to 0
1963 Paris
France 1G (5) to 1PG (3)
1964 Cardiff
Drawn 1G 2PG (11) each
1965 Paris
France 2G 1PG 1DG 2T (22) to 2G 1T (13)
1966 Cardiff
Wales 2PG 1T (9) to 1G 1T (8)
1967 Paris
France 1G 2DG 1PG 2T (20)
to 1G 2PG 1DG (14)

1968 Cardiff
France 1G 1PG 1DG 1T (14) to 2PG 1T (9)
1969 Paris
Drawn France 1G 1PG (8) Wales 1G 1T (8)
1970 Cardiff
Wales 1G 2PG (11) to 2T (6)
1971 Paris
Wales 1PG 2T (9) to 1G (5)
1972 Cardiff
Wales 4PG 2T (20) to 2PG (6)
1973 Paris
France 3PG 1DG (12) to 1DG (3)
1974 Cardiff
Drawn 3PG 1DG 1T (16) each
1975 Paris
Wales 1G 1PG 4T (25) to 2PG 1T (10)
1976 Cardiff
Wales 5PG 1T (19) to 1G 1PG 1T (13)

WALES v. NEW ZEALAND
Played 9
Wales won 3
New Zealand won 6
Drawn 0

1905 Cardiff
Wales 1T (3) to 0
1924 Swansea
New Zealand 2G 1PG 2T (19) to 0
1935 Cardiff
Wales 2G 1T (13) to 1G 1DG 1T (12)
1953 Cardiff
Wales 2G 1PG (13) to 1G 1PG (8)
1963 Cardiff
New Zealand 1DG 1PG (6) to 0
1967 Cardiff
New Zealand 2G 1PG (13) to 1DG 1PG (6)
1969 *1* Christchurch
New Zealand 2G 1PG 2T (19) to 0
2 Auckland
New Zealand 3G 1DG 5PG (33) to 2PG 2T (12)
New Zealand won series 2-0
1972 Cardiff
New Zealand 5PG 1T (19) to 4PG 1T (16)

WALES v. SOUTH AFRICA
Played 7
Wales won 0
South Africa won 6
Drawn 1

1906 Swansea
South Africa 1G 2T (11) to 0
1912 Cardiff
South Africa 1PG (3) to 0
1931 Swansea
South Africa 1G 1T (8) to 1T (3)
1951 Cardiff
South Africa 1DG 1T (6) to 1T (3)
1960 Cardiff
South Africa 1PG (3) to 0
1965 Durban
South Africa 3G 1DG 2PG (24) to 1PG (3)
1970 Cardiff
Drawn 1PG 1T (6) each

WALES v. AUSTRALIA
Played 7
Wales won 6
Australia won 1
Drawn 0

1908 Cardiff
Wales 1PG 2T (9) to 2T (6)
1947 Cardiff
Wales 2PG (6) to 0
1957 Cardiff
Wales 1DG 1PG 1T (9) to 1T (3)
1966 Cardiff
Australia 1G 1DG 1PG 1T (14)
to 1G 1PG 1T (11)
1969 Sydney
Wales 2G 2PG 1T (19) to 2G 2PG (16)
1973 Cardiff
Wales 4PG 3T (24) to 0
1975 Cardiff
Wales 3G 1PG 1DG 1T (28) to 1PG (3)

FRANCE v. SOUTH AFRICA
Played 18
France won 3
South Africa won 11
Drawn 4

1913 Bordeaux
South Africa 4G 1PG 5T (38) to 1G (5)
1952 Paris
South Africa 2G 1PG 4T (25) to 1DG (3)
1958 *1* Cape Town
Drawn South Africa 1T (3) France 1DG (3)
2 Johannesburg
France 2DG 1PG (9) to 1G (5)
France won series 1-0, with 1 draw
1961 Paris
Drawn no score
1964 Springs (SA)
France 1G 1PG (8) to 1PG 1T (6)
1967 *1* Durban
South Africa 4G 1PG 1T (26) to 1T (3)
2 Bloemfontein
South Africa 2G 1PG 1T (16) to 1PG (3)
3 Johannesburg
France 2G 2DG 1PG (19) to 1G 2PG 1T (14)
4 Cape Town
Drawn South Africa 1DG 1PG (6)
France 1PG 1T (6)
South Africa won series 2-1, with 1 draw
1968 *1* Bordeaux
South Africa 4PG (12) to 3T (9)
2 Paris
South Africa 2G 1PG 1T (16) to 1G 2DG (11)
South Africa won series 2-0
1971 *1* Bloemfontein
South Africa 2G 1DG 3PG (22)
to 2PG 1T (9)
2 Durban
Drawn 1G 1DG (8) each
South Africa won series 1-0, with 1 draw
1974 *1* Toulouse
South Africa 3PG 1T (13) to 1T (4)
2 Paris
South Africa 2PG 1T (10) to 2T (8)
South Africa won series 2-0
1975 *1* Bloemfontein
South Africa 3G 4PG 2T (38)
to 3G 1PG 1T (25)
2 Pretoria
South Africa 2G 7PG (33)
to 1G 3PG 1DG (8)
South Africa won series 2-0

FRANCE v. NEW ZEALAND
Played 12
France won 2
New Zealand won 10
Drawn 0

1906 Paris
New Zealand 4G 6T (38) to 1G 1T (8)
1925 Toulouse
New Zealand 3G 5T (30) to 2T (6)
1954 Paris
France 1T (3) to 0
1961 *1* Auckland
New Zealand 2G 1DG (13) to 2DG (6)
    2 Wellington
New Zealand 1G (5) to 1T (3)
    3 Christchurch
New Zealand 4G 3PG 1T (32) to 1T (3)
New Zealand won series 3–0
1964 Paris
New Zealand 1DG 2PG 1T (12) to 1PG (3)
1967 Paris
New Zealand 3G 1PG 1T (21)
to 3PG 1DG 1T (15)
1968 *1* Christchurch
New Zealand 3PG 1T (12) to 1DG 2PG (9)
    2 Wellington
New Zealand 3PG (9) to 1PG (3)
    3 Auckland
New Zealand 2G 1DG 2PG (19)
to 1DG 3T (12)
New Zealand won series 3–0

FRANCE v. AUSTRALIA
Played 9
France won 6
Australia won 2
Drawn 1

1948 Paris
France 2G 1T (13) to 2PG (6)
1958 Paris
France 2G 2DG 1T (19) to 0
1961 Sydney
France 2DG 3T (15) to 1G 1PG (8)
1967 Paris
France 1G 1DG 4PG (20)
to 1G 1DG 1PG 1T (14)
1968 Sydney
Australia 1G 1DG 1PG (11) to 2G (10)
1971 *1* Toulouse
Australia 1G 1PG 1T (13) to 1PG 2T (11)
    2 Paris
France 1G 4PG (18) to 3PG (9)
Series drawn 1–1
1972 *1* Sydney
Drawn Australia 2PG 2T (14) France 1G 2T (14)
    2 Brisbane
France 2G 1T (16) to 5PG (15)
France won series 1–0, with 1 draw

NEW ZEALAND v. SOUTH AFRICA
Played 30
New Zealand won 12
South Africa won 16
Drawn 2

1921 *1* Dunedin
New Zealand 2G 1T (13) to 1G (5)
    2 Auckland
South Africa 1G 1DG (9) to 1G (5)
    3 Wellington
Drawn no score
Series drawn 1–1, with 1 draw
1928 *1* Durban
South Africa 2DG 2PG 1T (17) to 0
    2 Johannesburg
New Zealand 1G 1PG (7) to 1PG 1GM (6)
    3 Port Elizabeth
South Africa 1G 2T (11) to 2T (6)
    4 Cape Town
New Zealand 1DG 2PG 1T (13) to 1G (5)
Series drawn 2–2
1937 *1* Wellington
New Zealand 1DG 2PG 1T (13) to 1DG 1T (7)
    2 Christchurch
South Africa 2G 1PG (13) to 2T (6)
    3 Auckland
South Africa 1G 4T (17) to 2PG (6)
South Africa won series 2–1
1949 *1* Cape Town
South Africa 5PG (15) to 1G 1DG 1PG (11)
    2 Johannesburg
South Africa 1DG 1PG 2T (12)
to 1DG 1PG (6)
    3 Durban
South Africa 3PG (9) to 1T (3)
    4 Port Elizabeth
South Africa 1G 1DG 1PG (11)
to 1G 1T (8)
South Africa won series 4–0
1956 *1* Dunedin
New Zealand 2G (10) to 1PG 1T (6)
    2 Wellington
South Africa 1G 1T (8) to 1T (3)
    3 Christchurch
New Zealand 1G 2PG 2T (17) to 2G (10)
    4 Auckland
New Zealand 1G 2PG (11) to 1G (5)
New Zealand won series 3–1
1960 *1* Johannesburg
South Africa 2G 1PG (13) to 0
    2 Cape Town
New Zealand 1G 1DG 1PG (11)
to 1PG (3)
    3 Bloemfontein
Drawn 1G 2PG (11) each
    4 Port Elizabeth
South Africa 1G 1PG (8) to 1PG (3)
South Africa won series 2–1, with 1 draw
1965 *1* Wellington
New Zealand 2T (6) to 1DG (3)
    2 Dunedin
New Zealand 2G 1T (13) to 0
    3 Christchurch
South Africa 2G 1PG 2T (19)
to 2G 1PG 1T (16)
    4 Auckland
New Zealand 1G 1DG 4T (20) to 1PG (3)
New Zealand won series 3–1
1970 *1* Pretoria
South Africa 1G 2PG 1DG 1T (17) to
1PG 1T (6)
    2 Cape Town
New Zealand 1PG 2T (9) to 1G 1PG (8)
    3 Port Elizabeth
South Africa 1G 2PG 1T (14) to 1PG (3)
    4 Johannesburg
South Africa 1G 4PG 1T (20) to 1G 4PG (17)
South Africa won series 3–1

NEW ZEALAND v. AUSTRALIA
Played 64
New Zealand won 47
Australia won 13
Drawn 4

1903 Sydney
New Zealand 1G 1PG 2GM 2T (22)
to 1PG (3)
1905 Dunedin
New Zealand 1G 3T (14) to 1T (3)
1907 *1* Sydney
New Zealand 4G 2T (26) to 1PG 1GM (6)
    2 Brisbane
New Zealand 1G 3T (14) to 1G (5)
    3 Sydney
Drawn 1G (5) each
New Zealand won series 2–0, with 1 draw
1910 *1* Sydney
New Zealand 2T (6) to 0
    2 Sydney
Australia 1G 2T (11) to 0
    3 Sydney
New Zealand 2G 6T (28) to 2G 1PG (13)
New Zealand won series 2–1
1913 *1* Wellington
New Zealand 3G 5T (30) to 1G (5)
    2 Dunedin
New Zealand 3G 1DG 2T (25)
to 2G 1T (13)
    3 Christchurch
Australia 2G 2T (16) to 1G (5)
New Zealand won series 2–1
1914 *1* Sydney
New Zealand 1G (5) to 0
    2 Brisbane
New Zealand 1G 4T (17) to 0
    3 Sydney
New Zealand 2G 4T (22) to 1DG 1T (7)
New Zealand won series 3–0
1929 *1* Sydney
Australia 2PG 1T (9) to 1G 1PG (8)
    2 Brisbane
Australia 1G 2PG 2T (17) to 1PG 2T (9)
    3 Sydney
Australia 3PG 2T (15) to 2G 1T (13)
Australia won series 3–0
1931 Auckland
New Zealand 1G 4PG 1T (20) to 2G 1T (13)
1932 *1* Sydney
Australia 2G 2PG 2T (22)
to 2G 1DG 1T (17)
    2 Brisbane
New Zealand 1G 1DG 1PG 3T (21) to 1T (3)
    3 Sydney
New Zealand 3G 2T (21) to 2G 1T (13)
New Zealand won series 2–1
1934 *1* Sydney
Australia 2G 3PG 2T (25) to 1G 2T (11)
    2 Sydney
Drawn 1T (3) each
Australia won series 1–0, with 1 draw
1936 *1* Wellington
New Zealand 1G 2T (11) to 1PG 1T (6)
    2 Dunedin
New Zealand 4G 1PG 5T (38)
to 2G 1PG (13)
New Zealand won series 2–0
1938 *1* Sydney
New Zealand 3G 2PG 1T (24) to 3PG (9)
    2 Brisbane
New Zealand 2G 1DG 2T (20)
to 1G 1PG 2T (14)
    3 Sydney
New Zealand 1G 2PG 1T (14)
to 1PG 1T (6)
New Zealand won series 3–0

1946 *1* Dunedin
New Zealand 5G 2T (31) to 1G 1T (8)
2 Auckland
New Zealand 1G 3PG (14) to 2G (10)
New Zealand won series 2–0
1947 *1* Brisbane
New Zealand 2G 1T (13) to 1G (5)
2 Sydney
New Zealand 3G 4PG (27) to 1G 3PG (14)
New Zealand won series 2–0
1949 *1* Wellington
Australia 1G 2T (11) to 1PG 1T (6)
2 Auckland
Australia 2G 1PG 1T (16)
to 1DG 1PG 1T (9)
Australia won series 2–0
1951 *1* Sydney
New Zealand 1G 1PG (8) to 0
2 Sydney
New Zealand 1G 1DG 3T (17)
to 1G 1PG 1T (11)
3 Brisbane
New Zealand 2G 2T (16) to 2PG (6)
New Zealand won series 3–0
1952 *1* Christchurch
Australia 1G 1DG 2T (14) to 1PG 2T (9)
2 Wellington
New Zealand 1DG 2PG 2T (15)
to 1G 1PG (8)
Series drawn 1–1
1955 *1* Wellington
New Zealand 2G 1PG 1T (16)
to 1G 1PG (8)
2 Dunedin
New Zealand 1G 1DG (8) to 0
3 Auckland
Australia 1G 1T (8) to 1T (3)
New Zealand won series 2–1

1957 *1* Sydney
New Zealand 2G 3PG 2T (25)
to 1G 2PG (11)
2 Brisbane
New Zealand 2G 1DG 1GM 2T (22)
to 2PG 1T (9)
New Zealand won series 2–0
1958 *1* Wellington
New Zealand 2G 5T (25) to 1T (3)
2 Christchurch
Australia 1PG 1T (6) to 1T (3)
3 Auckland
New Zealand 1G 4PG (17) to 1G 1PG (8)
New Zealand won series 2–1
1962 *1* Brisbane
New Zealand 1G 1DG 1PG 3T (20)
to 2PG (6)
2 Sydney
New Zealand 1G 2PG 1T (14) to 1G (5)
New Zealand won series 2–0
1962 *1* Wellington
Drawn New Zealand 2PG 1T (9)
Australia 3PG (9)
2 Dunedin
New Zealand 1PG (3) to 0
3 Auckland
New Zealand 2G 1DG 1T (16)
to 1G 1PG (8)
New Zealand won series 2–0, with 1 draw
1964 *1* Dunedin
New Zealand 1G 1DG 2PG (14)
to 2PG 1T (9)
2 Christchurch
New Zealand 3G 1T (18) to 1T (3)
3 Wellington
Australia 1G 1DG 3PG 1T (20) to 1G (5)
New Zealand won series 2–1
1967 Wellington
New Zealand 4G 1DG 2PG (29)
to 1PG 2T (9)

1968 *1* Sydney
New Zealand 3G 1PG 3T (27)
to 1G 2PG (11)
2 Brisbane
New Zealand 2G 2PG 1T (19)
to 5PG 1T (18)
New Zealand won series 2–0
1972 *1* Wellington
New Zealand 3G 1DG 2T (29) to 2PG (6)
2 Christchurch
New Zealand 2G 2PG 3T (30)
to 1G 1DG 2T (17)
3 Auckland
New Zealand 4G 2PG 2T (38) to 1PG (3)
New Zealand won series 3–0
1974 *1* Sydney
New Zealand 1PG 2T (11) to 1G (6)
2 Brisbane
Drawn 1G 2PG 1T (16) each
3 Sydney
New Zealand 2G 1T (16) to 2PG (6)
New Zealand won series 2–0, with 1 draw

SOUTH AFRICA *v.* AUSTRALIA
Played 28
South Africa won 21
Australia won 7
Drawn 0

1933 *1* Cape Town
South Africa 1G 1PG 3T (17) to 1PG (3)
2 Durban
Australia 3G 1PG 1T (21) to 1PG 1T (6)
3 Johannesburg
South Africa 1G 1DG 1T (12) to 1T (3)
4 Port Elizabeth
South Africa 1G 1PG 1T (11) to 0
5 Bloemfontein
Australia 1G 1DG 2T (15) to 1DG (4)
South Africa won series 3–2
1937 *1* Sydney
South Africa 1PG 2T (9) to 1G (5)
2 Sydney
South Africa 4G 2T (26)
to 1G 2PG 2T (17)
South Africa won series 2–0
1953 *1* Johannesburg
South Africa 2G 2PG 3T (25) to 1PG (3)
2 Cape Town
Australia 3G 1T (18) to 1G 3T (14)
3 Durban
South Africa 3G 1T (18) to 1G 1PG (8)
4 Port Elizabeth
South Africa 2G 2DG 2PG (22)
to 2PG 1T (9)
South Africa won series 3–1
1956 *1* Sydney
South Africa 1PG 2T (9) to 0
2 Brisbane
South Africa 1DG 2T (9) to 0
South Africa won series 2–0
1961 *1* Johannesburg
South Africa 2G 6T (28) to 1PG (3)
2 Port Elizabeth
South Africa 1G 1DG 3PG 2T (23)
to 1G 2PG (11)
South Africa won series 2–0

1963 *1* Pretoria
South Africa 1G 2PG 1T (14) to 1T (3)
2 Cape Town
Australia 1DG 1PG 1T (9) to 1G (5)
3 Johannesburg
Australia 1G 1DG 1PG (11) to 3PG (9)
4 Port Elizabeth
South Africa 2G 3PG 1T (22)
to 1DG 1PG (6)
Series drawn 2–2
1965 *1* Sydney
Australia 4PG 2T (18) to 1G 1PG 1T (11)
2 Brisbane
Australia 4PG (12) to 1G 1T (8)
Australia won series 2–0
1969 *1* Johannesburg
South Africa 3G 3PG 2T (30)
to 1G 2PG (11)
2 Durban
South Africa 2G 1PG 1T (16) to 3PG (9)
3 Cape Town
South Africa 1G 1PG 1T (11) to 1PG (3)
4 Bloemfontein
South Africa 2G 2PG 1T (19)
to 1G 1PG (8)
South Africa won series 4–0
1971 *1* Sydney
South Africa 2G 1DG 1PG 1T (19)
to 1G 2PG (11)
2 Brisbane
South Africa 1G 1PG 2T (14)
to 1DG 1PG (6)
3 Sydney
South Africa 3G 1PG (18) to 1PG 1T (6)
South Africa won series 3–0

GRAND SLAM WINNERS

England 7 times: 1913, 1914, 1921, 1923, 1924, 1928, 1957.
Wales 7 times: 1908, 1909, 1911, 1950, 1952, 1971, 1976.
Scotland once: 1925.
Ireland once: 1948.
France once: 1968.

TRIPLE CROWN WINNERS

England 13 times: 1884, 1892, 1913, 1914, 1921, 1923, 1924, 1928, 1934, 1937, 1954, 1957, 1960.
Wales 13 times: 1893, 1900, 1902, 1905, 1908, 1909, 1911, 1950, 1952, 1965, 1969, 1971, 1976.
Scotland 8 times: 1891, 1895, 1901, 1903, 1907, 1925, 1933, 1938.
Ireland 4 times: 1894, 1899, 1948, 1949.

INTERNATIONAL CHAMPIONSHIP WINNERS

Wales have won the title 19 times
England have won it 16 times
Scotland 11, Ireland 8, and France 5.

1884	England	1950	Wales
1885*	———	1951	Ireland
1886	England / Scotland	1952	Wales
1887	Scotland	1953	England
1888*	———	1954	England / France / Wales
1889*	———		
1890	England / Scotland	1955	France / Wales
1891	Scotland	1956	Wales
1892	England	1957	England
1893	Wales	1958	England
1894	Ireland	1959	France
1895	Scotland	1960	France / England
1896	Ireland		
1897*	———	1961	France
1898*	———	1962	France
1899	Ireland	1963	England
1900	Wales	1964	Scotland / Wales
1901	Scotland		
1902	Wales	1965	Wales
1903	Scotland	1966	Wales
1904	Scotland	1967	France
1905	Wales	1968	France
1906	Ireland / Wales	1969	Wales
1907	Scotland	1970	France / Wales
1908	Wales		
1909	Wales	1971	Wales
1910	England	1972*	———
1911	Wales	1973	Quintuple tie
1912	England / Ireland	1974	Ireland
1913	England	1975	Wales
1914	England	1976	Wales
1920	England / Scotland / Wales	*Matches not completed	
1921	England		
1922	Wales		
1923	England		
1924	England		
1925	Scotland		
1926	Scotland / Ireland		
1927	Scotland / Ireland		
1928	England		
1929	Scotland		
1930	England		
1931	Wales		
1932	England / Wales / Ireland		
1933	Scotland		
1934	England		
1935	Ireland		
1936	Wales		
1937	England		
1938	Scotland		
1939	England / Wales / Ireland		
1947	Wales / England		
1948	Ireland		
1949	Ireland		

INTERNATIONAL TOURS

BRITISH ISLES TO AUSTRALIA AND NEW ZEALAND

1888
Full record:
in Australia	Played 16 Won 14 Lost 0 Drawn 2
	Points for 218 Against 68
in New Zealand	Played 19 Won 13 Lost 2 Drawn 4
	Points for 82 Against 33

1899 (Australia only)
Full record:
	Played 21 Won 18 Lost 3 Drawn 0
	Points for 333 Against 90
International record:	Played 4 Won 3 Lost 1
Details	British Isles 3 Australia 13
	British Isles 11 Australia 0
	British Isles 13 Australia 0
	British Isles 11 Australia 10

1904
Full record:
in Australia	Played 14 Won 14 Lost 0 Drawn 0
	Points for 265 Against 51
in New Zealand	Played 5 Won 2 Lost 2 Drawn 1
	Points for 22 Against 33
International record:	v. Australia Played 3 Won 3
	v. New Zealand Played 1 Lost 1
Details:	
v. Australia	British Isles 17 Australia 0
	British Isles 17 Australia 3
	British Isles 16 Australia 0
v. New Zealand	British Isles 3 New Zealand 9

1908
Full record:
in Australia	Played 9 Won 7 Lost 2 Drawn 0
	Points for 139 Against 48
in New Zealand	Played 17 Won 9 Lost 7 Drawn 1
	Points for 184 Against 153
International record:	v. New Zealand Played 3 Lost 2 Drawn 1
Details:	British Isles 5 New Zealand 32
	British Isles 3 New Zealand 3
	British Isles 0 New Zealand 29

1930
Full record:
in New Zealand	Played 21 Won 15 Lost 6 Drawn 0
	Points for 420 Against 205
in Australia	Played 7 Won 5 Lost 2 Drawn 0
	Points for 204 Against 113
International record:	v. New Zealand Played 4 Won 1 Lost 3
	v. Australia Played 1 Won 0 Lost 1
Details:	
v. New Zealand	British Isles 6 New Zealand 3
	British Isles 10 New Zealand 13
	British Isles 10 New Zealand 15
	British Isles 8 New Zealand 22
v. Australia	British Isles 5 Australia 6

1950
Full record:
in New Zealand	Played 23 Won 17 Lost 5 Drawn 1
	Points for 420 Against 162
in Australia	Played 6 Won 5 Lost 1 Drawn 0
	Points for 150 Against 52
International record:	v. New Zealand Played 4 Won 0 Lost 3 Drawn 1
	v. Australia Played 2 Won 2 Lost 0 Drawn 0
Details:	
v. New Zealand	British Isles 9 New Zealand 9
	British Isles 0 New Zealand 8
	British Isles 3 New Zealand 6
	British Isles 8 New Zealand 11
v. Australia	British Isles 19 Australia 6
	British Isles 24 Australia 3

1959
Full record:

in Australia — Played 6 Won 5 Lost 1 Drawn 0
Points for 174 Against 70

in New Zealand — Played 25 Won 20 Lost 5 Drawn 0
Points for 582 Against 266

International record: — v. Australia Played 2 Won 2 Lost 0
v. New Zealand Played 4 Won 1 Lost 3

Details:

v. Australia — British Isles 17 Australia 6
British Isles 24 Australia 3

v. New Zealand — British Isles 17 New Zealand 18
British Isles 8 New Zealand 11
British Isles 8 New Zealand 22
British Isles 9 New Zealand 6

1966
Full record:

in Australia — Played 8 Won 7 Lost 0 Drawn 1
Points for 202 Against 48

in New Zealand — Played 25 Won 15 Lost 8 Drawn 2
Points for 300 Against 281

International record: — v. Australia Played 2 Won 2 Lost 0
v. New Zealand Played 4 Won 0 Lost 4

Details:

v. Australia — British Isles 11 Australia 8
British Isles 31 Australia 0

v. New Zealand — British Isles 3 New Zealand 20
British Isles 12 New Zealand 16
British Isles 6 New Zealand 19
British Isles 11 New Zealand 24

1971
Full record:

in Australia — Played 2 Won 1 Lost 1 Drawn 0
Points for 25 Against 27

in New Zealand — Played 24 Won 22 Lost 1 Drawn 1
Points for 555 Against 204

International record: — v. New Zealand Played 4 Won 2 Drawn 1 Lost 1
Details: — British Isles 9 New Zealand 3
British Isles 12 New Zealand 22
British Isles 13 New Zealand 3
British Isles 14 New Zealand 14

BRITISH ISLES to SOUTH AFRICA

1891
Full record: — Played 19 Won 19 Lost 0 Drawn 0
Points for 224 Against 1

International record: — Played 3 Won 3
Details: — British Isles 4 South Africa 0
British Isles 3 South Africa 0
British Isles 4 South Africa 0

1896
Full record: — Played 21 Won 19 Lost 1 Drawn 1
Points for 310 Against 45

International record: — Played 4 Won 3 Lost 1
Details: — British Isles 8 South Africa 0
British Isles 17 South Africa 8
British Isles 9 South Africa 3
British Isles 0 South Isles 5

1903
Full record: — Played 22 Won 11 Lost 8 Drawn 3
Points for 231 Against 138

International record: — Played 3 Won 0 Lost 1 Drawn 2
Details: — British Isles 10 South Africa 10
British Isles 0 South Africa 0
British Isles 0 South Africa 8

1910
Full record: — Played 24 Won 13 Lost 8 Drawn 3
Points for 290 Against 236

International record: — Played 3 Won 1 Lost 2
Details: — British Isles 10 South Africa 14
British Isles 8 South Africa 3
British Isles 5 South Africa 21

1924
Full record: — Played 21 Won 9 Lost 9 Drawn 3
Points for 175 Against 155

International record: — Played 4 Lost 3 Drawn 1
Details: — British Isles 3 South Africa 7
British Isles 0 South Africa 17
British Isles 3 South Africa 3
British Isles 9 South Africa 16

1938
Full record: — Played 23 Won 17 Lost 6 Drawn 0
Points for 407 Against 272

International record: — Played 3 Won 1 Lost 2
Details: — British Isles 12 South Africa 26
British Isles 3 South Africa 19
British Isles 21 South Africa 16

1955
Full record: — Played 24 Won 18 Lost 5 Drawn 1
Points for 418 Against 271

International record: — Played 4 Won 2 Lost 2
Details: — British Isles 23 South Africa 22
British Isles 9 South Africa 25
British Isles 9 South Africa 6
British Isles 8 South Africa 22

1962
Full record: — Played 24 Won 15 Lost 5 Drawn 4
Points for 351 Against 208

International record: — Played 4 Won 0 Lost 3 Drawn 1
Details: — British Isles 3 South Africa 3
British Isles 0 South Africa 3
British Isles 3 South Africa 8
British Isles 14 South Africa 34

1968
Full record: — Played 20 Won 15 Lost 4 Drawn 1
Points for 377 Against 181

International record: — Played 4 Won 0 Lost 3 Drawn 1
Details: — British Isles 20 South Africa 25
British Isles 6 South Africa 6
British Isles 6 South Africa 11
British Isles 6 South Africa 19

1974
Full record: — Played 22 Won 21 Drawn 1
Points for 729 Against 207

International record: — Played 4 Won 3 Drawn 1
Details: — British Isles 12 South Africa 3
British Isles 28 South Africa 9
British Isles 26 South Africa 9
British Isles 13 South Africa 13

NEW ZEALAND to BRITISH ISLES and FRANCE

1888-9 (The Maoris)
Full record: — Played 74 Won 49 Lost 20 Drawn 5
Points for 394 Against 188

International record: — Played 3 Won 1 Lost 2
Details: — Maoris 13 Ireland 4
Maoris 0 Wales 5
Maoris 0 England 7

1905-6
Full record: — Played 33 Won 32 Lost 1 Drawn 0
Points for 868 Against 47

International record: — Played 5 Won 4 Lost 1 Drawn 0
Details: — New Zealand 12 Scotland 7
New Zealand 15 Ireland 0
New Zealand 15 England 0
New Zealand 0 Wales 3
New Zealand 38 France 8

1924-5

Full record:	Played 30 Won 30 Lost 0 Drawn 0
	Points for 721 Against 112
International record:	Played 4 Won 4
Details:	New Zealand 6 Ireland 0
	New Zealand 19 Wales 0
	New Zealand 17 England 11
	New Zealand 30 France 6

1926-7 (The Maoris)

Full record:	Played 31 Won 22 Lost 7 Drawn 2
	Points for 459 Against 194
International record:	Played 1 Won 1
Details:	Maoris 12 France 3

1935-6

Full record:	Played 28 Won 24 Lost 3 Drawn 1
	Points for 431 Against 180
International record:	Played 4 Won 2 Lost 2
Details:	New Zealand 18 Scotland 8
	New Zealand 17 Ireland 9
	New Zealand 12 Wales 13
	New Zealand 0 England 13

1953-4

Full record:	Played 31 Won 25 Lost 4 Drawn 2
	Points for 446 Against 129
International record:	Played 5 Won 3 Lost 2
Details:	New Zealand 8 Wales 13
	New Zealand 14 Ireland 3
	New Zealand 5 England 0
	New Zealand 3 Scotland 0
	New Zealand 0 France 3

1963-4

Full record:	Played 34 Won 32 Lost 1 Drawn 1
	Points for 568 Against 153
International record:	Played 5 Won 4 Lost 0 Drawn 1
Details:	New Zealand 6 Ireland 5
	New Zealand 6 Wales 0
	New Zealand 14 England 0
	New Zealand 0 Scotland 0
	New Zealand 12 France 3

1967

Full record:	Played 15 Won 14 Lost 0 Drawn 1
	Points for 294 Against 129
International record:	Played 4 Won 4 Lost 0
	New Zealand 23 England 11
	New Zealand 13 Wales 6
	New Zealand 21 France 15
	New Zealand 14 Scotland 3

1972-3

Full record:	Played 30 Won 23 Lost 5 Drawn 2
	Points for 568 Against 254
International record:	Played 5 Won 3 Lost 1 Drawn 1
Details:	New Zealand 19 Wales 16
	New Zealand 14 Scotland 9
	New Zealand 9 England 0
	New Zealand 10 Ireland 10
	New Zealand 6 France 13

1974 (to Ireland, and UK)

Full record:	Played 8 Won 7 Lost O Drawn 1
	Points for 127 Against 50
in Ireland	Played 6 Won 6 Lost 0 Drawn 0
	Points for 102 Against 34
International record:	Played 1 Won 1
Details:	New Zealand 15 Ireland 6

NEW ZEALAND to SOUTH AFRICA

1928

Full record:	Played 22 Won 16 Lost 5 Drawn 1
	Points for 339 Against 144
International record:	Played 4 Won 2 Lost 2
Details:	New Zealand 0 South Africa 17
	New Zealand 7 South Africa 6
	New Zealand 6 South Africa 11
	New Zealand 13 South Africa 5

1949

Full record:	Played 24 Won 14 Lost 7 Drawn 3
	Points for 230 Against 146
International record:	Played 4 Lost 4
Details:	New Zealand 11 South Africa 15
	New Zealand 6 South Africa 12
	New Zealand 3 South Africa 9
	New Zealand 8 South Africa 11

1960

Full record:	Played 26 Won 20 Lost 4 Drawn 2
	Points for 441 Against 164
International record:	Played 4 Won 1 Lost 2 Drawn 1
Details:	New Zealand 0 South Africa 13
	New Zealand 11 South Africa 3
	New Zealand 11 South Africa 11
	New Zealand 3 South Africa 8

1970

Full record:	Played 24 Won 21 Lost 3 Drawn 0
	Points for 687 Against 228
International record:	Played 4 Won 1 Lost 3 Drawn 0
Details:	New Zealand 6 South Africa 17
	New Zealand 9 South Africa 8
	New Zealand 3 South Africa 14
	New Zealand 17 South Africa 20

1976

Full record:	Played 24 Won 18 Lost 6 Drawn 0
	Points for 591 Against 306
International record:	Played 4 Won 1 Lost 3
Details:	New Zealand 7 South Africa 16
	New Zealand 15 South Africa 9
	New Zealand 10 South Africa 15
	New Zealand 14 South Africa 15

SOUTH AFRICA to BRITISH ISLES and FRANCE

1906-7

Full record:	Played 28 Won 25 Lost 2 Drawn 1
	Points for 553 Against 81
International record:	Played 4 Won 2 Lost 1 Drawn 1
Details:	South Africa 0 Scotland 6
	South Africa 15 Ireland 12
	South Africa 11 Wales 0
	South Africa 3 England 3

1912-13

Full record:	Played 27 Won 24 Lost 3 Drawn 0
	Points for 441 Against 101
International record:	Played 5 Won 5 Lost 0
Details:	South Africa 16 Scotland 0
	South Africa 38 Ireland 0
	South Africa 3 Wales 0
	South Africa 9 England 3
	South Africa 38 France 5

1931-2 (British Isles only)

Full record:	Played 26 Won 23 Lost 1 Drawn 2
	Points for 407 Against 124
International record:	Played 4 Won 4
Details:	South Africa 8 Wales 3
	South Africa 8 Ireland 3
	South Africa 7 England 0
	South Africa 6 Scotland 3

1951-2

Full record:	Played 31 Won 30 Lost 1 Drawn 0
	Points for 562 Against 167
International record:	Played 5 Won 5
Details:	South Africa 44 Scotland 0
	South Africa 17 Ireland 5
	South Africa 6 Wales 3
	South Africa 8 England 3
	South Africa 25 France 3

1960-1

Full record:	Played 34 Won 31 Lost 1 Drawn 2
	Points for 567 Against 132
International record:	Played 5 Won 4 Lost 0 Drawn 1
Details:	South Africa 3 Wales 0
	South Africa 8 Ireland 3
	South Africa 5 England 0
	South Africa 12 Scotland 5
	South Africa 0 France 0

1965 (Ireland and Scotland only)

Full record:	Played 5 Won 0 Lost 4 Drawn 1
	Points for 37 Against 53
International record:	Played 2 Won 0 Lost 2 Drawn 0
Details:	South Africa 6 Ireland 9
	South Africa 5 Scotland 8

1968 (France only)

Full record:	Played 6 Won 5 Lost 1 Drawn 0
	Points for 84 Against 43
International record:	Played 2 Won 2
Details:	South Africa 12 France 9
	South Africa 16 France 11

1969-70 (British Isles only)

Full record:	Played 24 Won 15 Lost 5 Drawn 4
	Points for 232 Against 157
International record:	Played 4 Won 0 Lost 2 Drawn 2
Details:	South Africa 3 Scotland 6
	South Africa 8 England 11
	South Africa 8 Ireland 8
	South Africa 6 Wales 6

1974 (France only)

Full record:	Played 9 Won 8 Lost 1 Drawn 0
	Points for 170 Against 74
International record:	Played 2 Won 2
Details:	South Africa 13 France 4
	South Africa 10 France 8

SOUTH AFRICA to AUSTRALIA and NEW ZEALAND

1921

Full record:	
in Australia	Played 5 Won 5 Lost 0 Drawn 0
	Points for 134 Against 38
in New Zealand	Played 19 Won 15 Lost 2 Drawn 2
	Points for 224 Against 81
International record:	
v. New Zealand	Played 3 Won 1 Lost 1 Drawn 1
Details:	South Africa 5 New Zealand 13
	South Africa 9 New Zealand 5
	South Africa 0 New Zealand 0

1937

Full record:	
in Australia	Played 11 Won 10 Lost 1 Drawn 0
	Points for 444 Against 76
in New Zealand	Played 17 Won 16 Lost 1 Drawn 0
	Points for 411 Against 104
International record:	
v. Australia	Played 2 Won 2 Lost 0
v. New Zealand	Played 3 Won 2 Lost 1
Details:	
v. Australia	South Africa 9 Australia 5
	South Africa 26 Australia 17
v. New Zealand	South Africa 7 New Zealand 13
	South Africa 13 New Zealand 6
	South Africa 17 New Zealand 6

1956

Full record:	
in Australia	Played 6 Won 6 Lost 0 Drawn 0
	Points for 150 Against 26
in New Zealand	Played 23 Won 16 Lost 6 Drawn 1
	Points for 370 Against 177
International record:	
v. Australia	Played 2 Won 2 Lost 0
v. New Zealand	Played 4 Won 1 Lost 3
Details:	
v. Australia	South Africa 9 Australia 0
	South Africa 9 Australia 0
v. New Zealand	South Africa 6 New Zealand 10
	South Africa 8 New Zealand 3
	South Africa 10 New Zealand 17
	South Africa 5 New Zealand 11

1965

Full record:	
in Australia	Played 6 Won 3 Lost 3 Drawn 0
	Points for 184 Against 53
in New Zealand	Played 24 Won 19 Lost 5 Drawn 0
	Points for 485 Against 232
International record:	
v. Australia	Played 2 Won 0 Lost 2
v. New Zealand	Played 4 Won 1 Lost 3
Details:	
v. Australia	South Africa 11 Australia 18
	South Africa 8 Australia 12
v. New Zealand	South Africa 3 New Zealand 6
	South Africa 0 New Zealand 13
	South Africa 19 New Zealand 16
	South Africa 3 New Zealand 20

1971 (Australia only)

Full record:	Played 13 Won 13 Lost 0 Drawn 0
	Points for 396 Against 102
International record:	Played 3 Won 3
Details:	South Africa 19 Australia 11
	South Africa 14 Australia 6
	South Africa 18 Australia 6

AUSTRALIA to BRITISH ISLES and FRANCE

1908-9

Full record:	Played 31 Won 25 Lost 5 Drawn 1
	Points for 438 Against 146
International record:	Played 2 Won 1 Lost 1
Details:	Australia 6 Wales 9
	Australia 9 England 3

1927-8 (New South Wales, 'The Waratahs')

Full record:	Played 31 Won 24 Lost 5 Drawn 2
	Points for 432 Against 207
'International' record:	Played 5 Won 3 Lost 2
Details:	New South Wales 5 Ireland 3
	New South Wales 18 Wales 8
	New South Wales 8 Scotland 10
	New South Wales 11 England 18
	New South Wales 11 France 8

1947-8

Full record:	Played 35 Won 29 Lost 6 Drawn 0
	Points for 500 Against 243
International record:	Played 5 Won 3 Lost 2
Details:	Australia 16 Scotland 7
	Australia 16 Ireland 3
	Australia 0 Wales 6
	Australia 11 England 0
	Australia 6 France 13

1957-8

Full record:	Played 34 Won 16 Lost 15 Drawn 3
	Points for 285 Against 224
International record:	Played 5 Lost 5
Details:	Australia 3 Wales 9
	Australia 6 Ireland 9
	Australia 6 England 9
	Australia 8 Scotland 12
	Australia 0 France 19

1966-7

Full record:	Played 34 Won 16 Lost 15 Drawn 3
	Points for 348 Against 324
International record:	Played 5 Won 2 Lost 3
Details:	Australia 14 Wales 11
	Australia 5 Scotland 11
	Australia 23 England 11
	Australia 8 Ireland 15
	Australia 14 France 20

1968 (Ireland and Scotland only)

Full record:	Played 5 Won 2 Lost 3 Drawn 0
	Points for 38 Against 40
International record:	Played 2 Lost 2
Details:	Australia 3 Ireland 10
	Australia 3 Scotland 9

1971 (France only)

Full record:	Played 8 Won 4 Lost 4 Drawn 0
	Points for 110 Against 101
International record:	Played 2 Won 1 Lost 1
Details:	Australia 13 France 11
	Australia 9 France 18

1973 (England and Wales only)

Full record:	Played 8 Won 2 Lost 5 Drawn 1
	Points for 85 Against 131
International record:	Played 2 Lost 2
Details:	Australia 0 Wales 24
	Australia 3 England 20

1975-6 (including one match in USA)

Full record:	Played 26 Won 19 Lost 6 Drawn 1
	Points for 496 Against 349
International record:	Played 5 Won 2 Lost 3
Details:	Australia 3 Scotland 10
	Australia 3 Wales 28
	Australia 6 England 23
	Australia 20 Ireland 10
	Australia 24 USA 12

AUSTRALIA to SOUTH AFRICA

1933

Full record:	Played 23 Won 12 Lost 10 Drawn 1
	Points for 229 Against 195
International record:	Played 5 Won 2 Lost 3
Details:	Australia 3 South Africa 17
	Australia 21 South Africa 6
	Australia 3 South Africa 12
	Australia 0 South Africa 11
	Australia 15 South Africa 4

1953

Full record:	Played 27 Won 16 Lost 10 Drawn 1
	Points for 450 Against 413
International record:	Played 4 Won 1 Lost 3
Details:	Australia 3 South Africa 25
	Australia 18 South Africa 14
	Australia 8 South Africa 18
	Australia 9 South Africa 22

1961

Full record:	Played 6 Won 3 Lost 2 Drawn 1
	Points for 90 Against 80
International record:	Played 2 Lost 2
Details:	Australia 3 South Africa 28
	Australia 11 South Africa 23

1963

Full record:	Played 24 Won 15 Lost 8 Drawn 1
	Points for 303 Against 233
International record:	Played 4 Won 2 Lost 2
Details:	Australia 3 South Africa 14
	Australia 9 South Africa 5
	Australia 11 South Africa 9
	Australia 6 South Africa 22

1969

Full record:	Played 26 Won 15 Lost 11 Drawn 0
	Points for 465 Against 353
International record:	Played 4 Won 0 Lost 4 Drawn 0
Details:	Australia 11 South Africa 30
	Australia 9 South Africa 16
	Australia 3 South Africa 11
	Australia 8 South Africa 19

ENGLAND to AUSTRALIA and NEW ZEALAND

1963

in New Zealand	Played 4 Won 1 Lost 4 Drawn 0
	Points for 45 Against 73
in Australia	Played 1 Won 0 Lost 1 Drawn 0
	Points for 9 Against 18
International record:	
v. New Zealand	Played 2 Lost 2
v. Australia	Played 1 Lost 1
Details:	
v. New Zealand	England 11 New Zealand 21
	England 6 New Zealand 9
v. Australia	England 9 Australia 18

ENGLAND to SOUTH AFRICA

1972

Full record:	Played 7 Won 6 Lost 0 Drawn 1
	Points for 166 Against 58
International record:	Played 1 Won 1
Details:	England 18 South Africa 9

ENGLAND to FIJI and NEW ZEALAND

1973

in Fiji	Played 1 Won 1 Lost 0 Drawn 0
	Points for 13 Against 12
in New Zealand	Played 4 Won 1 Lost 3 Drawn 0
	Points for 47 Against 60
International record:	
v. New Zealand	Played 1 Won 1
Details:	England 16 New Zealand 10

ENGLAND to AUSTRALIA

1975

Full record:	Played 8 Won 4 Lost 4 Drawn 0
	Points for 217 Against 110
International record:	Played 2 Lost 2
Details:	England 9 Australia 16
	England 21 Australia 30

IRELAND to SOUTH AFRICA

1961

Full record:	Played 4 Won 3 Lost 1 Drawn 0
	Points for 59 Against 36
International record:	Played 1 Lost 1
Details:	Ireland 8 South Africa 24

IRELAND to AUSTRALIA

1967
Full record: Played 6 Won 4 Lost 2 Drawn 0
                                Points for 119 Against 80

International record: Played 1 Won 1
Details: Ireland 11 Australia 5

IRELAND TO NEW ZEALAND

1976
Full record: Played 7 Won 4 Lost 4 Drawn 0
                                Points for 88 Against 68

International record: Played 1 Lost 1
Details: Ireland 3 New Zealand 11

WALES to SOUTH AFRICA

1964
Full record: Played 4 Won 2 Lost 2 Drawn 0
                                Points for 43 Against 58

International record: Played 1 Lost 1
Details: Wales 3 South Africa 24

WALES to AUSTRALIA, NEW ZEALAND and FIJI

1969
Full record:
  in New Zealand   Played 5 Won 2 Lost 2 Drawn 1
                                Points for 62 Against 76
  in Australia   Played 1 Won 1 Lost 0 Drawn 0
                                Points for 19 Against 16
  in Fiji   Played 1 Won 1 Lost 0 Drawn 0
                                Points for 31 Against 11

International record:
  v. New Zealand   Played 2 Lost 2
Details: Wales 0 New Zealand 19
                                Wales 12 New Zealand 33

FRANCE to SOUTH AFRICA

1958
Full record: Played 10 Won 5 Lost 3 Drawn 2
                                Points for 137 Against 124

International record: Played 2 Won 1 Drawn 1
Details: France 3 South Africa 3
                                France 9 South Africa 5

1964
Full record: Played 6 Won 5 Lost 1 Drawn 0
                                Points for 117 Against 55

International record: Played 1 Won 1
Details: France 8 South Africa 6

1967
Full record: Played 13 Won 8 Lost 4 Drawn 1
                                Points for 209 Against 161

International record: Played 4 Won 1 Lost 2 Drawn 1
Details: France 3 South Africa 26
                                France 3 South Africa 16
                                France 19 South Africa 14
                                France 6 South Africa 6

1971
Full record: Played 9 Won 7 Lost 1 Drawn 1
                                Points for 228 Against 92

International record: Played 2 Lost 1 Drawn 1
Details: France 9 South Africa 22
                                France 8 South Africa 8

1975
Full record: Played 11 Won 6 Lost 4 Drawn 1
                                Points for 282 Against 190

International record: Played 2 Lost 2
Details: France 25 South Africa 38
                                France 18 South Africa 33

FRANCE to AUSTRALIA and NEW ZEALAND

1961
Full record:
  in New Zealand   Played 13 Won 6 Lost 7 Drawn 0
                                Points for 150 Against 149
  in Australia   Played 2 Won 2 Lost 0 Drawn 0
                                Points for 30 Against 20

International record:
  v. New Zealand   Played 3 Lost 3
  v. Australia   Played 1 Won 1
Details:
  v. New Zealand   France 6 New Zealand 13
                                France 3 New Zealand 5
                                France 3 New Zealand 32
  v. Australia   France 15 Australia 8

1968
Full record:
  in New Zealand   Played 12 Won 8 Lost 4 Drawn 0
                                Points for 154 Against 120
  in Australia   Played 2 Won 1 Lost 1 Drawn 0
                                Points for 41 Against 22

International record:
  v. New Zealand   Played 3 Lost 3
  v. Australia   Played 1 Lost 1
Details:
  v. New Zealand   France 9 New Zealand 12
                                France 3 New Zealand 9
                                France 12 New Zealand 19
  v. Australia   France 10 Australia 11

1972 (Australia only)
Full record: Played 9 Won 8 Lost 0 Drawn 1
                                Points for 254 Against 122
International record: Played 2 Won 1 Drawn 1
Details: France 14 Australia 14
                                France 16 Australia 15

SCOTLAND to SOUTH AFRICA

1960
Full record: Played 3 Won 2 Lost 1 Drawn 0
                                Points for 61 Against 45
International record: Played 1 Lost 1
Details: Scotland 10 South Africa 18

SCOTLAND to AUSTRALIA

1970
Full record: Played 6 Won 3 Lost 2 Drawn 0
                                Points for 109 Against 94
International record: Played 1 Lost 1
Details: Scotland 3 Australia 23

SCOTLAND to NEW ZEALAND

1975
Full record: Played 7 Won 4 Lost 3 Drawn 0
                                Points for 157 Against 104
International record: Played 1 Lost 1
Details: Scotland 0 New Zealand 24

INTERNATIONAL RECORDS

AUSTRALIA

Team records
Highest score:
 30 v. England (30–21) Brisbane 1975
Biggest winning points margin:
 20 v. Scotland (23–3) Sydney 1970
Highest score by opposing team:
 38 New Zealand (13–38) Dunedin 1936
 38 New Zealand (3–38) Auckland 1972
Biggest losing points margin:
 35 v. New Zealand (3–38) Auckland 1972
Most tries by Australia in an international:
 6 v. Scotland (23–3) Sydney 1970
Most tries against Australia in an international:
 8 by South Africa (3–28) Johannesburg 1961
Most points on overseas tour:
 500 in British Isles and France (35 matches)
 1947-8
Most tries on overseas tour:
 115 in British Isles and France (35 matches)
 1947-8

Individual records
Most capped players:
 P. G. Johnson 39 1959-71
 G. V. Davis 39 1963-72
Most points in internationals:
 65 A. N. McGill (19 appearances) 1968-73
 (excluding 2 appearances against Tonga)
Most points in an international:
 15 A. N. McGill v. New Zealand Brisbane 1968
 15 R. L. Fairfax v. France Brisbane 1972
Most tries in internationals:
 7 C. J. Windon (15 appearances) 1946-52
 (excluding 5 appearances against Maoris
 and Fiji)
Most points on overseas tour:
 154 P. E. McLean (18 appearances) British
 Isles 1975-6
Most tries on overseas tour:
 23 C. Russell British Isles 1908-9
Most points in international series on tour:
 28 P. F. Hawthorne (4 appearances) 1966-7
 British Isles and France
Most points in any match on tour:
 23 J. C. Hindmarsh v. Glamorgan Neath 1975
Most tries in any match on tour:
 6 J. S. Boyce v. Wairarapa (NZ)
 Masterton 1962

BRITISH ISLES

Team records
Highest score:
 31 v. Australia (31–0) Brisbane 1966
Biggest winning points margin:
 31 v. Australia (31–0) Brisbane 1966
Highest score by opposing team:
 34 v. South Africa (14–34) Bloemfontein 1962
Biggest losing points margin:
 20 v. South Africa (14–34) Bloemfontein 1962
Most tries by British Isles in an international:
 5 v. Australia (24–3) Sydney 1950
 5 v. South Africa (23–22) Johannesburg 1955
 5 v. Australia (24–3) Sydney 1959
 5 v. Australia (31–0) Brisbane 1966
 5 v. South Africa (28–9) Pretoria 1974
Most tries against British Isles in an international:
 7 by South Africa (9–25) Cape Town 1955
Most points on overseas tour:
 842 in Australia, New Zealand and Canada
 (33 matches) 1959

Most tries on overseas tour:
 165 in Australia, New Zealand and Canada
 (33 matches) 1959

Individual records
Most capped player:
 W. J. McBride 17 1962-74
Most points in internationals:
 35 T. J. Kiernan (5 appearances) 1962-8
Most points in an international:
 17 T. J. Kiernan v. South Africa Pretoria 1968
Most tries in internationals:
 6 A. J. F. O'Reilly (10 appearances) 1955-9
Most tries in an international:
 C. D. Aarvold v. New Zealand
 Christchurch 1930
 2 J. E. Nelson v. Australia Sydney 1950
 2 M. J. Price v. New Zealand Dunedin 1959
 2 M. J. Price v. Australia Sydney 1959
 2 D. K. Jones v. Australia Brisbane 1966
 2 T. G. R. Davies v. New Zealand
 Christchurch 1971
 2 J. J. Williams v. South Africa Pretoria 1974
 2 J. J. Williams v. South Africa
 Port Elizabeth 1974
Most points for British Isles on overseas tour:
 188 B. John (17 appearances) Australia and
 New Zealand 1971
Most tries for British Isles on overseas tour:
 22 A. J. F. O'Reilly (23 appearances)
 Australia, New Zealand and Canada 1959
Most points for British Isles in an international
series:
 35 T. J. Kiernan (4 appearances)
 South Africa 1968
Most tries for British Isles in an international
series:
 J. J. Williams (4 appearances)
 South Africa 1974
Most points for British Isles in any match on
tour:
 37 A. G. B. Old v. South Western Districts
 Mossel Bay (SA) 1974
Most tries for British Isles in any match on tour:
 6 D. J. Duckham v. West-Coast-Buller
 Greymouth (NZ) 1971
 6 J. J. Williams v. South Western Districts
 Mossel Bay (SA) 1974

ENGLAND

Team records
Highest score:
 41 v. France (41–13) Richmond 1907
Biggest winning points margin:
 37 v. France (37–0) Twickenham 1911
Highest score by opposing team:
 37 France (12–37) Colombes 1972
Biggest losing points margin:
 25 v. Wales (0–25) Cardiff 1905
 25 v. France (12–37) Colombes 1972
Most tries by England in an international:
 9 v. France (35–8) Parc des Princes 1906
 9 v. France (41–13) Richmond 1907
 9 v. France (39–13) Colombes 1914
Most tries against England in an international:
 8 by Wales (6–28) Cardiff 1922

Individual records
Most capped player:
 J. V. Pullin 42 1966-76
Most points in internationals:
 138 R. Hiller (19 appearances) 1968-72
Most points in an international:
 22 D. Lambert v. France Twickenham 1911
Most tries in internationals:
 13 J. G. G. Birkett (21 appearances) 1906-12

Most tries in an international:
 4 A. Hudson v. France Parc des Princes 1906
 4 D. Lambert v. France Richmond 1907
Most points in International Championship in a
season:
 38 R. W. Hosen 1966-7
Most points in any tour match:
 36 W. N. Bennet v. Western Australia
 Perth 1975

FRANCE

Team records
Highest score:
 37 v. England (37–12) Colombes 1972
Biggest winning points margin:
 25 v. England (37–12) Colombes 1972
Highest score by opposing team:
 49 Wales (14–49) Swansea 1910
Biggest losing points margin:
 42 v. Wales (5–47) Colombes 1909
Most tries by France in an international:
 6 v. Ireland (27–6) Colombes 1964
 6 v. England (35–13) Colombes 1970
 6 v. England (37–12) Colombes 1972
 6 v. England (30–9) Parc des Princes 1976
Most tries against France in an international:
 11 by Wales (5–47) Colombes 1909
Most points on a tour (all matches):
 282 in South Africa (11 matches) 1975

Individual records
Most capped player:
 B. Dauga 50 1964-72
Most points in internationals:
 133 P. Villepreux (29 appearances) 1967-72
Most points in an international:
 17 G. Camberabero v. Australia
 Colombes 1967
Most tries in internationals:
 14 C. Darrouy (28 appearances) 1957-67
Most tries in an international:
 3 M. Crauste v. England Colombes 1962
 3 C. Darrouy v. Ireland Dublin 1963
Most points in International Championship in a
season:
 32 G. Camberabero (3 appearances) 1966-7
Most tries in International Championship in a
season:
 4 M. Crauste (4 appearances) 1961-2
 4 C. Darrouy (3 appearances) 1964-5
Most points on overseas tour:
 71 J.-P. Romeu (7 appearances)
 South Africa 1971
Most points in any match on tour:
 19 J. L. Dehez v. South Western Districts
 George (SA) 1967
Most tries in any match on tour:
 4 R. Bertranne v. West Transvaal
 Potchefstroom 1971

IRELAND

Team records
Highest score:
 26 v. Scotland (26–8) Murrayfield 1953
 26 v. England (26–21) Twickenham 1974
Biggest winning points margin:
 24 v. France (24–0) Cork 1913
Highest score by opposing team:
 38 South Africa (0–38) Dublin 1912
Biggest losing points margin:
 38 v. South Africa (0–38) Dublin 1912

Most tries by Ireland in an international:
6 v. France (24–0) Cork 1913
6 v. Scotland (26–8) Murrayfield 1953
Most tries against Ireland in an international:
10 by South Africa (0–38) Dublin 1912

Individual records
Most capped players:
W. J. McBride 63 1962-75
Most points in internationals:
158 T. J. Kiernan (54 appearances) 1960-73
Most points in an international:
14 J. C. M. Moroney v. France Dublin 1969
Most tries in internationals:
11 A. T. A. Duggan (25 appearances) 1964-72
Most tries in an international:
3 A. R. V. Jackson v. France Cork 1911
3 J. P. Quinn v. France Cork 1911
3 E. O'D. Davy v. Scotland Murrayfield 1930
3 S. Byrne v. Scotland Murrayfield 1953
Most points in International Championship in a season:
26 G. W. Norton 1948-9
26 W. M. McCombe 1974-5
Most points for Ireland on overseas tour:
53 T. J. Kiernan (6 appearances)
Australia 1967
Most points in any match on tour:
17 T. J. Kiernan v. Queensland Brisbane 1967

NEW ZEALAND

Team records
Highest score:
38 v. France (38–8) Parc des Princes 1906
38 v. Australia (38–13) Dunedin 1936
38 v. Australia (38–3) Auckland 1972
Biggest winning points margin:
35 v. Australia (38–3) Auckland 1972
Highest score by opposing team:
25 Australia (11–25) Sydney 1934
Biggest losing points margin:
17 v. South Africa (0–17) Durban 1928
Most tries by New Zealand in an international:
10 v. France (38–8) Parc des Princes 1906
Most tries against New Zealand in an international:
5 by South Africa (6–17) Auckland 1937
Most points on overseas tour (all matches):
868 in British Isles and France (33 matches) 1905-6
Most tries on overseas tour (all matches):
215 in British Isles and France (33 matches) 1905-6

Individual records
Most capped player:
C. E. Meads 55 1957-71
Most points in internationals:
207 D. B. Clarke (31 appearances) 1956-64
Most points in an international:
24 W. F. McCormick v. Wales Auckland 1969
Most tries in internationals:
13 I. A. Kirkpatrick (30 appearances) 1967-75
Most tries in an international:
4 D. McGregor v. England Crystal Palace 1905
Most points for New Zealand on overseas tour:
230 W. J. Wallace (25 appearances)
British Isles and France 1905-6
Most tries for New Zealand on overseas tour:
42 J. Hunter (23 appearances) British Isles and France 1905-6
Most points for New Zealand in International Series on tour:
32 W. F. McCormick (4 appearances)
British Isles and France 1967

Most tries for New Zealand in International Series on tour:
5 K. S. Svenson (4 appearances)
British Isles and France 1924-5
Most points for New Zealand in any match on tour:
41 J. F. Karam v. South Australia
Adelaide 1974
Most tries for New Zealand in any match on tour:
8 T. R. Heeps v. Northern NSW Quirindi 1962

SCOTLAND

Team records
Highest score:
35 v. Wales (35–10) Inverleith 1924
Biggest winning points margin:
28 v. France (31–3) Inverleith 1912
Highest score by opposing team:
44 South Africa (0–44) Murrayfield 1951
Biggest losing points margin:
44 v. South Africa (0–44) Murrayfield 1951
Most tries by Scotland in an international:
8 v. Wales (35–10) Inverleith 1924
Most tries against Scotland in an international:
9 by South Africa (0–44) Murrayfield 1951

Individual records
Most capped player:
A. B. Carmichael 45 1967-76
Most points in internationals:
82 A. R. Irvine (20 appearances) 1973-6
Most points in an international:
13 F. H. Turner v. France Inverleith 1912
13 P. C. Brown v. England Murrayfield 1972
Most tries in internationals:
23 I. S. Smith (32 appearances) 1924-33
Most tries in an international:
4 W. A. Stewart v. Ireland Inverleith 1913
4 I. S. Smith v. France Inverleith 1925
4 I. S. Smith v. Wales Swansea 1925
Most points in International Championship in a season:
26 A. R. Irvine 1973-4 and 1975-6
Most tries in International Championship in a season:
8 I. S. Smith 1924-5

SOUTH AFRICA

Team records
Highest score:
44 v. Scotland (44–0) Murrayfield 1951
Biggest winning points margin:
44 v. Scotland (44–0) Murrayfield 1951
Highest score by opposing team:
28 British Isles (9–28) Pretoria 1974
Biggest losing points margin:
19 v. British Isles (9–28) Pretoria 1974
Most tries by South Africa in an international:
10 v. Ireland (38–0) Dublin 1912
Most tries against South Africa in an international:
5 by British Isles (22–23) Johannesburg 1955
5 by New Zealand (3–20) Auckland 1965
5 by British Isles (9–28) Pretoria 1974
Most points on overseas tour (all matches):
753 in Australia and New Zealand (26 matches) 1937
Most tries on overseas tour (all matches):
161 in Australia and New Zealand (26 matches) 1937

Individual records
Most capped player:
F. C. H. du Preez 38 1960-71
Most points in internationals:
130 P. J. Visagie (25 appearances) 1967-71
Most points in an international:
22 G. R. Bosch v. France Pretoria 1975
Most tries in internationals:
8 J. L. Gainsford (33 appearances) 1960-7
8 J. P. Englebrecht (35 appearances) 1960-9
Most tries in an international:
3 E. E. McHardy v. Ireland Dublin 1912
3 J. A. Stegmann v. Ireland Dublin 1912
3 K. T. van Vollenhoven v. British Isles
Cape Town 1955
3 H. J. van Zyl v. Australia Johannesburg 1961
Most points for South Africa on overseas tour:
190 G. H. Brand (20 appearances)
Australia and New Zealand 1937
Most tries for South Africa on overseas tour:
22 J. A. Loubser (20 appearances) British
Isles and France 1906-7
Most points for South Africa in International Series on tour:
19 P. J. Visagie (2 appearances) France 1968
Most tries for South Africa in International Series on tour:
5 J. A. Stegmann (5 appearances) British
Isles and France 1912-13
Most points for South Africa in any match on tour:
25 P. J. Visagie v. S. Australia Adelaide 1971
Most tries for South Africa in any match on tour:
6 R. G. Dryburgh v. Queensland Brisbane 1956

WALES

Team records
Highest score:
49 v. France (49–14) Swansea 1910
Biggest winning points margin:
42 v. France (47–5) Colombes 1909
Highest score by opposing team:
35 Scotland (10–35) Inverleith 1924
Biggest losing points margin:
25 v. England (0–25) Blackheath 1896
25 v. Scotland (10–35) Inverleith 1924
Most tries by Wales in an international:
11 v. France (47–5) Colombes 1909
Most tries against Wales in an international:
8 by Scotland (10–35) Inverleith 1924

Individual records
Most capped player:
G. O. Edwards 45 1967-76
Most points in internationals:
117 P. Bennett (21 appearances) 1969-76
Most points in an international:
19 J. Bancroft v. France Swansea 1910
19 K. S. Jarrett v. England Cardiff 1967
19 P. Bennett v. Ireland Dublin 1976
Most tries in internationals:
18 G. O. Edwards (45 appearances) 1967-76
Most tries in an international:
4 W. Llewellyn v. England Swansea 1899
4 R. A. Gibbs v. France Cardiff 1908
4 M. C. R. Richards v. England Cardiff 1969
Most points in International Championship in a season:
38 P. Bennett (4 appearances) 1975-76
Most tries in International Championship in a season:
6 R. A. Gibbs 1907-8
6 M. C. R. Richards 1968-9

ENGLISH COUNTY CHAMPIONSHIPS

	Winners	Runners-up
1889	Yorkshire	
1890	Yorkshire	
1891	Lancashire	
1892	Yorkshire	
1893	Yorkshire	
1894	Yorkshire	
1895	Yorkshire	
1896	Yorkshire	Surrey
1897	Kent	Cumberland
1898	Northumberland	Midlands
1899	Devon	Northumberland
1900	Durham	Devon
1901	Devon	Durham
1902	Durham	Gloucestershire
1903	Durham	Kent
1904	Kent	Durham
1905	Durham	Middlesex
1906	Devon	Durham
1907	Devon and Durham joint champions	
1908	Cornwall	Durham
1909	Durham	Cornwall
1910	Gloucestershire	Yorkshire
1911	Devon	Yorkshire
1912	Devon	Northumberland
1913	Gloucestershire	Cumberland
1914	Midlands	Durham
1920	Gloucestershire	Yorkshire
1921	Gloucestershire	Leicestershire
1922	Gloucestershire	North Midlands
1923	Somerset	Leicestershire
1924	Cumberland	Kent
1925	Leicestershire	Gloucestershire
1926	Yorkshire	Hampshire
1927	Kent	Leicestershire
1928	Yorkshire	Cornwall
1929	Middlesex	Lancashire
1930	Gloucestershire	Lancashire
1931	Gloucestershire	Warwickshire
1932	Gloucestershire	Durham
1933	Hampshire	Lancashire
1934	East Midlands	Gloucestershire
1935	Lancashire	Somerset
1936	Hampshire	Northumberland
1937	Gloucestershire	East Midlands
1938	Lancashire	Surrey
1939	Warwickshire	Somerset
1947	Lancashire	Gloucestershire
1948	Lancashire	Eastern Counties
1949	Lancashire	Gloucestershire
1950	Cheshire	East Midlands
1951	East Midlands	Middlesex
1952	Middlesex	Lancashire
1953	Yorkshire	East Midlands
1954	Middlesex	Lancashire
1955	Lancashire	Middlesex
1956	Middlesex	Devon
1957	Devon	Yorkshire
1958	Warwickshire	Cornwall
1959	Warwickshire	Gloucestershire
1960	Warwickshire	Surrey
1961	Cheshire	Devon
1962	Warwickshire	Hampshire
1963	Warwickshire	Yorkshire
1964	Warwickshire	Lancashire
1965	Warwickshire	Durham
1966	Middlesex	Lancashire
1967	Surrey and Durham joint champions	
1968	Middlesex	Warwickshire
1969	Lancashire	Cornwall
1970	Staffordshire	Gloucestershire
1971	Surrey	Gloucestershire
1972	Gloucestershire	Warwickshire
1973	Lancashire	Gloucestershire
1974	Gloucestershire	Lancashire
1975	Gloucestershire	Eastern Counties
1976	Gloucestershire	Middlesex

RUGBY FOOTBALL UNION CLUB COMPETITION

	Winners	Runners-up
1972	Gloucester	Moseley
1973	Coventry	Bristol
1974	Coventry	London Scottish
1975	Bedford	Rosslyn Park
1976	Gosforth	Rosslyn Park

SCOTTISH CLUB CHAMPIONS

1974	Hawick
1975	Hawick
1976	Hawick

FRENCH CHAMPIONSHIPS

1892	Racing Club de France 4 Stade Français 3
1893	Stade Français 7 Racing Club de France 3
1894	Stade Français 18 Inter-nos 0
1895	Stade Français 16 Olympique de Paris 0
1896	Olympique de Paris 12 Stade Français 0
1897	Stade Français
1898	Stade Français
1899	Stade Bordelais U.C. 5 Stade Français 3
1900	Racing Club de France 37
1901	Stade Français Stade Bordelais U.C.
1902	Racing Club de France 6 Stade Bordelais U.C. 0
1903	Stade Français 16 Stade Olympique E.T. 8
1904	Stade Bordelais U.C. 3 Stade Français 0
1905	Stade Bordelais U.C. 12 Stade Français 3
1906	Stade Bordelais U.C. 9 Stade Français 0
1907	Stade Bordelais U.C. 14 Stade Français 3
1908	Stade Français 16 Stade Bordelais U.C. 3
1909	Stade Bordelais U.C. 17 Stade Toulousain 0
1910	F.C. Lyon 13 Stade Bordelais U.C. 8
1911	Stade Bordelais U.C. 14 S.C.U.F. 0
1912	Stade Toulousain 8 Racing Club de France 6
1913	Aviron Bayonnais 31 S.C.U.F. 8
1914	U.S. Perpignan 8 S. Tarbais 7
1920	S. Tarbais 8 Racing Club de France 3
1921	U.S. Perpignan 5 S. Toulousain 0
1922	S. Toulousain 6 A. Bayonnais 0
1923	S. Toulousain 3 A. Bayonnais 0
1924	S. Toulousain 3 U.S. Perpignan 0
1925	U.S. Perpignan 5 S.A. Carcassone 0
1926	S. Toulousain 11 U.S. Perpignan 0

1927	S. Toulousain 19	S. Français 9
1928	Section Paloise 6	U.S. Quillan 4
1929	U.S. Quillan 11	F.C. Lezignan 8
1930	S.U. Agen 4	U.S. Quillan 0
1931	R.C. Toulon 6	Lyon O.U. 3
1932	Lyon O.U. 9	R.C. Narbonne 3
1933	Lyon O.U. 10	R.C. Narbonne 3
1934	Aviron Bayonnais 13	Biarritz Olympique 8
1935	Biarritz Olympique 3	U.S.A. Perpignan 0
1936	R.C. Narbonne 6	AS. Montferand 3
1937	C.S. Vienne 13	AS. Montferand 7
1938	U.S.A. Perpignan 11	Biarritz Olympique 6
1939	Biarritz Olympique 6	U.S.A. Perpignan 0
1943	A. Bayonnais 3	S.U. Agen 0
1944	U.S.A. Perpignan 20	A. Bayonnais 5
1945	S.U. Agen 7	F.C. Lourdes 3
1946	S. Paloise 11	F.C. Lourdes 0
1947	S. Toulousain 10	S.U. Agen 3
1948	F.C. Lourdes 11	R.C. Toulon 3
*1949	Castres Olympique 14	S. Montois 3
1950	Castres Olympique 11	Racing Club de France 8
1951	U.S. Carmaux 14	S. Tarbais 12
1952	F.C. Lourdes 20	U.S.A. Perpignan 11
1953	F.C. Lourdes 21	S. Montois 16
1954	F.C. Grenoble 5	U.S. Cognac 3
1955	U.S.A. Perpignan 11	F.C. Lourdes 6
1956	F.C. Lourdes 20	U.S. Dax 0
1957	F.C. Lourdes 16	Racing Club de France 13
1958	F.C. Lourdes 25	S.C. Mazamet 8
1959	Racing Club de France 8	S. Montais 3
1960	F.C. Lourdes 14	AS. Béziers 11
1961	AS. Béziers 6	U.S. Dax 3
1962	S.U. Agen 14	AS. Béziers 11
1963	S. Montais 9	U.S. Dax 6
1964	S. Paloise 14	AS. Béziers 0
1965	S.U. Agen 15	C.A. Brive 8
1966	S.U. Agen 9	U.S. Dax 8
1967	U.S. Montauban 11	C.A. Bègles 3
**1968	F.C. Lourdes 9	R.C. Toulon 9
1969	C.A. Bègles 11	S. Toulousain 9
1970	La Voulte S.P. 3	AS. Montferrand 0
1971	A.S. Béziers 15	R.C. Toulon 9
1972	AS. Béziers 9	C.A. Brive 0
1973	S. Tarbes 18	U.S. Dax 12
1974	S. Béziers 16	Narbonne 14
1975	S. Béziers 13	Brive 12
1976	S.U. Agen 13	Béziers 10

*After a draw
**Lourdes won on tries

CURRIE CUP (SOUTH AFRICA)

1889	Western Province
1892	Western Province
1893	Western Province
1894	Western Province
1895	Western Province
1897	Western Province
1898	Western Province
1899	Griqualand West
1904	Western Province
1906	Western Province
1908	Western Province
1911	Griqualand West
1914	Western Province
1920	Western Province
1922	Transvaal
1925	Western Province
1927	Western Province
1929	Western Province
1932	Western Province and Border
1934	Western Province and Border
1936	Western Province
1939	Transvaal
1946	Northern Transvaal
1947	Western Province
1950	Transvaal
1952	Transvaal
1954	Western Province
1956	Northern Transvaal
1957	Western Province
1959	Western Province
1964	Western Province
1966	Western Province
1968	Northern Transvaal
1969	Northern Transvaal
1970	Griqualand West
1971	Northern Tranvaal and Transvaal
1972	Transvaal
1973	Northern Transvaal
1974	Northern Transvaal
1975	Northern Transvaal
1976	Orange Free State

There was no Currie Cup competition when major tours took place in South Africa, and on other occasions, when the competition was expanded to include all provinces playing at home and away, a competition would cover two, and sometimes three, seasons.

RANFURLY SHIELD (NEW ZEALAND)

Year	Winner	Challengers Resisted
1902	Auckland	
1903	Auckland	
1904	Wellington	4
1905	Wellington	
1906-13	Auckland	23
1914-20	Wellington	15
1920	Southland	
1921	Southland	1
1921	Wellington	
1922	Wellington	2
1922-27	Hawkes Bay	24
1927	Wairarapa	1
1927	Hawkes Bay (win disallowed)	
1927	Manawhenua	2
1927	Canterbury	
1928	Canterbury	2
1928	Wairarapa	
1929	Wairarapa	8
1929	Southland	
1930	Southland	3
1930	Wellington	
1931	Wellington	1
1931-34	Canterbury	15
1934	Hawkes Bay	2
1934	Auckland	
1935	Auckland	1
1935	Canterbury	4
1935-37	Otago	8
1937	Southland	
1938	Southland	
1938	Otago	5
1938	Southland	2
1939	Southland	4
1939-46	Southland	5
1947	Otago	4
1948	Otago	7
1949	Otago	6
1950	Otago	1
1950	Canterbury	
1950	Wairarapa	
1950	South Canterbury	
1950	North Auckland	
1951	North Auckland	2
1951	Waikato	4
1952	Waikato	2
1952	Auckland	
1952	Waikato	3
1953	Waikato	3
1953	Wellington	5
1953	Canterbury	
1954	Canterbury	9
1955	Canterbury	7
1956	Canterbury	6
1956	Wellington	1
1957	Wellington	3
1957	Otago	1
1957	Taranaki	
1958	Taranaki	9
1959	Taranaki	4
1959	Southland	
1959	Auckland	
1960	Auckland	2
1960	North Auckland	1
1960	Auckland	5
1961	Auckland	8
1962	Auckland	9
1963	Auckland	3
1963	Wellington	
1963	Taranaki	1
1964	Taranaki	9

1965	Taranaki	5
1965	Auckland	1
1966	Auckland	2
1966	Waikato	1
1966	Hawkes Bay	
1967	Hawkes Bay	7
1968	Hawkes Bay	7
1969	Hawkes Bay	7
1969	Canterbury	
1970	Canterbury	8
1971	Canterbury	1
1971	Auckland	1
1971	North Auckland	1
1972	North Auckland	5
1972	Auckland	
1972	Canterbury	2
1973	Marlborough	5
1974	Marlborough	1
1974	South Canterbury	1
1974	Wellington	1
1974	Auckland	1
1975	Auckland	7
1976	Manawatu	

The shield is played on a challenge basis among the provincial rugby teams of New Zealand. Any team has the right to challenge at the beginning of each season and it is for the union who holds the shield to decide which of the challenges they will accept.

UNIVERSITY MATCH (OXFORD AND CAMBRIDGE)

1871-2	Oxford	1G 1T to 0
1872-3	Cambridge	1G 2T to 0
1873-4	Drawn	1T each
*1874-5	Drawn	Oxford 2T to 0
1875-6	Oxford	1T to 0
1876-7	Cambridge	1G 2T to 0
1877-8	Oxford	2T to 0
1878-9	Drawn	
1879-80	Cambridge	1G 1DG to 1DG
1880-1	Drawn	1T each
1881-2	Oxford	2G 1T to 1G
1882-3	Oxford	1T to 0
1883-4	Oxford	3G 4T to 1G
1884-5	Waikato	3G 1T to 1T
1885-6	Cambridge	2T to 0
1886-7	Cambridge	3T to 0
1887-8	Cambridge	1DG 1T to 0
1888-9	Cambridge	1G 2T to 0
1889-90	Oxford	1G 1T to 0
1890-1	Drawn	1G each
1891-2	Cambridge	2T to 0
1892-3	Drawn	No score
1893-4	Oxford	1T to 0
1894-5	Drawn	1G each
1895-6	Cambridge	1G to 0
1896-7	Oxford	1G 1DG to 1G 1T
1897-8	Oxford	2T to 0
1898-9	Cambridge	1G 2T to 0
1899-1900	Cambridge	2G 4T to 0
1900-1	Oxford	2G to 1G 1T
1901-2	Oxford	1G 1T to 0
1902-3	Drawn	1G 1T each
1903-4	Oxford	3G 1T to 2G 1T
1904-5	Cambridge	3G to 2G
1905-6	Cambridge	3G (15) to 2G 1T (13)

1906-7	Oxford	4T (12) to 1G 1T (8)
1907-8	Oxford	1G 4T (17) to 0
1908-9	Drawn	1G (5) each
1909-10	Oxford	4G 5T (35) to 1T (3)
1910-11	Oxford	4G 1T (23) to 3G 1T (18)
1911-12	Oxford	2G 3T (19) to 0
1912-13	Cambridge	2G (10) to 1T (3)
1913-14	Cambridge	1DG 3T (13) to 1T (3)
1919-20	Cambridge	1DG 1PG (7) to 1G (5)
1920-1	Oxford	1G 4T (17) to 1G 3T (14)
1921-2	Oxford	1G 2T (11) to 1G (5)
1922-3	Cambridge	3G 2T (21) to 1G 1T (8)
1923-4	Oxford	3G 2T (21) to 1G 1PG 2T (14)
1924-5	Oxford	1G 2T (11) to 2T (6)
1925-6	Cambridge	3G 6T (33) to 1T (3)
1926-7	Cambridge	3G 5T (30) to 1G (5)
1927-8	Cambridge	2G 2PG 2T (22) to 1G 3T (14)
1928-9	Cambridge	1G 3T (14) to 1DG 1PG 1T (10)
1929-30	Oxford	1G 1DG (9) to 0
1930-1	Drawn	Oxford 1PG (3) to Cambridge 1T (3)
1931-2	Oxford	1DG 2T (10) to 1T (3)
1932-3	Oxford	1G 1T (8) to 1T (3)
1933-4	Oxford	1G (5) to 1T (3)
1934-5	Cambridge	2G 1DG 1PG 4T (29) to 1DG (4)
1935-6	Drawn	No score
1936-7	Cambridge	2T (6) to 1G (5)
1937-8	Oxford	1G 4T (17) to 1DG (4)
1938-9	Cambridge	1G 1PG (8) to 2PG (6)
1939-40	Oxford at Cambridge	1G 1DG 2T (15) to 1T (3)
1940-1	Cambridge at Oxford	1G 2T (11) to 1G 1DG (9)
	Cambridge at Cambridge	2G 1T (13) to 0
1941-2	Cambridge at Cambridge	1PG 2T (9) to 1PG 1T (6)
	Cambridge at Oxford	1G 2PG 2T (17) to 1G 1T (8)
1942-3	Cambridge at Oxford	1G 1DG (9) to 0
	Cambridge at Oxford	1G 3T (14) to 2G 1T (13)
1943-4	Cambridge at Cambridge	2G 2T (16) to 1T (3)
	Cambridge at Cambridge	2G 1T (13) to 1DG (4)
	Oxford at Oxford	2T (6) to 1G (5)
1944-5	Drawn at Oxford	1T (3) each
	Cambridge at Cambridge	2G 2T (16) to 1DG (4)
1945-6	Cambridge	1G 2T (11) to 1G 1PG (8)
1946-7	Oxford	1G 1DG 2T (15) to 1G (5)
1947-8	Cambridge	2PG (6) to 0
1948-9	Oxford	1G 1DG 2T (14) to 1G 1PG (8)
1949-50	Oxford	1T (3) to 0
1950-1	Oxford	1G 1PG (8) to 0
1951-2	Oxford	2G 1T (13) to 0
1952-3	Cambridge	1PG 1T (6) to 1G (5)
1953-4	Drawn	Oxford 1PG 1T (6) Cambridge 2PG (6)
1954-5	Cambridge	1PG (3) to 0
1955-6	Oxford	1PG 2T (9) to 1G (5)
1956-7	Cambridge	1G 1DG 1PG 1T (14) to 2PG 1T (9)
1957-8	Oxford	1T (3) to 0
1958-9	Cambridge	1G 1PG 3T (17) to 1PG 1T (6)
1959-60	Oxford	3PG (9) to 1PG (3)
1960-1	Cambridge	2G 1T (13) to 0
1961-2	Cambridge	1DG 2T (9) to 1DG (3)
1962-3	Cambridge	1G 1DG 1PG 1T (14) to 0
1963-4	Cambridge	2G 1PG 2T (19) to 1G 1DG 1PG (11)
1964-5	Oxford	2G 1PG 2T (19) to 1PG 1GM (6)
1965-6	Drawn	1G each
1966-7	Oxford	1G 1T (8) to 1DG 1T (6)
1967-8	Cambridge	1T 1PG (6) to 0
1968-9	Cambridge	1T 1PG 1DG (9) to 2T (6)
1969-70	Oxford	3PG (9) to 2PG (6)
1970-1	Oxford	1G 1DG 2T (14) to 1PG (3)
1971-2	Oxford	3PG 3T (21) to 1PG (3)
1972-3	Cambridge	1G 1PG 1DG 1T (16) to 2PG (6)
1973-4	Cambridge	1DG 1PG 2T (14) to 1G 2PG (12)
1974-5	Cambridge	1G 2PG 1T (16) to 5PG (15)
1975-6	Cambridge	2G 5PG 1DG 1T (34) to 3PG 1DG (12)

* At this period matches were drawn if no goals had been scored.

INDEX

ACKNOWLEDGEMENTS

Front cover—Gerry Cranham. 2-3 Colorsport. 7 Gerry Cranham. 9 James Gilbert of Rugby (top right); Radio Times Hulton Picture Library (bottom). 10-11 Victoria & Albert Museum. 13 Mary Evans. 15 Radio Times Hulton Picture Library (top); Mary Evans (bottom). 18-19, 21 Rugby Football Union. 22 Sport & General. 23 Press Association. 24 Radio Times Hulton Picture Library. 26 Sport & General (left); Keystone (right). 27 Sport & General (bottom). 28 Visnews. 29 British Broadcasting Corporation (left); Sport & General (right). 30, 31, 33 Colorsport. 34 Syndication International. 36-7 E. R. Yerbury & Son. 39 Scottish Rugby Union. 40-1 Radio Times Hulton Picture Library; Sport & General (inset). 42-3 Radio Times Hulton Picture Library. 44 Sport & General. 45 Scottish Rugby Union. 46 Radio Times Hulton Picture Library (top); Keystone (bottom). 48 Popperfoto. 49 Colorsport. 50 Press Association. 53 Gerry Cranham. 55, 56, 58-9 Radio Times Hulton Picture Library. 61 Sport & General. 63 Ed Lacey. 64 Sport & General. 65 Colorsport (top); Irish Times (bottom). 67 Colorsport. 69 (bottom), 70 Western Mail & Echo. 71 Popperfoto (top); Sport & General (bottom). 73 Popperfoto (top); Western Mail & Echo (bottom). 74-5 Western Mail & Echo. 77 Sport & General. 78 Western Mail & Echo (top); Sport & General (bottom). 79 Colorsport (top); Ed Lacey (bottom). 81 Western Mail & Echo. 82, 83, 84 Colorsport. 85 Ed Lacey. 86, 87, 88, 89, 90-1 Colorsport. 92 Radio Times Hulton Picture Library 94-5 Colorsport. 96, 97 (top), 98, 99 Radio Times Hulton Picture Library. 100 Central Press. 101 New Zealand Herald-Weekly News. 103 Popperfoto. 104-5 New Zealand High Commission. 106 The Scotsman. 107 Sport & General. 108-9 Colorsport. 113 Central Press. 114-5 Radio Times Hulton Picture Library. 116 Sydney Morning Herald. 117 Radio Times Hulton Picture Library. 118, 119 Sydney Morning Herald. 120, 122 (top) Australian Information Service, London. 122 (bottom), 124 Colorsport. 126, 129 Ed Lacey. 133, 135 Radio Times Hulton Picture Library. 136 South African Embassy, London. 137 Radio Times Hulton Picture Library. 139 Central Press. 141 Associated Press. 143 Central Press (top); Press Association (bottom). 144 Argus South African Newspapers. 146-7 Gerry Cranham. 148 Colorsport (top); Argus South African Newspapers (bottom). 150-1 Republican Publications of South Africa. 152 Radio Times Hulton Picture Library. 154, 155 Gerry Cranham. 158, 159 Colorsport. 160, 161 Presse Sports. 162 Presse Sports (left & bottom right); Paris Match (top right). 163 Presse Sports (top); Paris Match (bottom). 164, 165 Paris Match. 166 Presse Sports. 167 Colorsport (top); Presse Sports (bottom). 169 Scottish Rugby Union (top); Radio Times Hulton Picture Library (bottom). 170, 171 New Zealand Herald Weekly News. 172 British Broadcasting Corporation (left); Associated Press (right). 173 Central Press (top). 174 Popperfoto (top); John Reason (bottom). 175 Central Press (top); New Zealand High Commission (bottom). 176 Peter Bush (top); Tom Lloyd (bottom). 177 D. J. Roy. 178, 179 Colorsport. 180 Argus South African Newspapers. 183 Radio Times Hulton Picture Library. 185 Western Mail & Echo. 186 Ed Lacey. 187 Ed Lacey (top); Colorsport (bottom). 189 Colorsport. 190, 191 British Broadcasting Corporation.

My thanks also to Cliff Morgan, Sandy Thorburn, Alf Wright, Henri Garcia and Reg Sweet for their help and encouragement, and to Norman Mair for allowing me to pinch some of his best stories.